BBC

DOCTOR WHO

A TALE OF TWO TIME LORDS

"As the Doctor would say, brilliant!"

BIG COMIC PAGE

"I can't say enough good things about this. It's everything that *Doctor Who* does best."

BUT WHY THO?

"This is one book newcomers and old fans alike are sure to enjoy. 9/10!"

EXPLORE THE MULTIVERSE

"This comic captures the energy and dramatic elements of the recent *Doctor Who* series. All of the creative team work together to produce a solid adventure which is sure to win the hearts of the fans."

MONKEYS FIGHTING ROBOTS

"Perfectly captures the look and voices of the characters!"

ADVENTURES IN POOR TASTE

"If you're a fan overflowing with love for the new Doctor, this is a great place to get an extra dose of *Doctor Who*."

COMICBOOK.COM

"Highly recommended... Bold, sassy, intelligent, and accessible to new fans. 5 out of 5!"

GEEK SYNDICATE

"A perfect continuation of what we've come to love about Series 11. 5 out of 5!"

KABOOOOOM

"A radical romp through time and space!"

NERDIST

"Houser nails it."

NEWSARAMA

"The art team continues to excel!"

SCIFI PULSE

Doctor Who Backlist

See Reader's Guide (page 110) for full list of titles

TENTH DOCTOR:
YEAR ONE
Hardback: 9781785863998

ELEVENTH DOCTOR:
YEAR ONE
Hardback: 9781785864001

TWELFTH DOCTOR:
YEAR ONE
Hardback: 9781785864018

Editor
Jake Devine

Senior Designer
Andrew Leung

Titan Comics

Managing Editor
Martin Eden

Senior Creative Editor
David Leach

Production Controller
Caterina Falqui

Senior Production Controller
Jackie Flook

Art Director
Oz Browne

Sales & Circulation Manager
Steve Tothill

Publicist
Imogen Harris

Press & Publicity Assistant
George Wickenden

Marketing Manager
Ricky Claydon

Head Of Rights
Jenny Boyce

Editorial Director
Duncan Baizley

Operations Director
Leigh Baulch

Executive Director
Vivian Cheung

Publisher
Nick Landau

For rights information contact Jenny Boyce
jenny.boyce@titanemail.com

Special thanks to Chris Chibnall, Matt Strevens, Sam Hoyle, Mandy Thwaites, Suzy L. Raia, Gabby De Matteis, Ross McGlinchey, David Wilson-Nunn, Kirsty Mullan and Kate Bush for their invaluable assistance.

BBC Studios

Chair, Editorial Review Boards **Nicholas Brett** | Managing Director, Consumer Products and Licensing **Stephen Davies**
Head of Publishing **Mandy Thwaites** | Compliance Manager **Cameron McEwan** | UK Publishing Co-Ordinator **Eva Abramik**

DOCTOR WHO: A TALE OF TWO TIME LORDS VOL. 1: A LITTLE HELP FROM MY FRIENDS
ISBN: 9781787733107

Published by Titan Comics, a division of Titan Publishing Group, Ltd. 144 Southwark Street, London, SE1 0UP.
Titan Comics is a registered trademark. All rights reserved.

A CIP catalogue record for this title is available from the British Library.
First edition: July 2020.

10 9 8 7 6 5 4 3 2 1

Printed in China

Titan Comics does not read or accept unsolicited DOCTOR WHO submissions of ideas, stories or artwork.

BBC
DOCTOR WHO

A TALE OF TWO TIME LORDS

WRITER
JODY HOUSER

ARTIST
ROBERTA INGRANATA

COLORIST
ENRICA EREN ANGIOLINI

COLOR ASSISTANT
SHARI CHANKHAMMA

LETTERERS
RICHARD STARKINGS & COMICRAFT'S SARAH HEDRICK

TITAN®
COMICS

BBC

BBC

DOCTOR WHO

A TALE OF TWO TIME LORDS

PREVIOUSLY...

Not so long ago, The Tenth Doctor and companion Martha were attacked by the menacing Weeping Angels – aliens that feed off of the potential energy of their victim's lost future by stranding them in the past. Now, the Thirteenth Doctor and fam travel to 1969 to party at Woodstock! Or so they think...

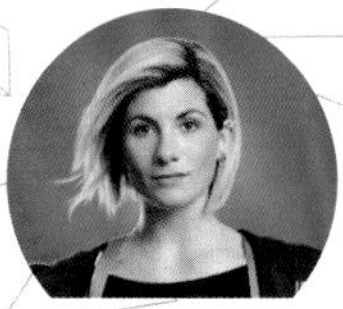

Thirteenth **Doctor**

The Thirteenth Doctor is a live wire, full of energy and fizzing with excitement and wit! She is a charismatic and confident explorer, dedicated to seeing all the wonders of the universe, championing fairness and kindness wherever she can.

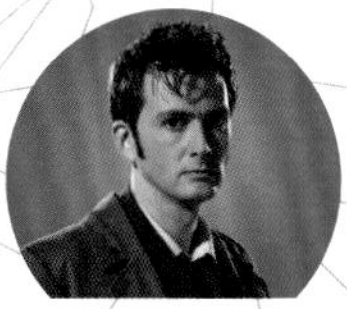

Tenth **Doctor**

The Tenth Doctor still hides his post-Time War guilt beneath a happy-go-lucky guise. While oftentimes plucky and adventurous, he feels a deep loss for those he has loved. Never cruel or cowardly, he champions the oppressed across time and space.

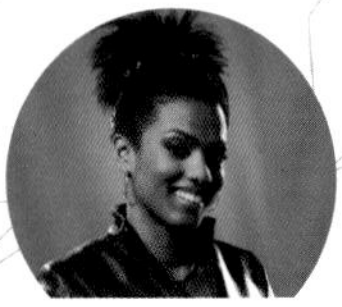

Martha Jones

Martha is a 23-year-old medical student from London, who's very independent, but remains close with her family. She's strong-willed and not afraid when things get tough!

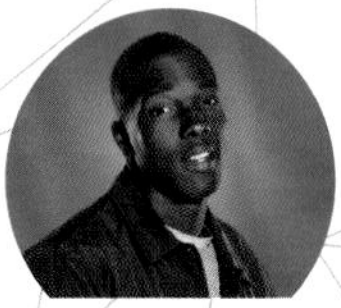

Ryan Sinclair

19-year-old Ryan is from Sheffield. He is studying to become a mechanic and is great with technology! Though dyspraxic, his curiosity and energy wins out over fear.

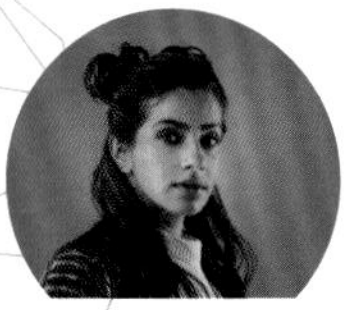

Yasmin 'Yaz' Khan

Yaz is a 19-year-old Sheffielder, friendly and self-assured, a quick logical thinker and a natural leader – which is why she loves her job as a probationary police officer!

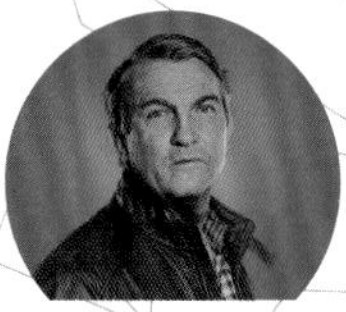

Graham O'Brien

Graham is a funny, charming and cheeky chap – a family man from Essex, with a sharp sense of humor and a caring nature. He's brave, selfless, and wise too.

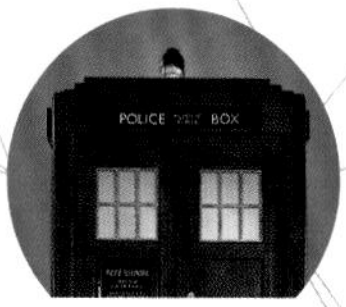

The **TARDIS**

'Time and Relative Dimension in Space'. Bigger on the inside, this unassuming blue police box is your ticket to amazing adventures across time and space!

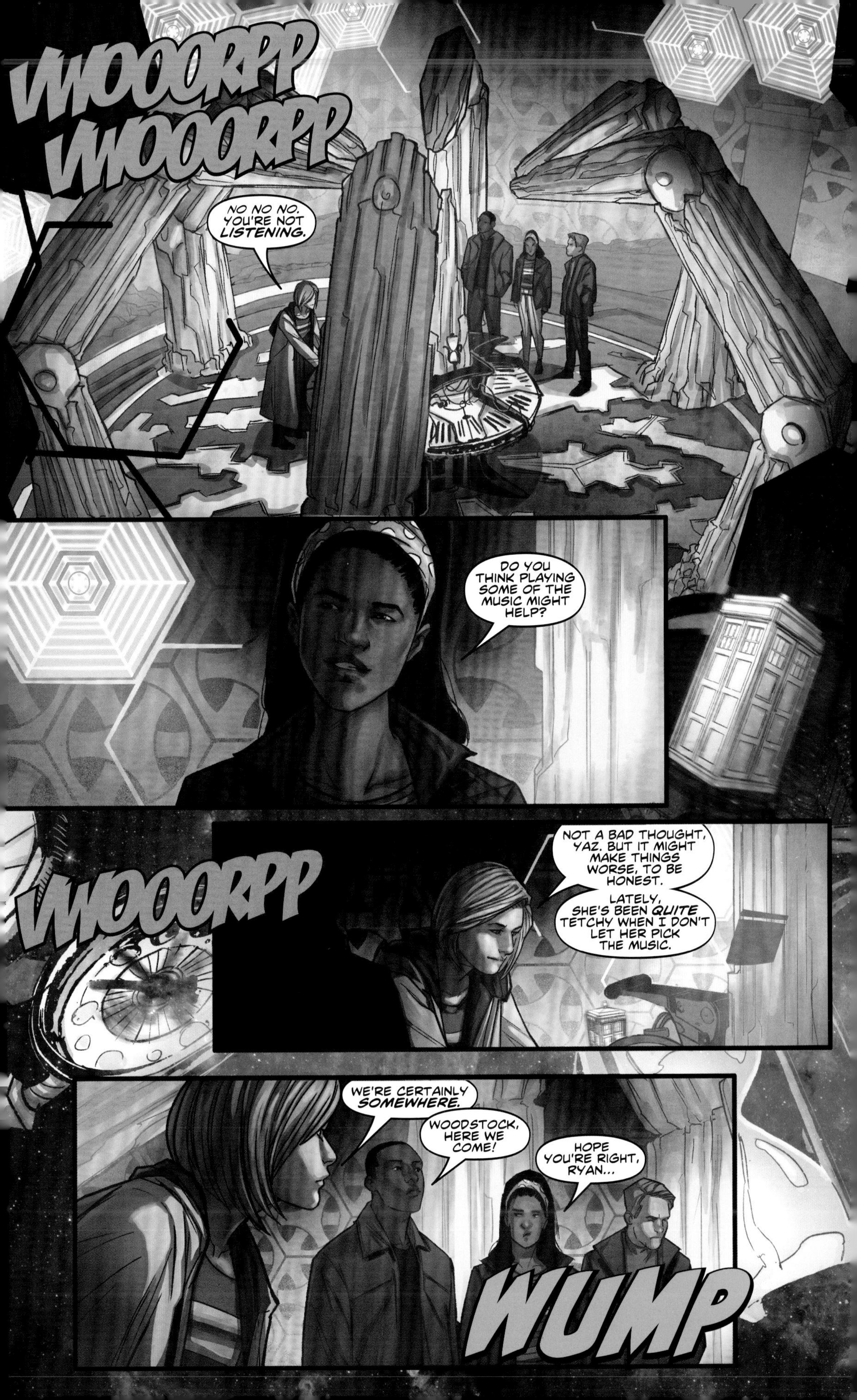
VWOOORPP
VWOOORPP
NO NO NO. YOU'RE NOT LISTENING.
DO YOU THINK PLAYING SOME OF THE MUSIC MIGHT HELP?
VWOOORPP
NOT A BAD THOUGHT, YAZ. BUT IT MIGHT MAKE THINGS WORSE, TO BE HONEST.
LATELY, SHE'S BEEN QUITE TETCHY WHEN I DON'T LET HER PICK THE MUSIC.
WE'RE CERTAINLY SOMEWHERE.
WOODSTOCK, HERE WE COME!
HOPE YOU'RE RIGHT, RYAN...
WUMP

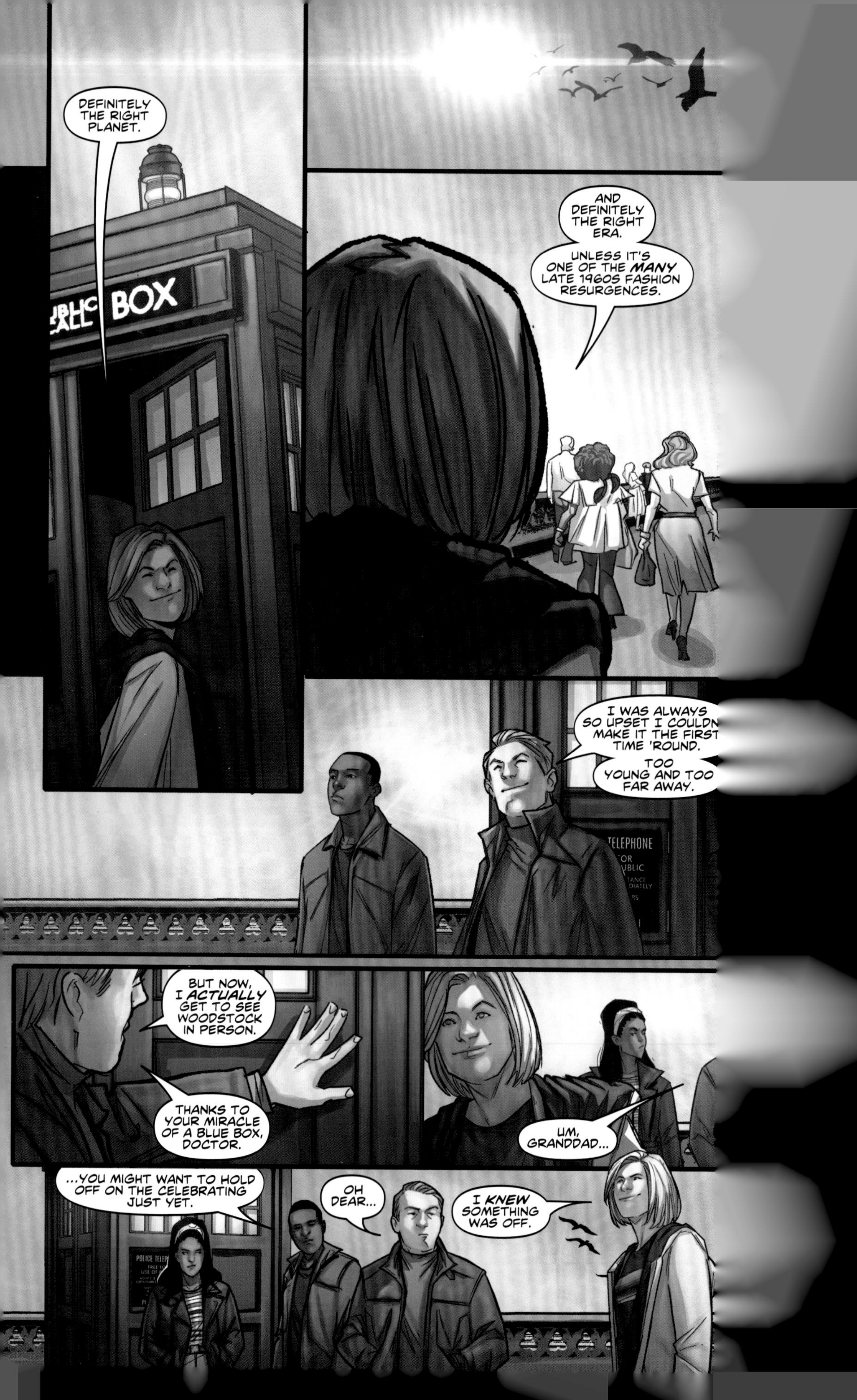

DEFINITELY THE RIGHT PLANET.
AND DEFINITELY THE RIGHT ERA.
UNLESS IT'S ONE OF THE MANY LATE 1960S FASHION RESURGENCES.
PUBLIC CALL BOX
I WAS ALWAYS SO UPSET I COULDN MAKE IT THE FIRST TIME 'ROUND.
TOO YOUNG AND TOO FAR AWAY.
TELEPHONE
BUT NOW, I ACTUALLY GET TO SEE WOODSTOCK IN PERSON.
THANKS TO YOUR MIRACLE OF A BLUE BOX, DOCTOR.
UM, GRANDDAD...
...YOU MIGHT WANT TO HOLD OFF ON THE CELEBRATING JUST YET.
OH DEAR...
I KNEW SOMETHING WAS OFF.

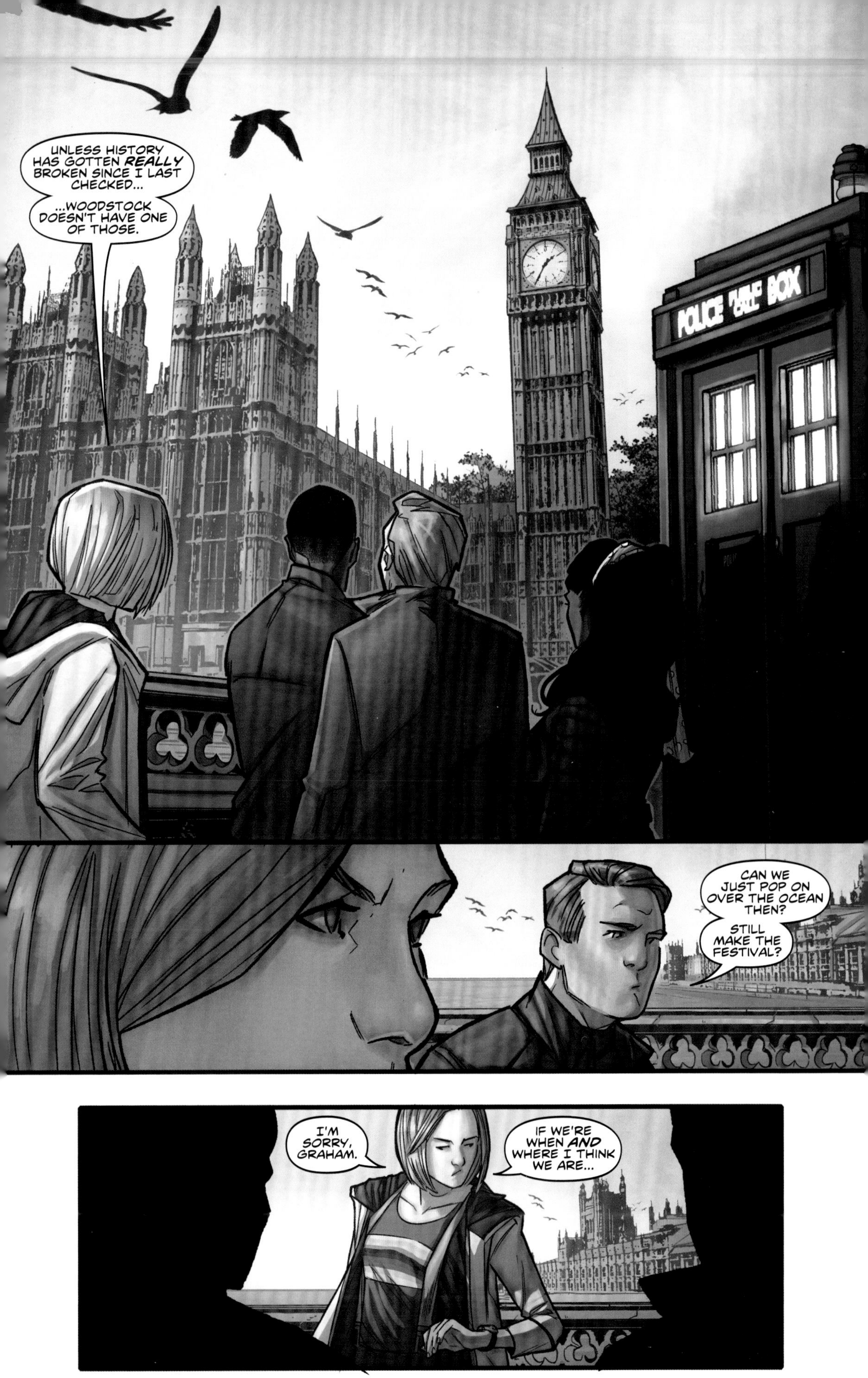
UNLESS HISTORY HAS GOTTEN REALLY BROKEN SINCE I LAST CHECKED...
...WOODSTOCK DOESN'T HAVE ONE OF THOSE.
POLICE PUBLIC CALL BOX
CAN WE JUST POP ON OVER THE OCEAN THEN?
STILL MAKE THE FESTIVAL?
I'M SORRY, GRAHAM.
IF WE'RE WHEN AND WHERE I THINK WE ARE...

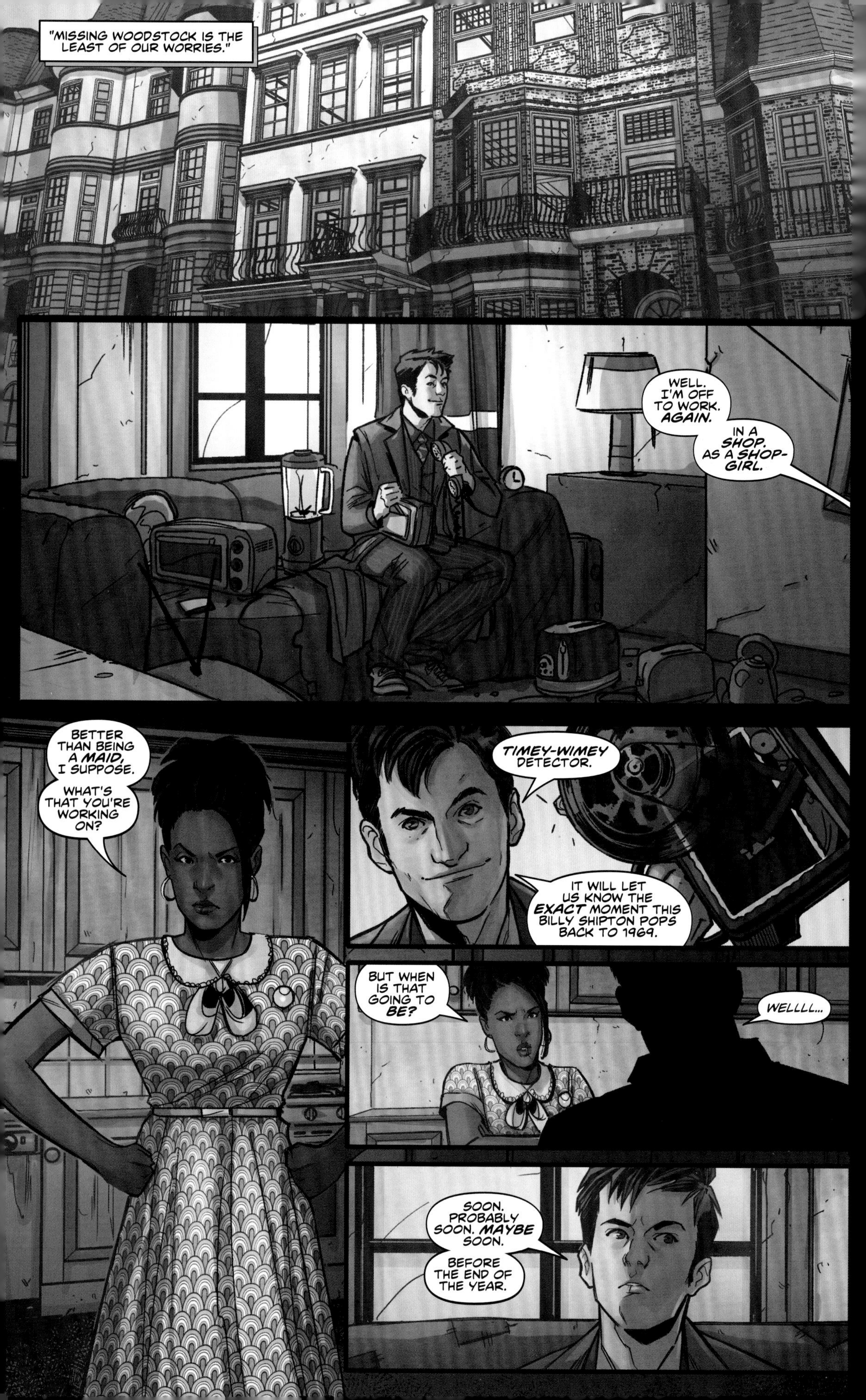
"MISSING WOODSTOCK IS THE LEAST OF OUR WORRIES."
WELL. I'M OFF TO WORK. AGAIN.
IN A SHOP. AS A SHOP-GIRL.
BETTER THAN BEING A MAID, I SUPPOSE.
WHAT'S THAT YOU'RE WORKING ON?
TIMEY-WIMEY DETECTOR.
IT WILL LET US KNOW THE EXACT MOMENT THIS BILLY SHIPTON POPS BACK TO 1969.
BUT WHEN IS THAT GOING TO BE?
WELLLL...
SOON. PROBABLY SOON. MAYBE SOON.
BEFORE THE END OF THE YEAR.

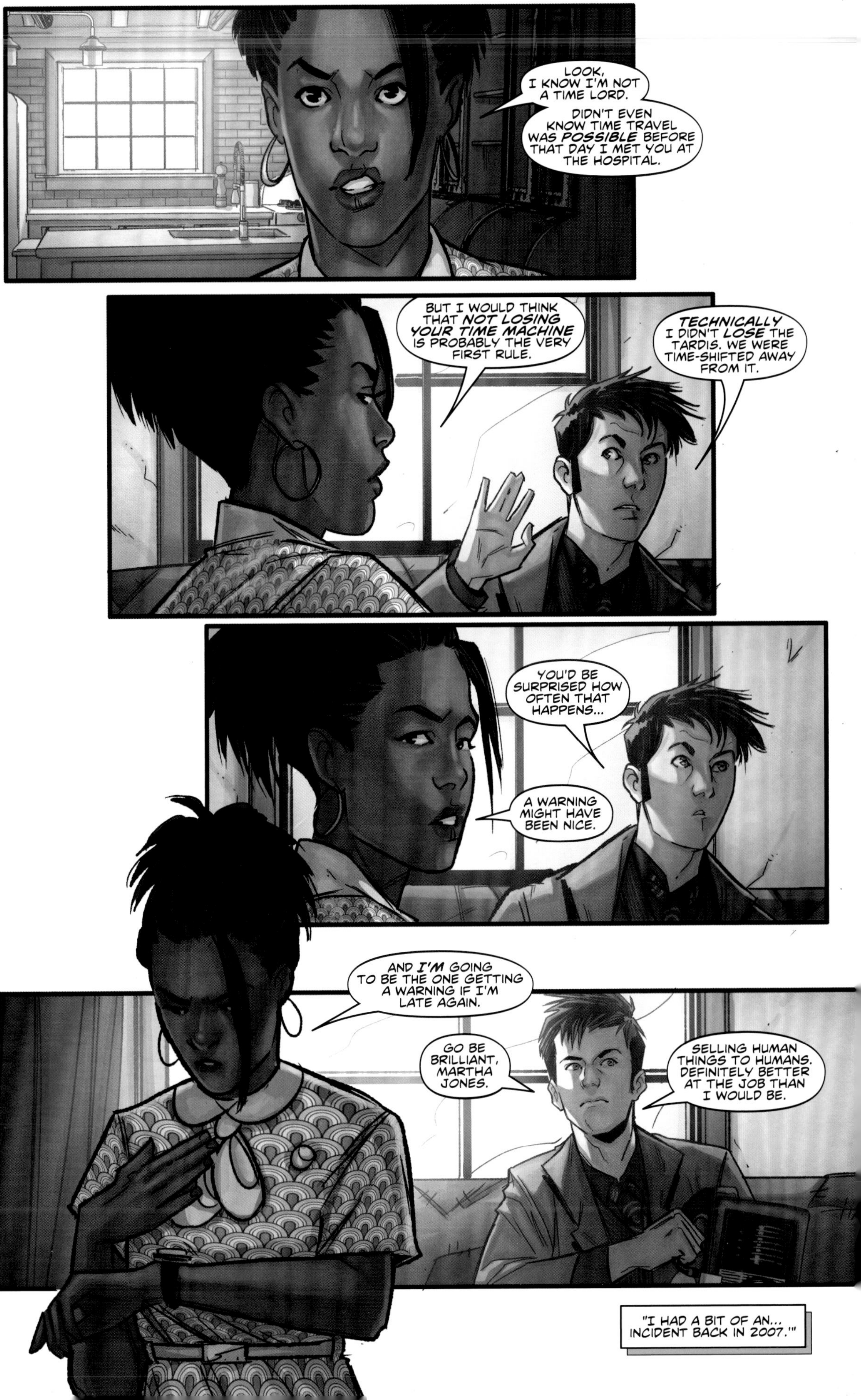
LOOK, I KNOW I'M NOT A TIME LORD.
DIDN'T EVEN KNOW TIME TRAVEL WAS *POSSIBLE* BEFORE THAT DAY I MET YOU AT THE HOSPITAL.
BUT I WOULD THINK THAT *NOT LOSING YOUR TIME MACHINE* IS PROBABLY THE VERY FIRST RULE.
TECHNICALLY I DIDN'T *LOSE* THE TARDIS. WE WERE TIME-SHIFTED AWAY FROM IT.
YOU'D BE SURPRISED HOW OFTEN THAT HAPPENS...
A WARNING MIGHT HAVE BEEN NICE.
AND *I'M* GOING TO BE THE ONE GETTING A WARNING IF I'M LATE AGAIN.
GO BE BRILLIANT, MARTHA JONES.
SELLING HUMAN THINGS TO HUMANS. DEFINITELY BETTER AT THE JOB THAN I WOULD BE.
"I HAD A BIT OF AN... INCIDENT BACK IN 2007.'"

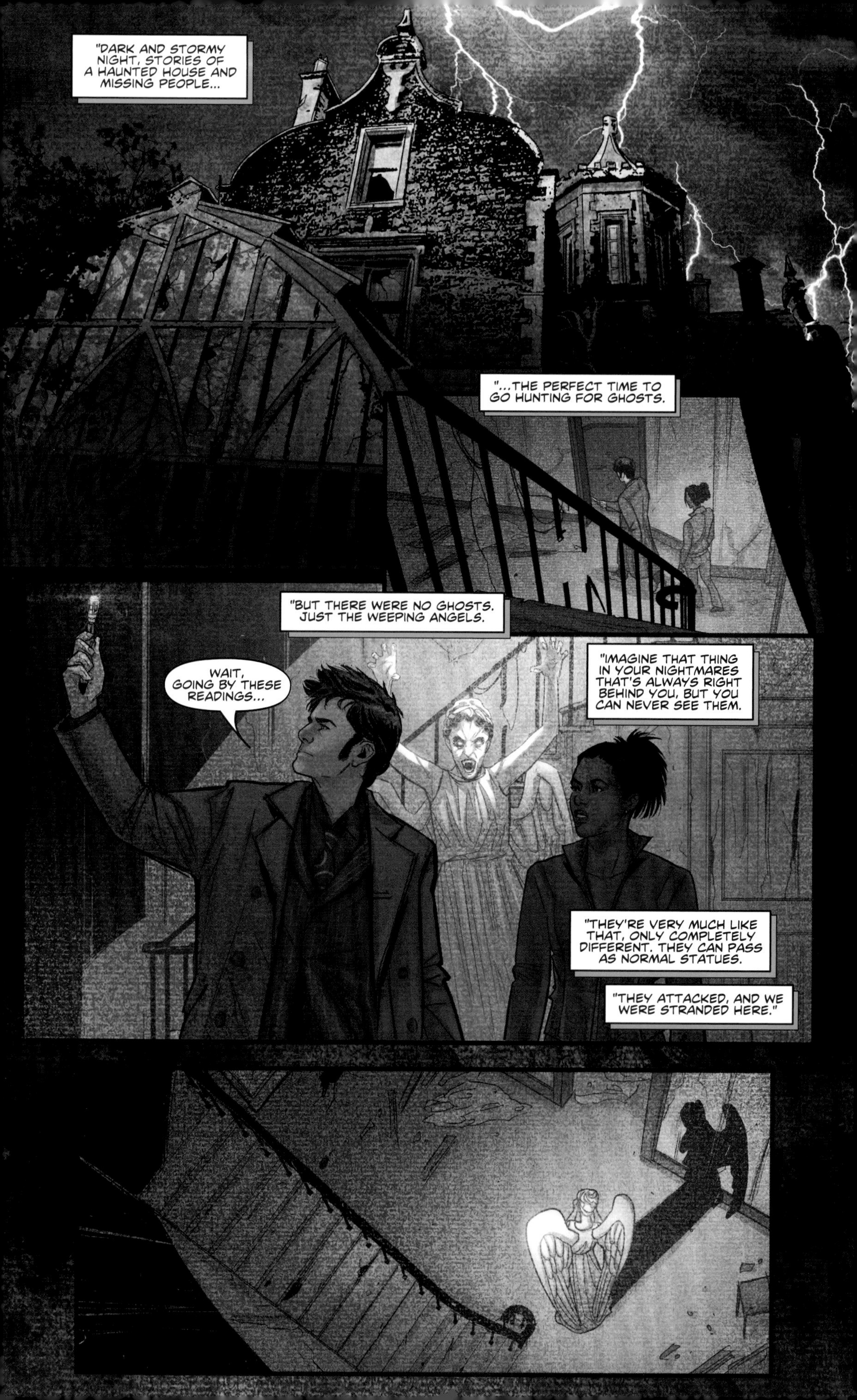
"DARK AND STORMY NIGHT, STORIES OF A HAUNTED HOUSE AND MISSING PEOPLE...
"...THE PERFECT TIME TO GO HUNTING FOR GHOSTS.
"BUT THERE WERE NO GHOSTS. JUST THE WEEPING ANGELS.
WAIT, GOING BY THESE READINGS...
"IMAGINE THAT THING IN YOUR NIGHTMARES THAT'S ALWAYS RIGHT BEHIND YOU, BUT YOU CAN NEVER SEE THEM.
"THEY'RE VERY MUCH LIKE THAT, ONLY COMPLETELY DIFFERENT. THEY CAN PASS AS NORMAL STATUES.
"THEY ATTACKED, AND WE WERE STRANDED HERE."

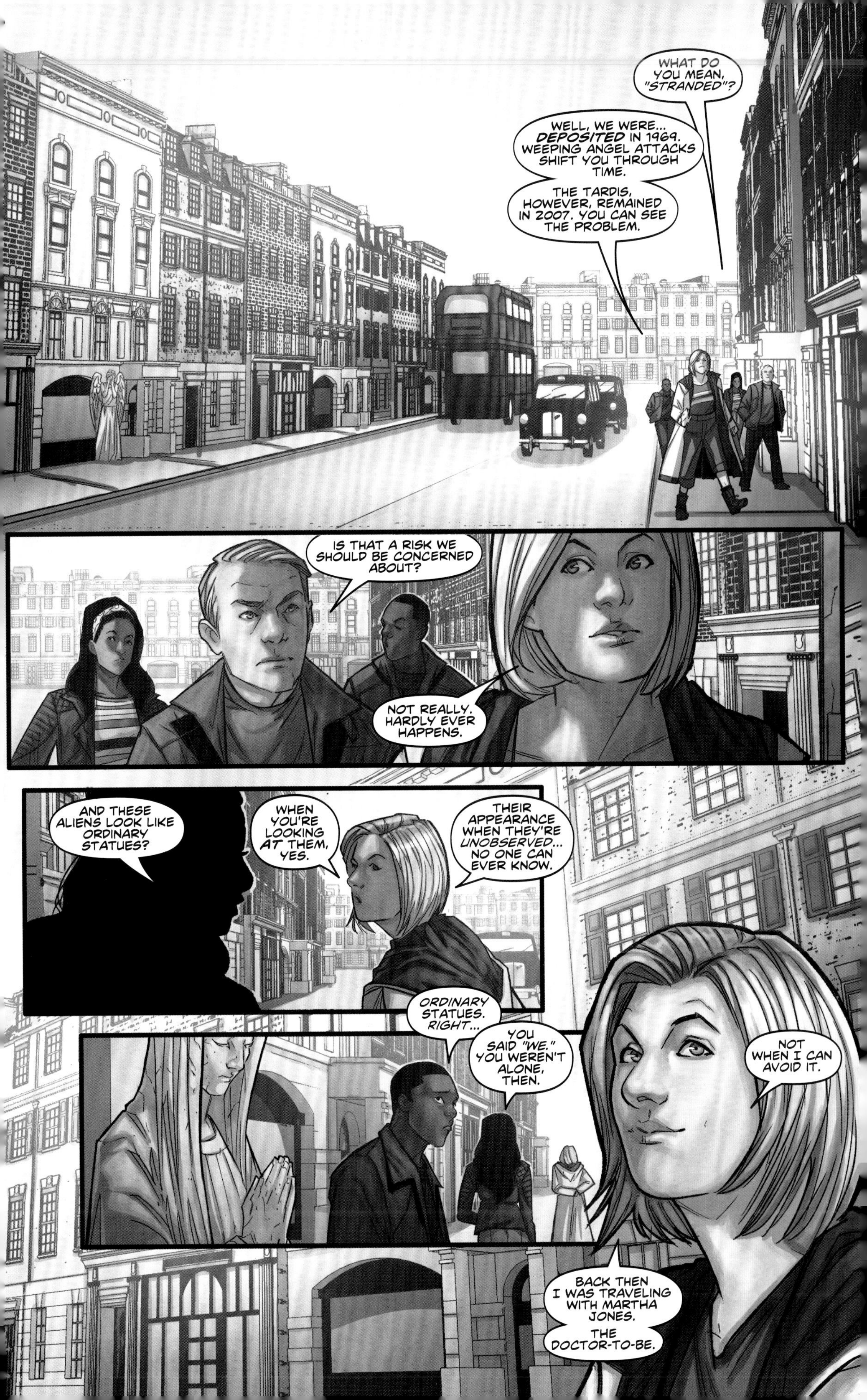
WHAT DO YOU MEAN, "STRANDED"?
WELL, WE WERE... DEPOSITED IN 1969. WEEPING ANGEL ATTACKS SHIFT YOU THROUGH TIME.
THE TARDIS, HOWEVER, REMAINED IN 2007. YOU CAN SEE THE PROBLEM.
IS THAT A RISK WE SHOULD BE CONCERNED ABOUT?
NOT REALLY. HARDLY EVER HAPPENS.
AND THESE ALIENS LOOK LIKE ORDINARY STATUES?
WHEN YOU'RE LOOKING AT THEM, YES.
THEIR APPEARANCE WHEN THEY'RE UNOBSERVED... NO ONE CAN EVER KNOW.
ORDINARY STATUES. RIGHT...
YOU SAID "WE." YOU WEREN'T ALONE, THEN.
NOT WHEN I CAN AVOID IT.
BACK THEN I WAS TRAVELING WITH MARTHA JONES.
THE DOCTOR-TO-BE.

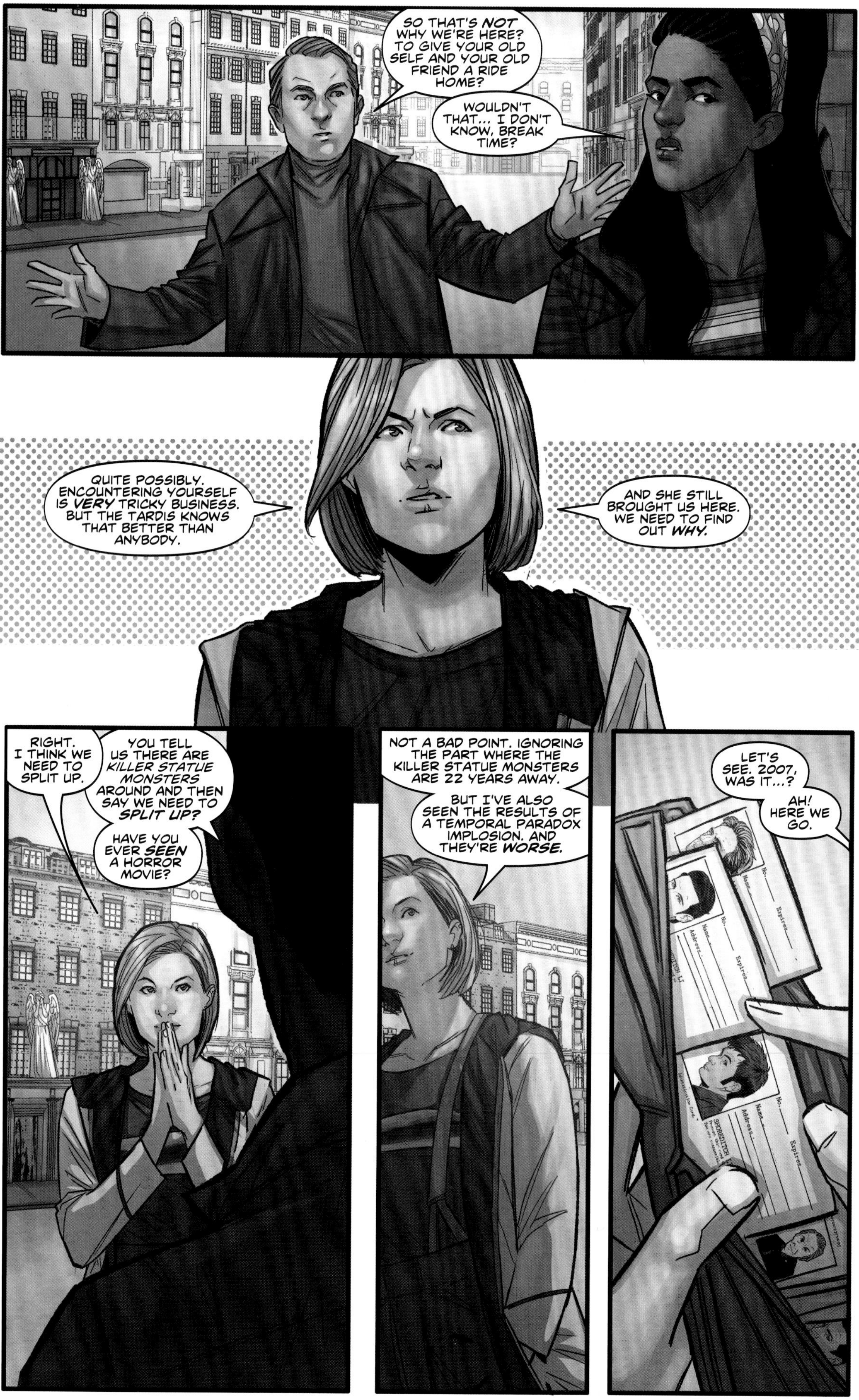
SO THAT'S *NOT* WHY WE'RE HERE? TO GIVE YOUR OLD SELF AND YOUR OLD FRIEND A RIDE HOME?
WOULDN'T THAT... I DON'T KNOW, BREAK TIME?
QUITE POSSIBLY. ENCOUNTERING YOURSELF IS *VERY* TRICKY BUSINESS. BUT THE TARDIS KNOWS THAT BETTER THAN ANYBODY.
AND SHE STILL BROUGHT US HERE. WE NEED TO FIND OUT *WHY.*
RIGHT. I THINK WE NEED TO SPLIT UP.
YOU TELL US THERE ARE *KILLER STATUE MONSTERS* AROUND AND THEN SAY WE NEED TO *SPLIT UP?*
HAVE YOU EVER *SEEN* A HORROR MOVIE?
NOT A BAD POINT. IGNORING THE PART WHERE THE KILLER STATUE MONSTERS ARE 22 YEARS AWAY.
BUT I'VE ALSO SEEN THE RESULTS OF A TEMPORAL PARADOX IMPLOSION. AND THEY'RE *WORSE.*
LET'S SEE. 2007, WAS IT...?
AH! HERE WE GO.

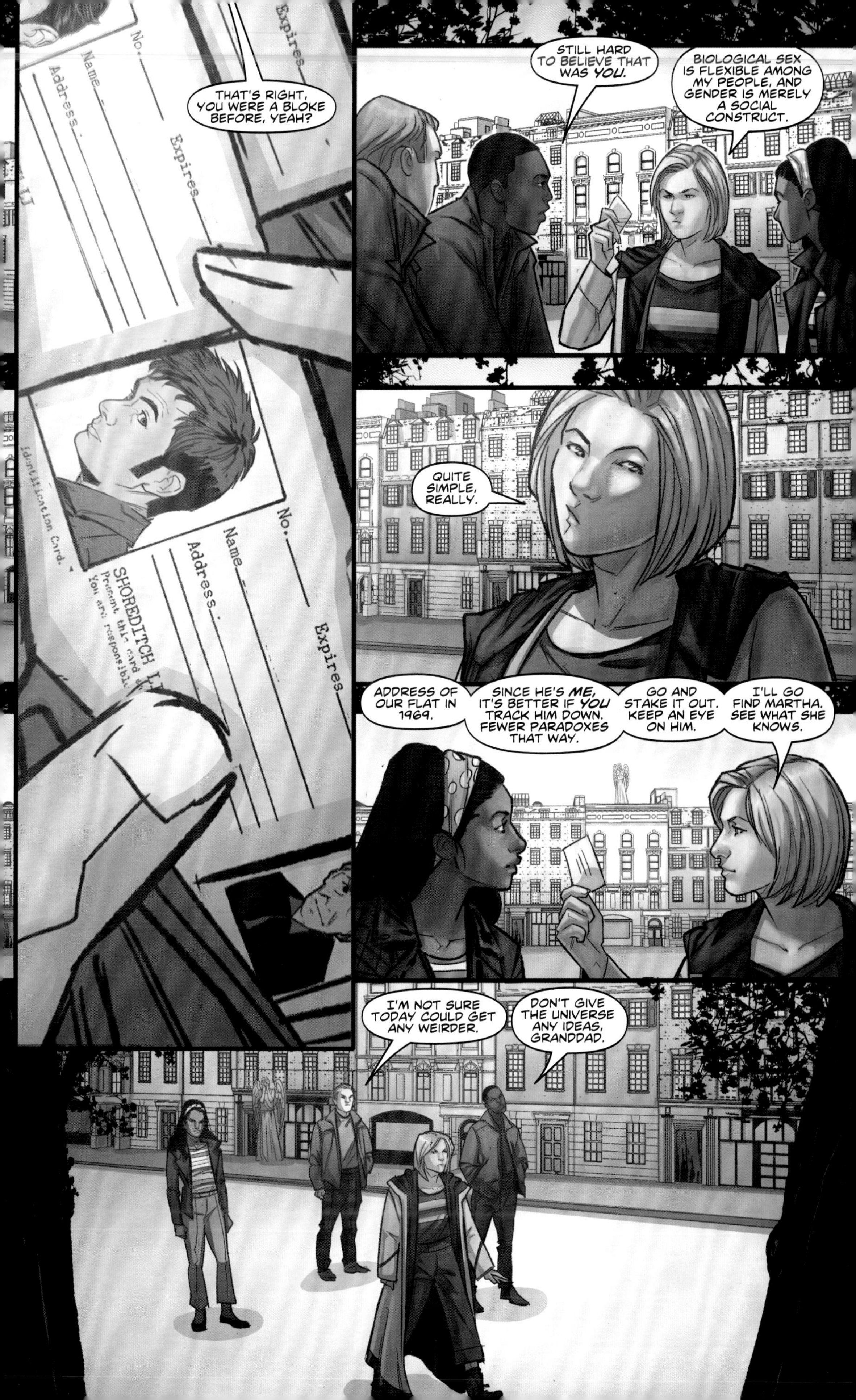
THAT'S RIGHT, YOU WERE A BLOKE BEFORE, YEAH?
STILL HARD TO BELIEVE THAT WAS YOU.
BIOLOGICAL SEX IS FLEXIBLE AMONG MY PEOPLE, AND GENDER IS MERELY A SOCIAL CONSTRUCT.
QUITE SIMPLE, REALLY.
ADDRESS OF OUR FLAT IN 1969.
SINCE HE'S ME, IT'S BETTER IF YOU TRACK HIM DOWN. FEWER PARADOXES THAT WAY.
GO AND STAKE IT OUT. KEEP AN EYE ON HIM.
I'LL GO FIND MARTHA. SEE WHAT SHE KNOWS.
I'M NOT SURE TODAY COULD GET ANY WEIRDER.
DON'T GIVE THE UNIVERSE ANY IDEAS, GRANDDAD.

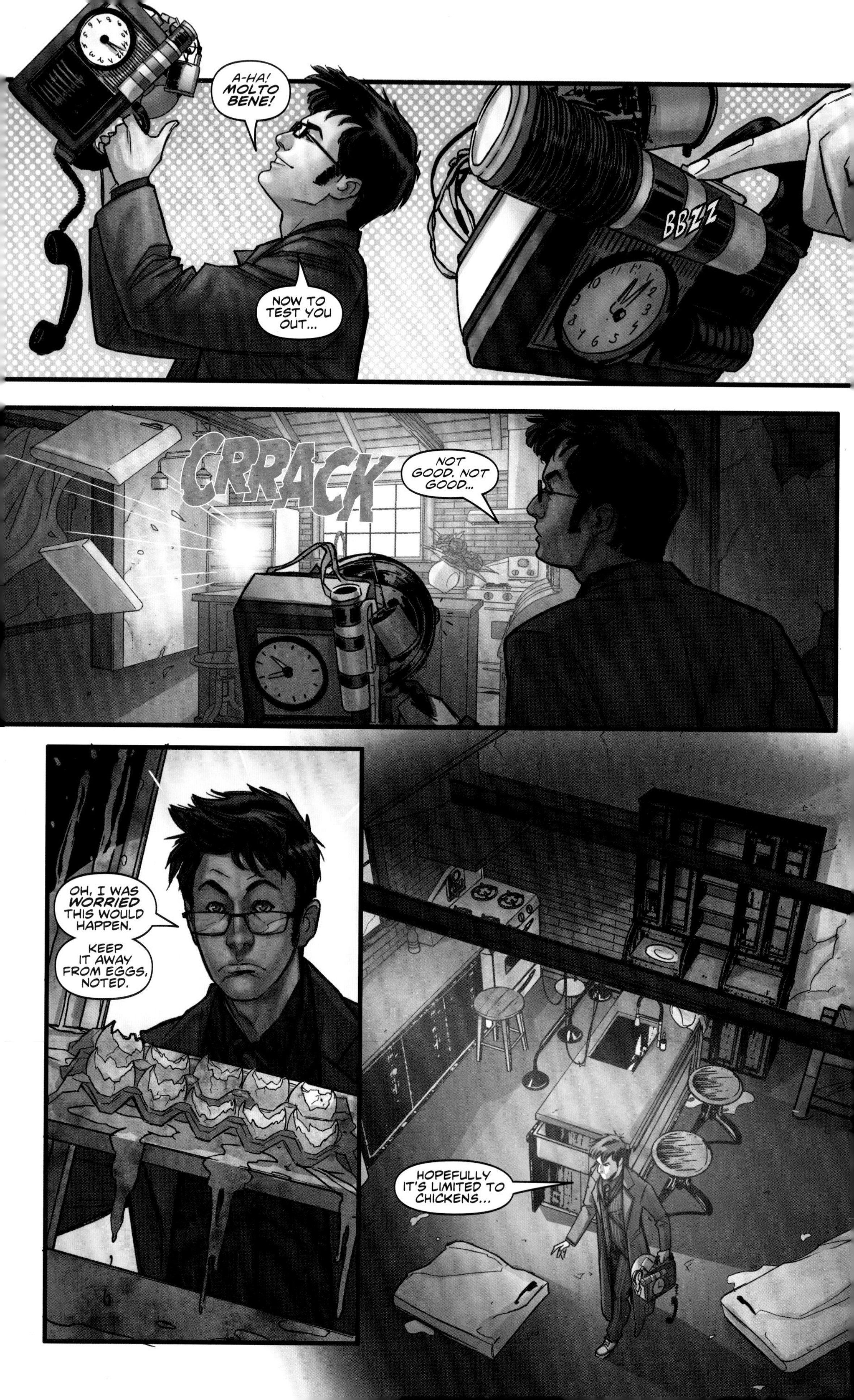
A-HA! MOLTO BENE!
NOW TO TEST YOU OUT...
BBZZ
CRRACK
NOT GOOD. NOT GOOD...
OH, I WAS WORRIED THIS WOULD HAPPEN.
KEEP IT AWAY FROM EGGS, NOTED.
HOPEFULLY IT'S LIMITED TO CHICKENS...

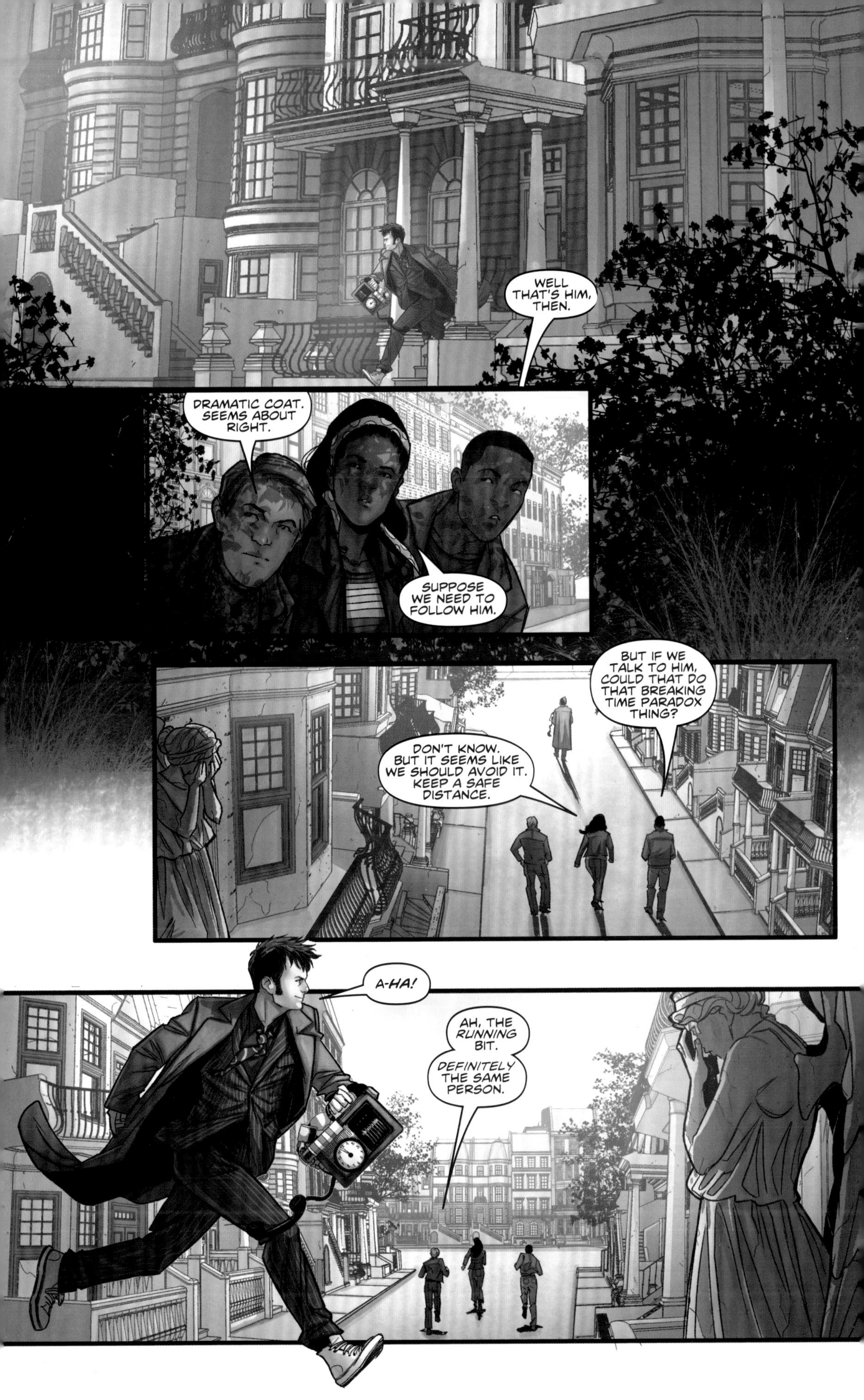
WELL THAT'S HIM, THEN.
DRAMATIC COAT. SEEMS ABOUT RIGHT.
SUPPOSE WE NEED TO FOLLOW HIM.
BUT IF WE TALK TO HIM, COULD THAT DO THAT BREAKING TIME PARADOX THING?
DON'T KNOW. BUT IT SEEMS LIKE WE SHOULD AVOID IT. KEEP A SAFE DISTANCE.
A-HA!
AH, THE RUNNING BIT.
DEFINITELY THE SAME PERSON.

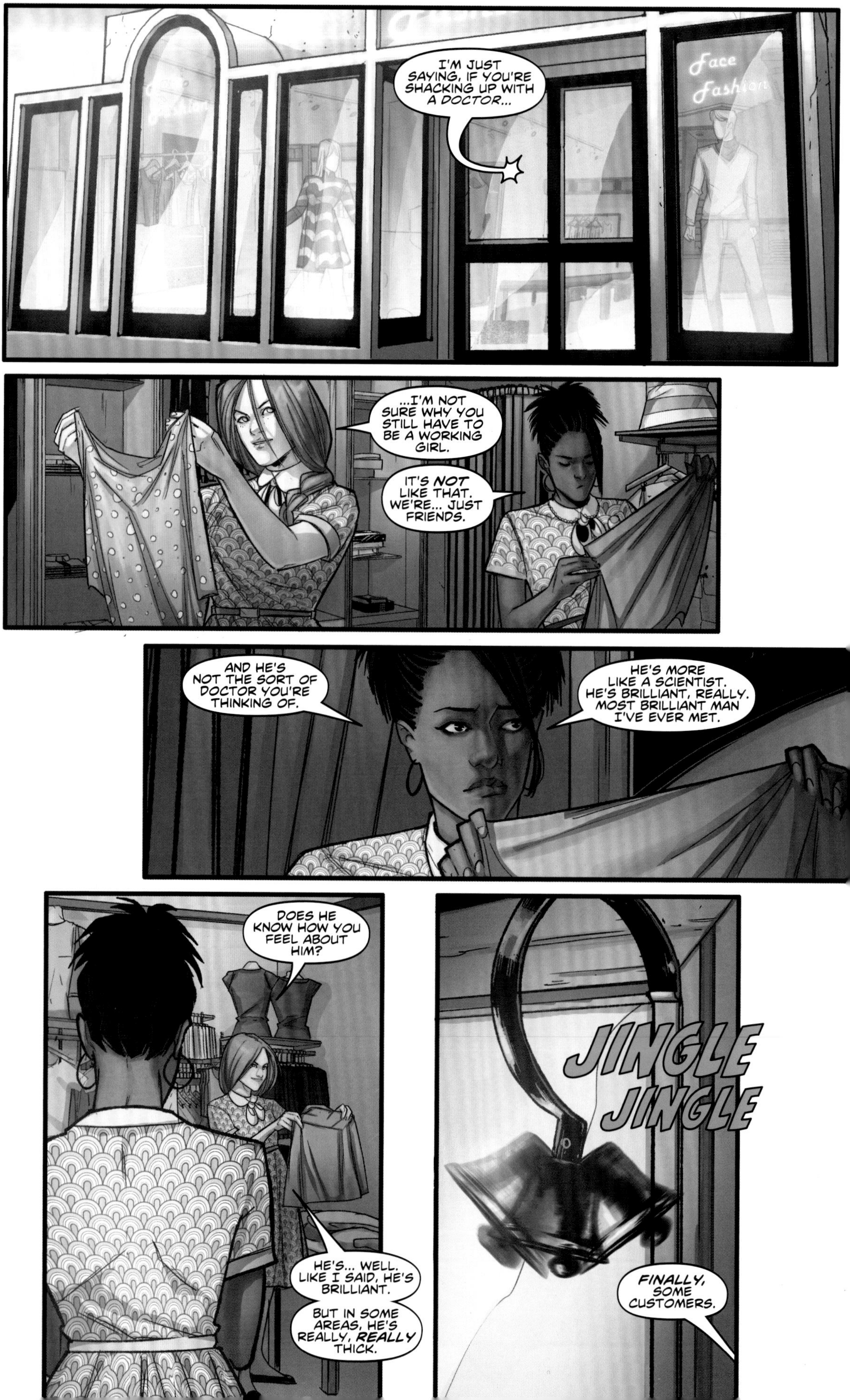
Face Fashion
I'M JUST SAYING, IF YOU'RE SHACKING UP WITH A DOCTOR...
...I'M NOT SURE WHY YOU STILL HAVE TO BE A WORKING GIRL.
IT'S NOT LIKE THAT. WE'RE... JUST FRIENDS.
AND HE'S NOT THE SORT OF DOCTOR YOU'RE THINKING OF.
HE'S MORE LIKE A SCIENTIST. HE'S BRILLIANT, REALLY. MOST BRILLIANT MAN I'VE EVER MET.
DOES HE KNOW HOW YOU FEEL ABOUT HIM?
HE'S... WELL. LIKE I SAID, HE'S BRILLIANT.
BUT IN SOME AREAS, HE'S REALLY, REALLY THICK.
JINGLE JINGLE
FINALLY, SOME CUSTOMERS.

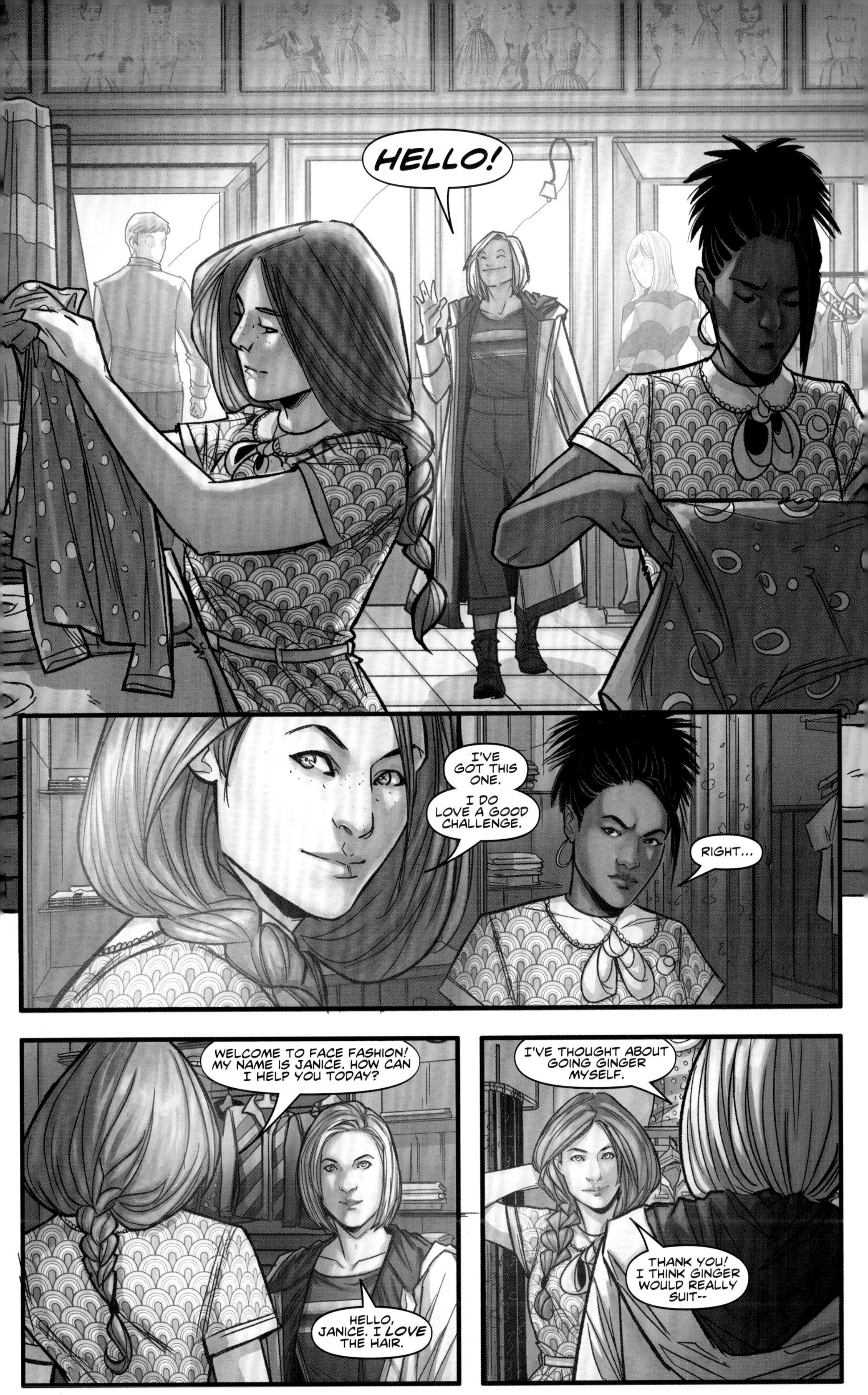
HELLO!
I'VE GOT THIS ONE.
I DO LOVE A GOOD CHALLENGE.
RIGHT...
WELCOME TO FACE FASHION! MY NAME IS JANICE. HOW CAN I HELP YOU TODAY?
HELLO, JANICE. I LOVE THE HAIR.
I'VE THOUGHT ABOUT GOING GINGER MYSELF.
THANK YOU! I THINK GINGER WOULD REALLY SUIT--

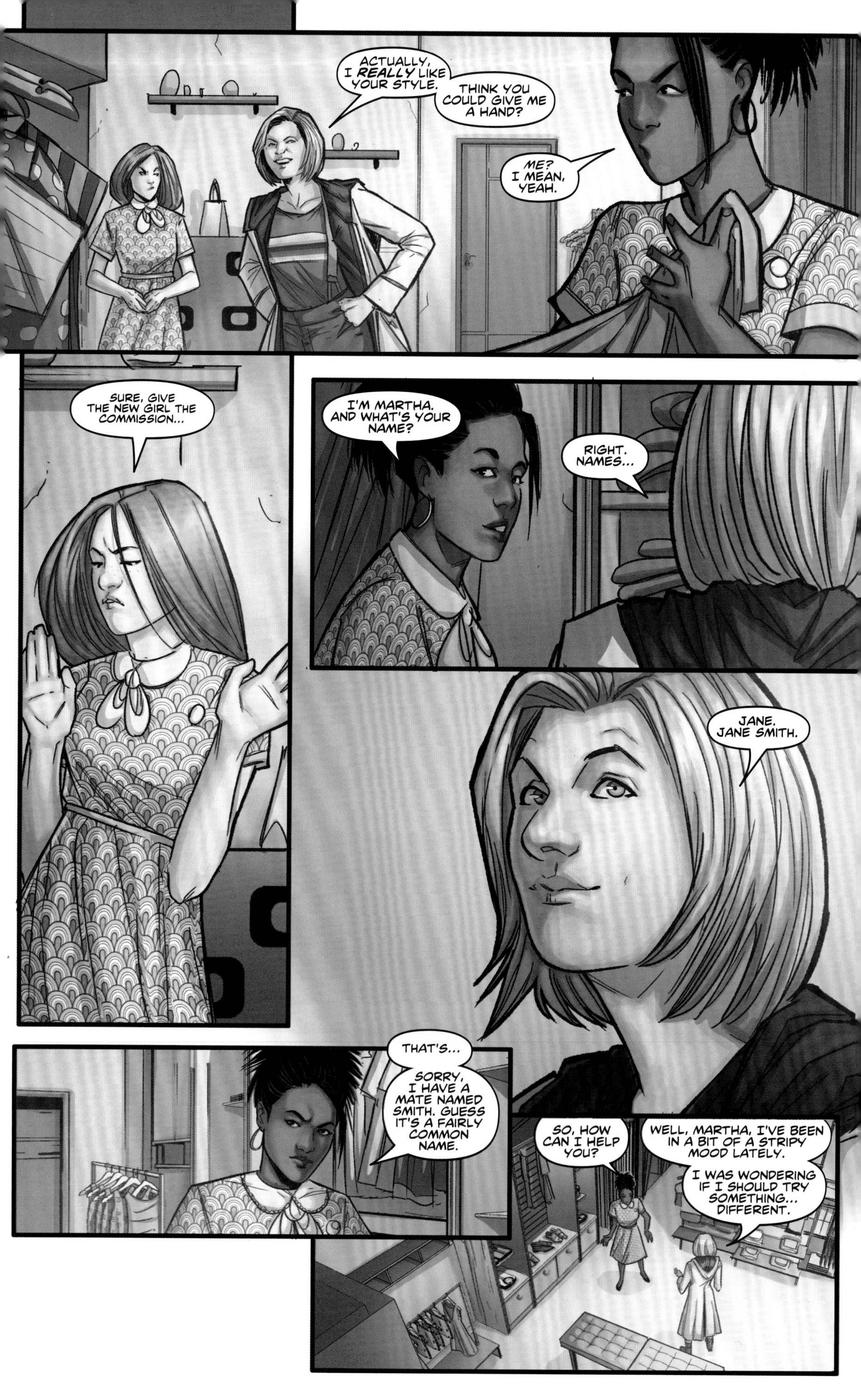
ACTUALLY, I REALLY LIKE YOUR STYLE.
THINK YOU COULD GIVE ME A HAND?
ME? I MEAN, YEAH.
SURE, GIVE THE NEW GIRL THE COMMISSION...
I'M MARTHA. AND WHAT'S YOUR NAME?
RIGHT. NAMES...
JANE. JANE SMITH.
THAT'S...
SORRY, I HAVE A MATE NAMED SMITH. GUESS IT'S A FAIRLY COMMON NAME.
SO, HOW CAN I HELP YOU?
WELL, MARTHA, I'VE BEEN IN A BIT OF A STRIPY MOOD LATELY.
I WAS WONDERING IF I SHOULD TRY SOMETHING... DIFFERENT.

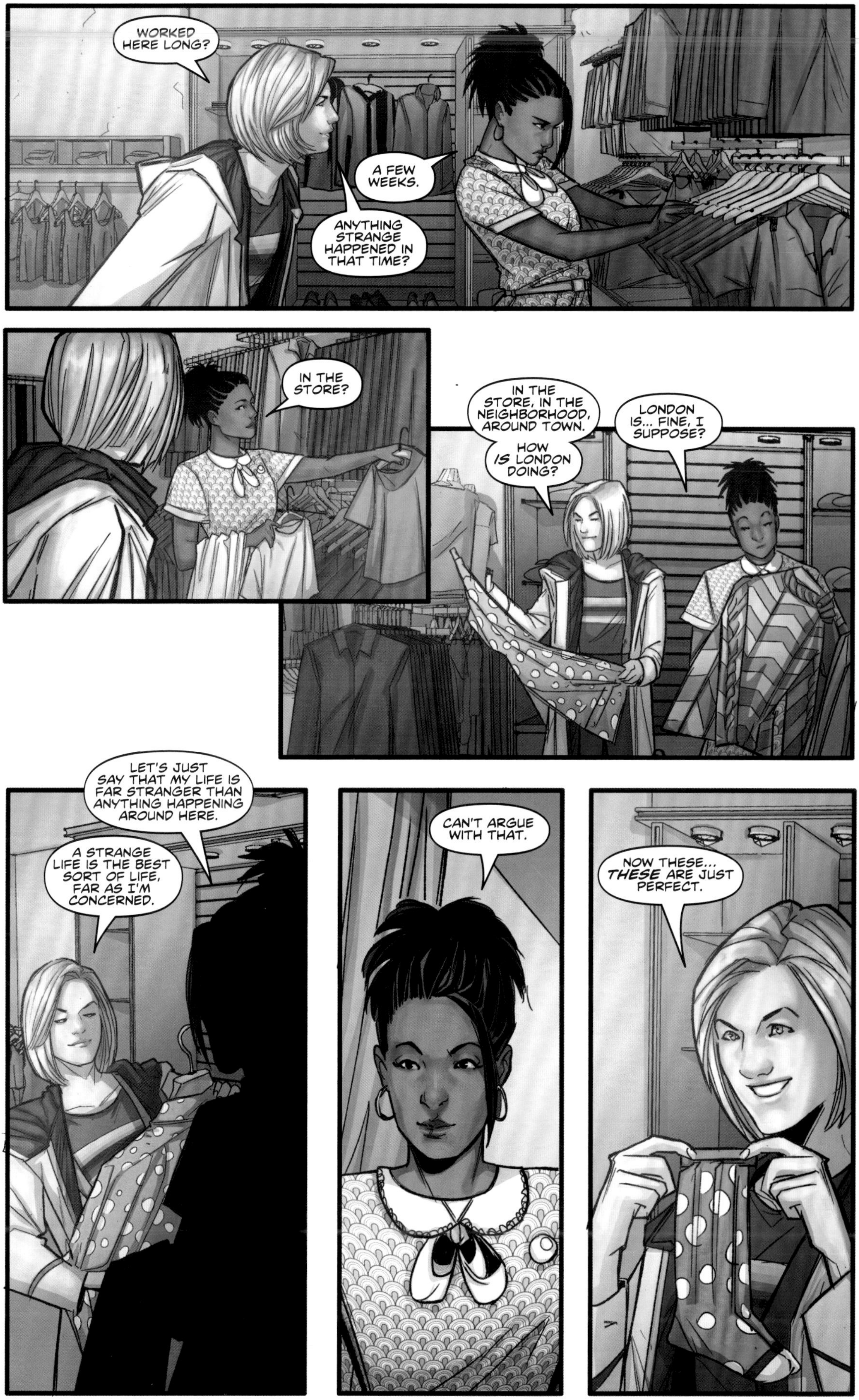
WORKED HERE LONG?
A FEW WEEKS.
ANYTHING STRANGE HAPPENED IN THAT TIME?
IN THE STORE?
IN THE STORE, IN THE NEIGHBORHOOD, AROUND TOWN.
HOW *IS* LONDON DOING?
LONDON IS... FINE, I SUPPOSE?
LET'S JUST SAY THAT MY LIFE IS FAR STRANGER THAN ANYTHING HAPPENING AROUND HERE.
A STRANGE LIFE IS THE BEST SORT OF LIFE, FAR AS I'M CONCERNED.
CAN'T ARGUE WITH THAT.
NOW THESE... *THESE* ARE JUST PERFECT.

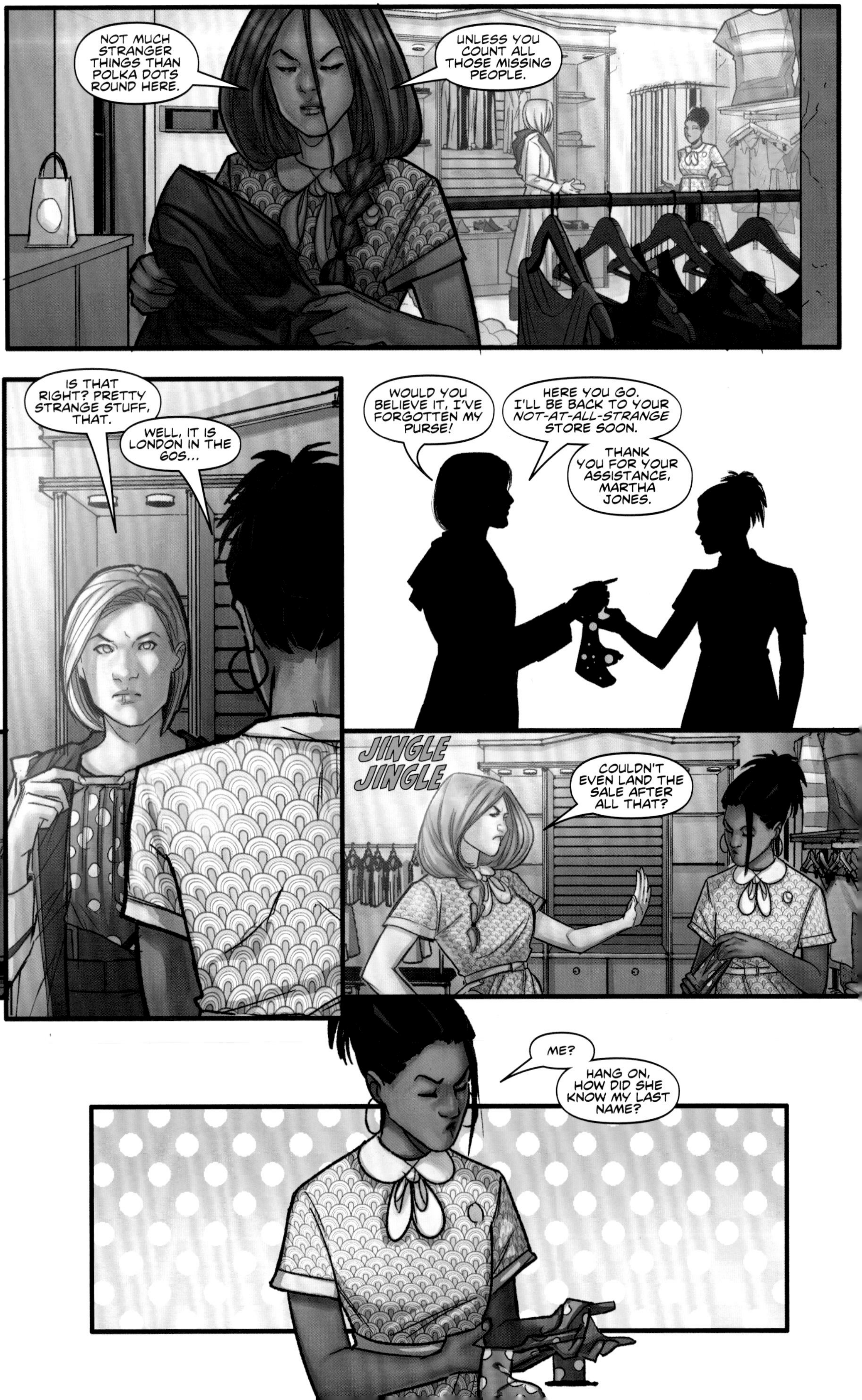
NOT MUCH STRANGER THINGS THAN POLKA DOTS ROUND HERE.
UNLESS YOU COUNT ALL THOSE MISSING PEOPLE.
IS THAT RIGHT? PRETTY STRANGE STUFF, THAT.
WELL, IT IS LONDON IN THE 60S...
WOULD YOU BELIEVE IT, I'VE FORGOTTEN MY PURSE!
HERE YOU GO. I'LL BE BACK TO YOUR *NOT-AT-ALL-STRANGE* STORE SOON.
THANK YOU FOR YOUR ASSISTANCE, MARTHA JONES.
JINGLE JINGLE
COULDN'T EVEN LAND THE SALE AFTER ALL THAT?
ME?
HANG ON, HOW DID SHE KNOW MY LAST NAME?

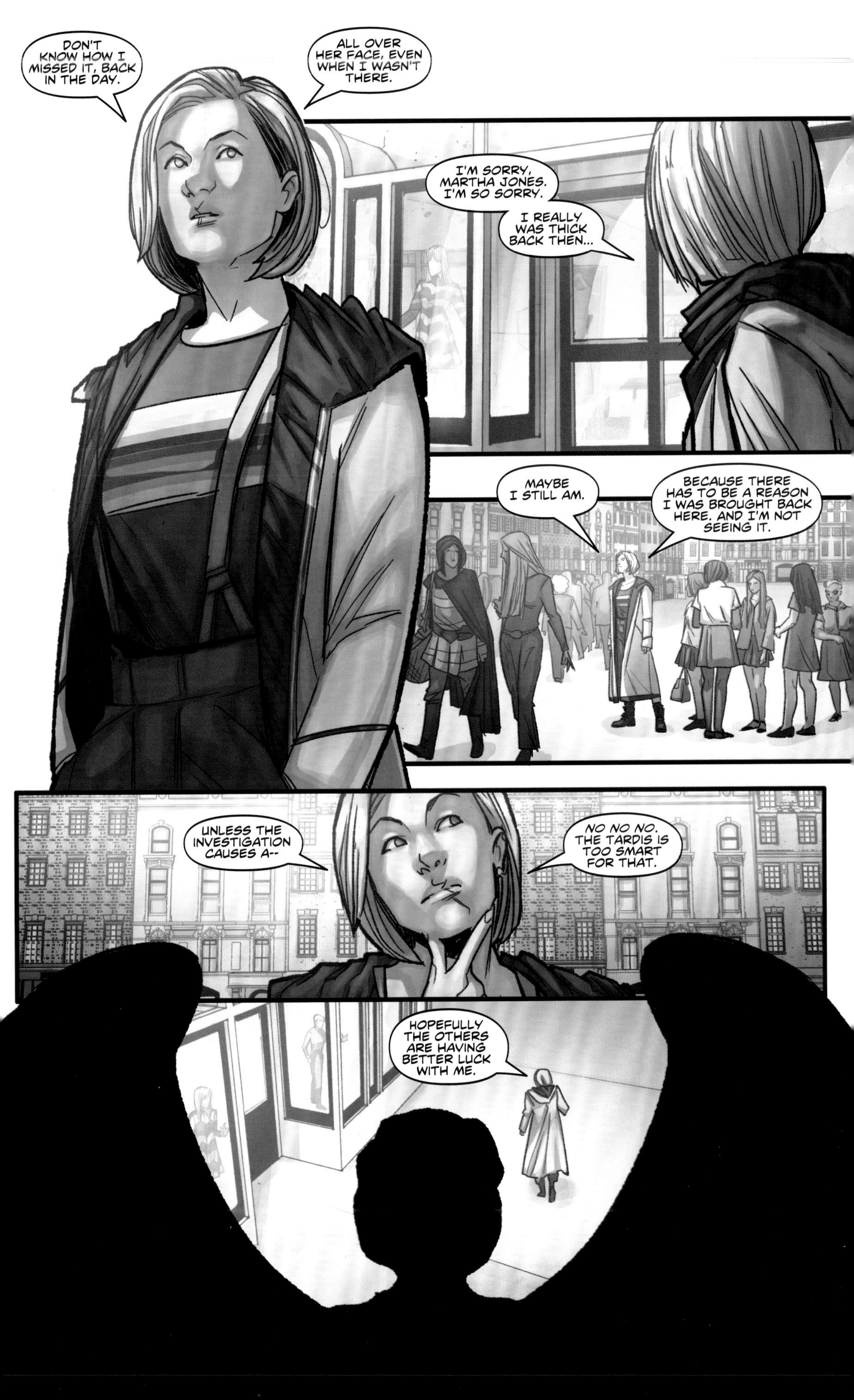
DON'T KNOW HOW I MISSED IT, BACK IN THE DAY.
ALL OVER HER FACE, EVEN WHEN I WASN'T THERE.
I'M SORRY, MARTHA JONES. I'M SO SORRY.
I REALLY WAS THICK BACK THEN...
MAYBE I STILL AM.
BECAUSE THERE HAS TO BE A REASON I WAS BROUGHT BACK HERE. AND I'M NOT SEEING IT.
UNLESS THE INVESTIGATION CAUSES A--
NO NO NO. THE TARDIS IS TOO SMART FOR THAT.
HOPEFULLY THE OTHERS ARE HAVING BETTER LUCK WITH ME.

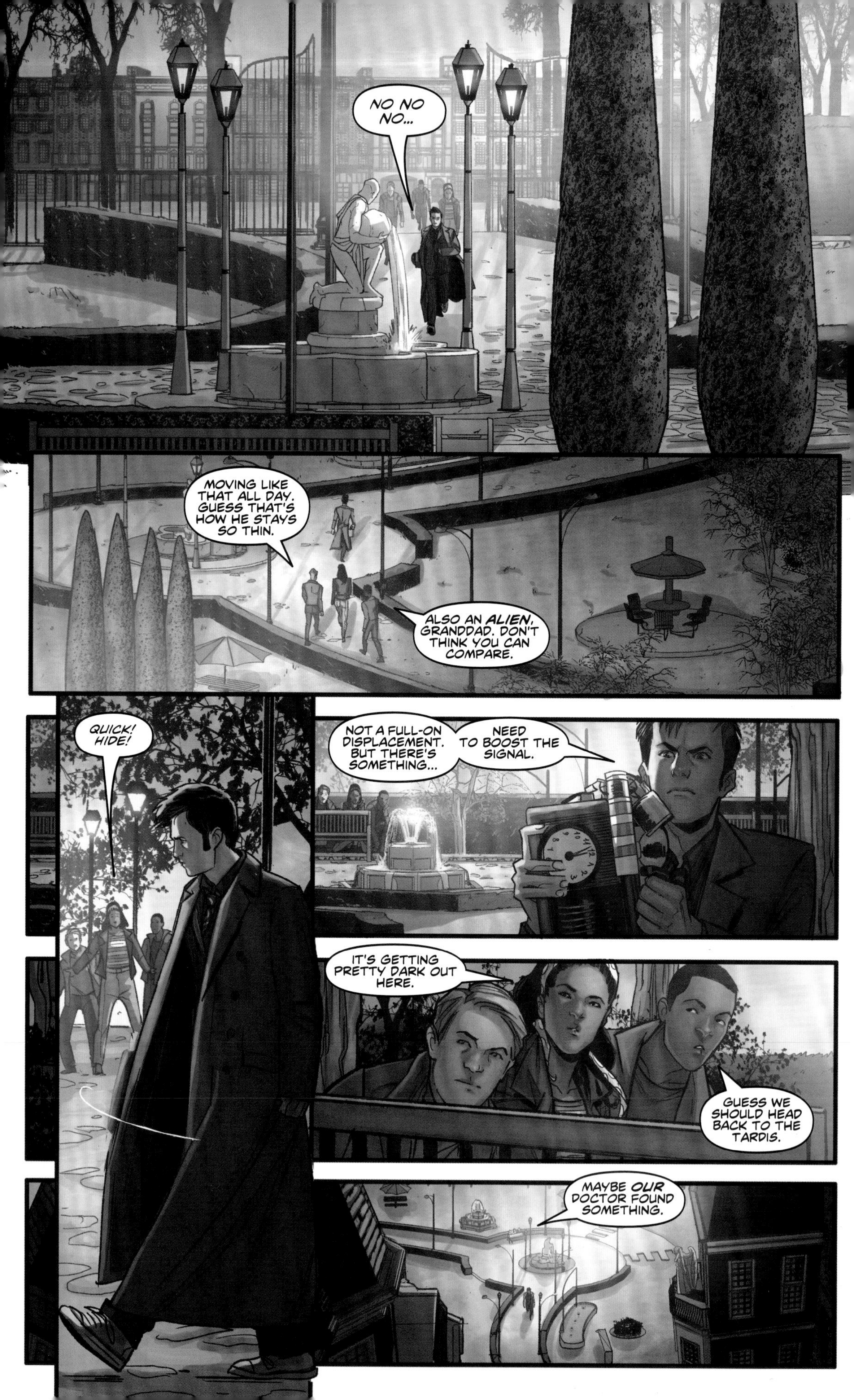
NO NO NO...
MOVING LIKE THAT ALL DAY. GUESS THAT'S HOW HE STAYS SO THIN.
ALSO AN ALIEN, GRANDDAD. DON'T THINK YOU CAN COMPARE.
QUICK! HIDE!
NOT A FULL-ON DISPLACEMENT. BUT THERE'S SOMETHING...
NEED TO BOOST THE SIGNAL.
IT'S GETTING PRETTY DARK OUT HERE.
GUESS WE SHOULD HEAD BACK TO THE TARDIS.
MAYBE OUR DOCTOR FOUND SOMETHING.

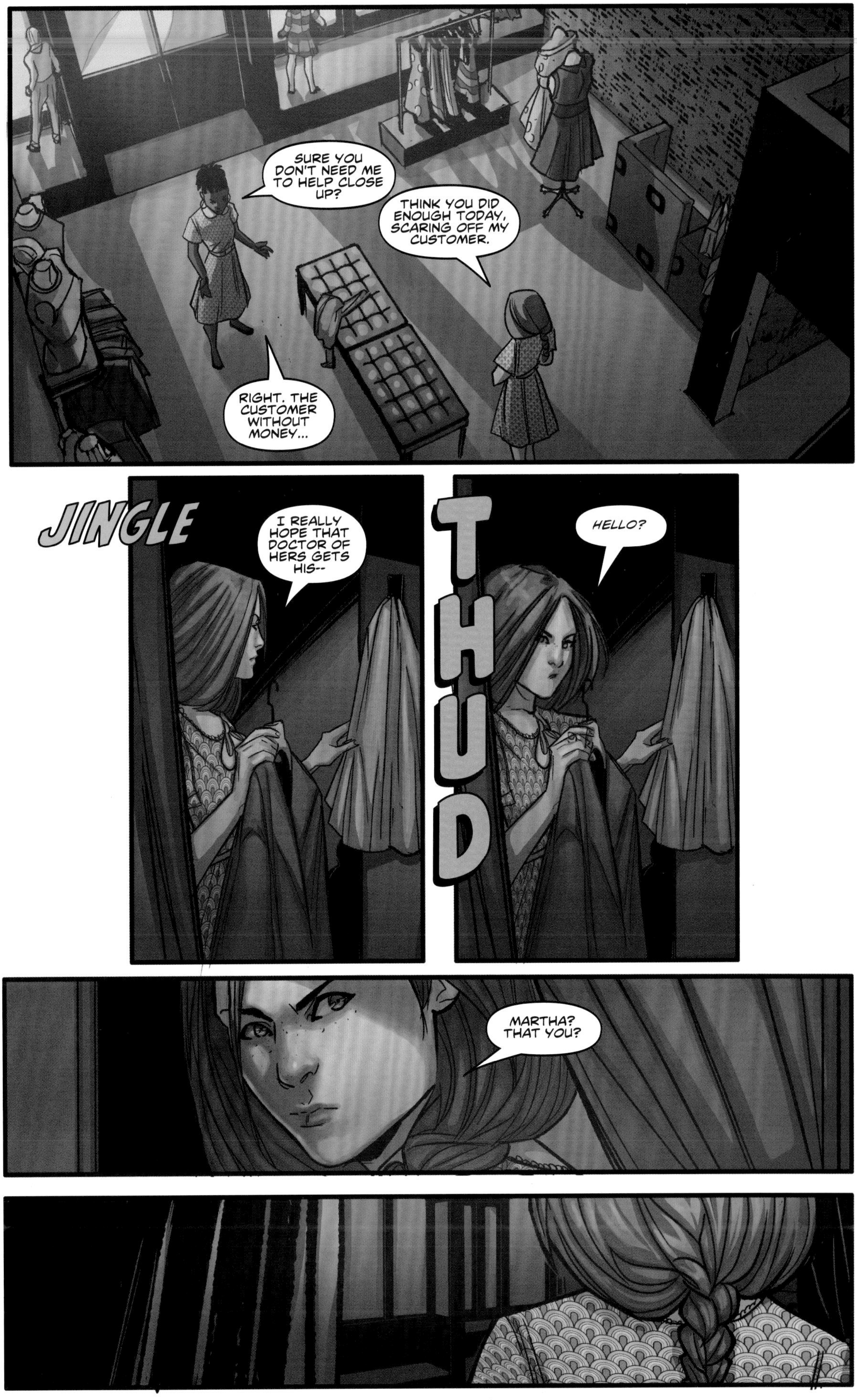

SURE YOU DON'T NEED ME TO HELP CLOSE UP?
THINK YOU DID ENOUGH TODAY, SCARING OFF MY CUSTOMER.
RIGHT. THE CUSTOMER WITHOUT MONEY...
JINGLE
I REALLY HOPE THAT DOCTOR OF HERS GETS HIS--
THUD
HELLO?
MARTHA? THAT YOU?

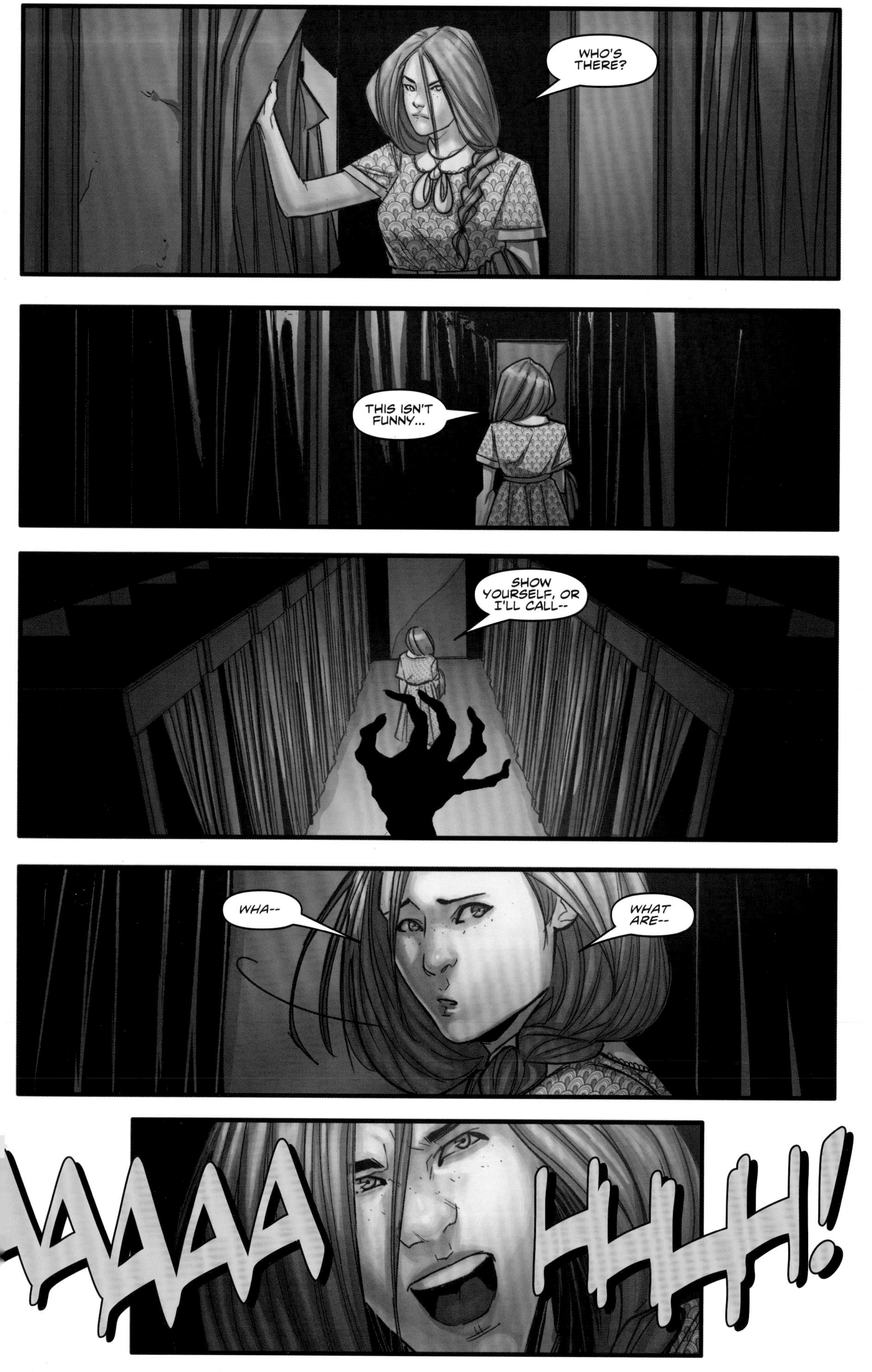
WHO'S THERE?
THIS ISN'T FUNNY...
SHOW YOURSELF, OR I'LL CALL--
WHA--
WHAT ARE--
AAAAHHHH!

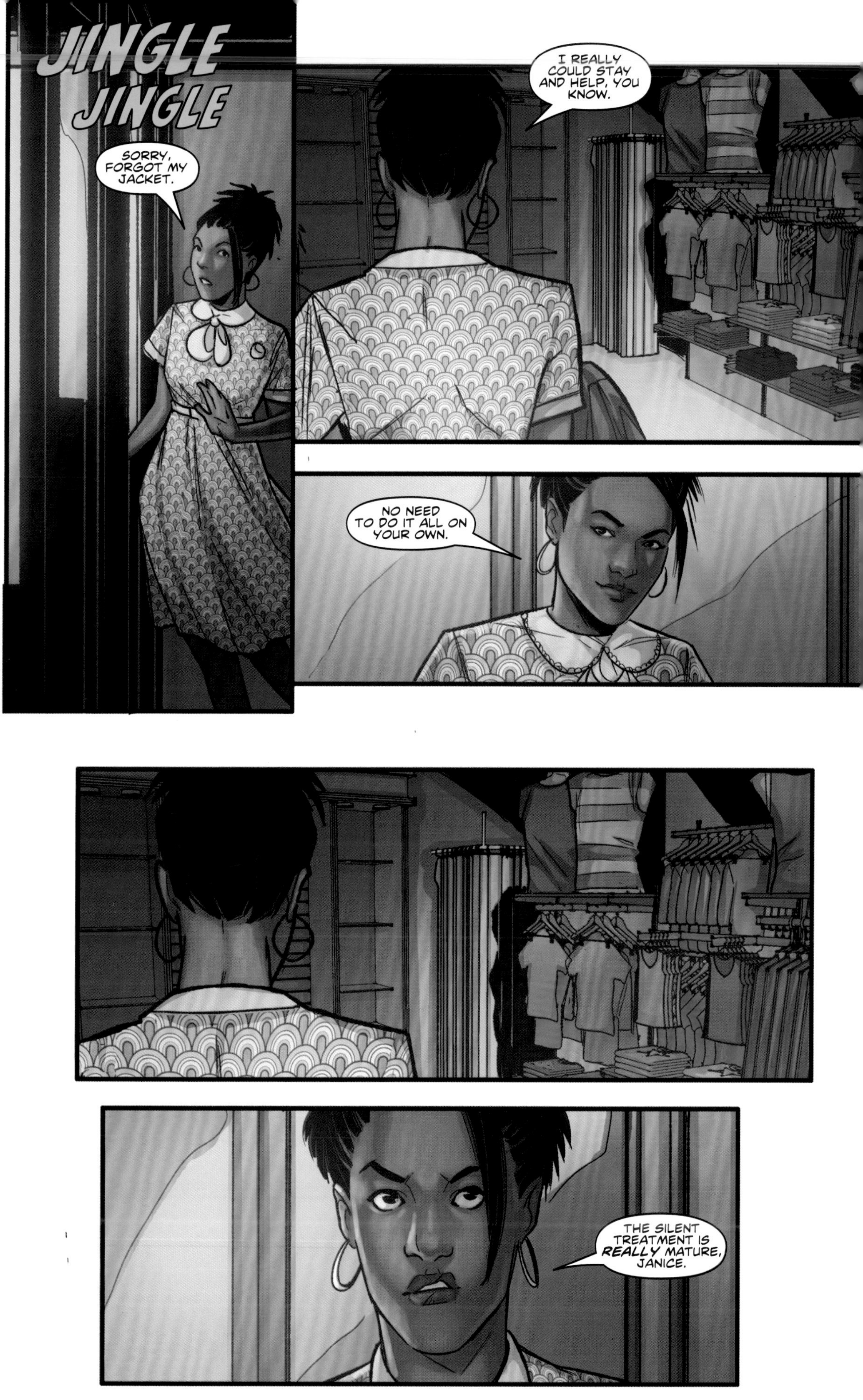
JINGLE JINGLE
SORRY, FORGOT MY JACKET.
I REALLY COULD STAY AND HELP, YOU KNOW.
NO NEED TO DO IT ALL ON YOUR OWN.
THE SILENT TREATMENT IS REALLY MATURE, JANICE.

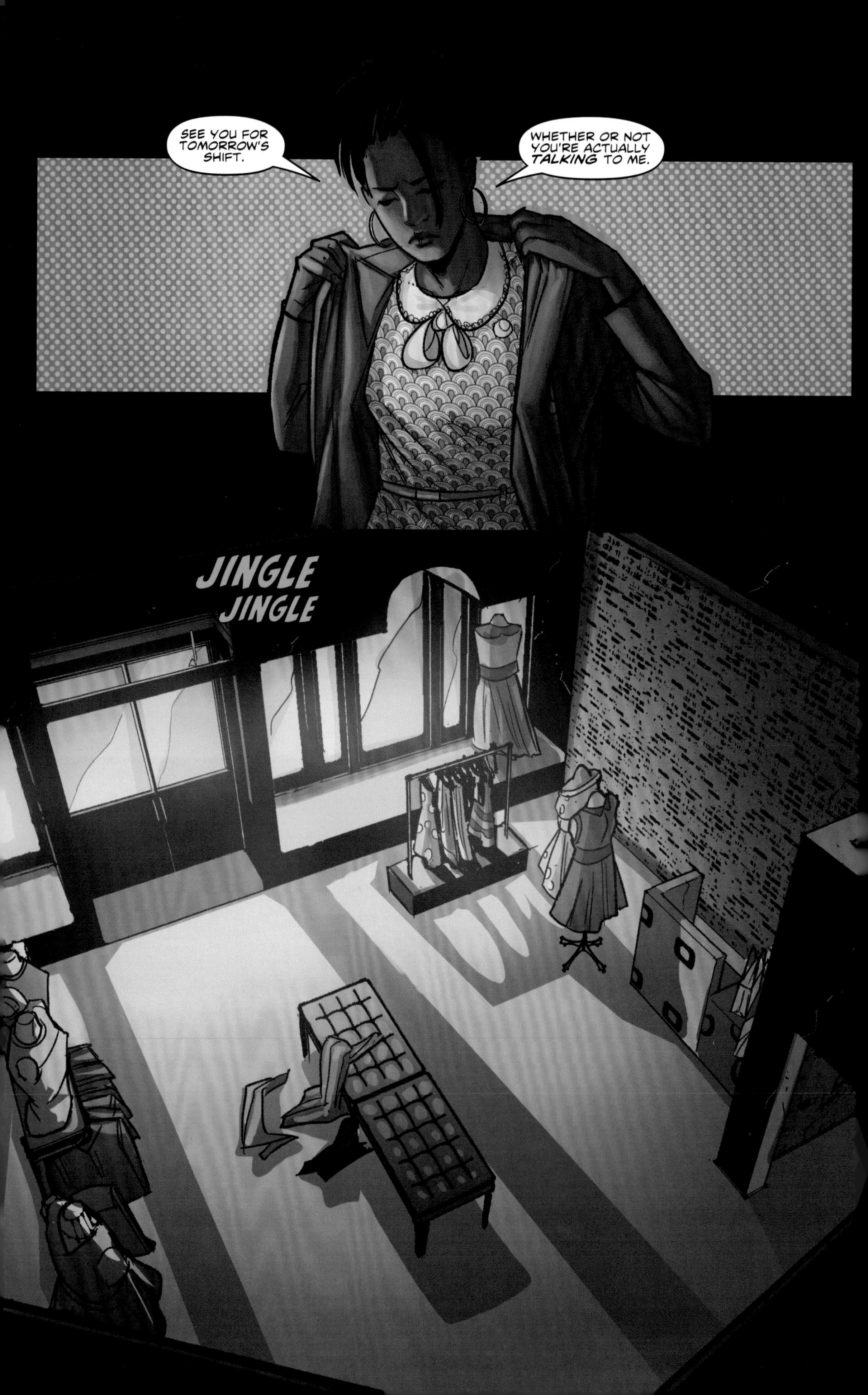
SEE YOU FOR TOMORROW'S SHIFT.
WHETHER OR NOT YOU'RE ACTUALLY *TALKING* TO ME.
JINGLE JINGLE

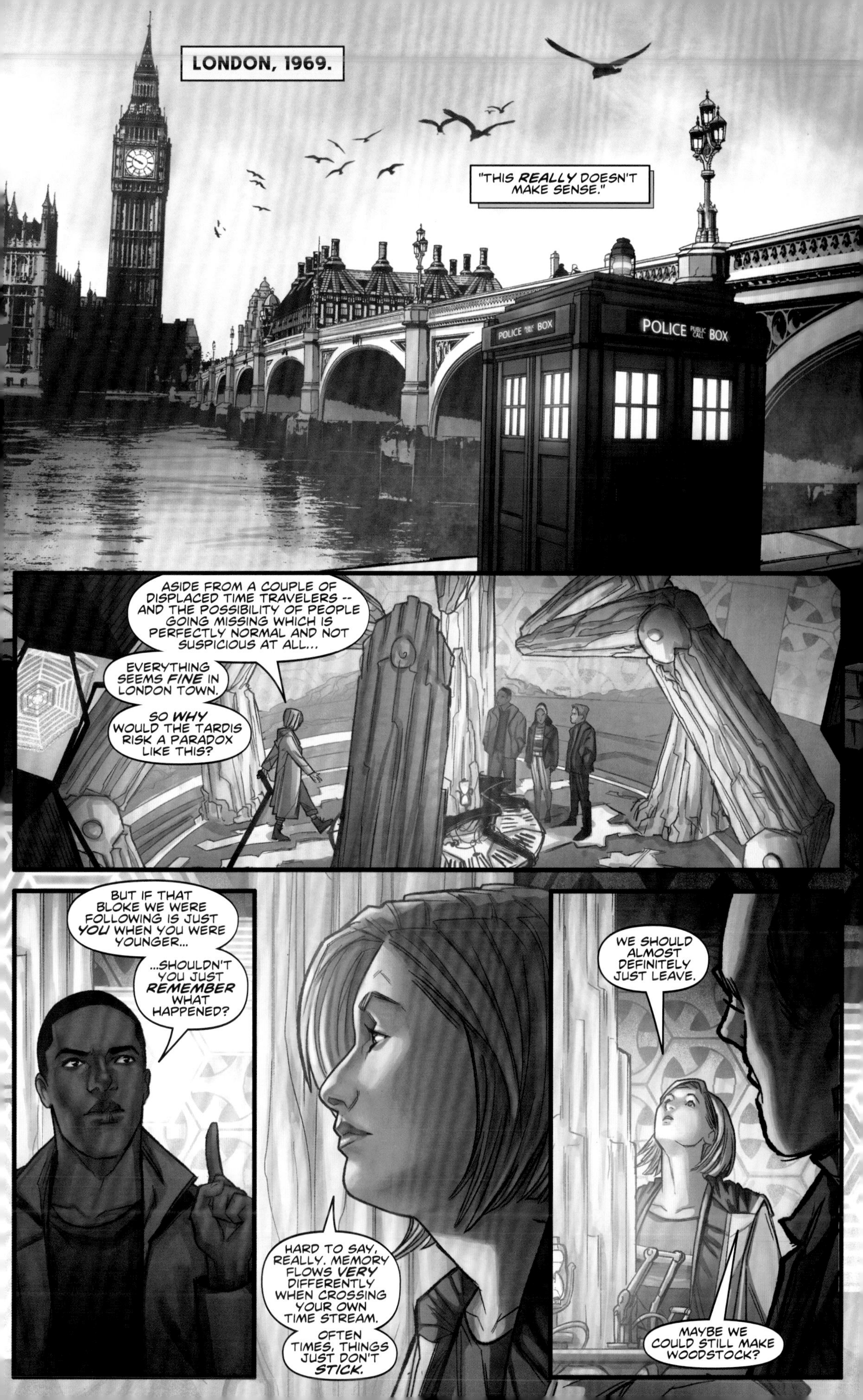
LONDON, 1969.
"THIS REALLY DOESN'T MAKE SENSE."
POLICE PUBLIC CALL BOX
POLICE PUBLIC CALL BOX
ASIDE FROM A COUPLE OF DISPLACED TIME TRAVELERS -- AND THE POSSIBILITY OF PEOPLE GOING MISSING WHICH IS PERFECTLY NORMAL AND NOT SUSPICIOUS AT ALL...
EVERYTHING SEEMS FINE IN LONDON TOWN.
SO WHY WOULD THE TARDIS RISK A PARADOX LIKE THIS?
BUT IF THAT BLOKE WE WERE FOLLOWING IS JUST YOU WHEN YOU WERE YOUNGER...
...SHOULDN'T YOU JUST REMEMBER WHAT HAPPENED?
HARD TO SAY, REALLY. MEMORY FLOWS VERY DIFFERENTLY WHEN CROSSING YOUR OWN TIME STREAM.
OFTEN TIMES, THINGS JUST DON'T STICK.
WE SHOULD ALMOST DEFINITELY JUST LEAVE.
MAYBE WE COULD STILL MAKE WOODSTOCK?

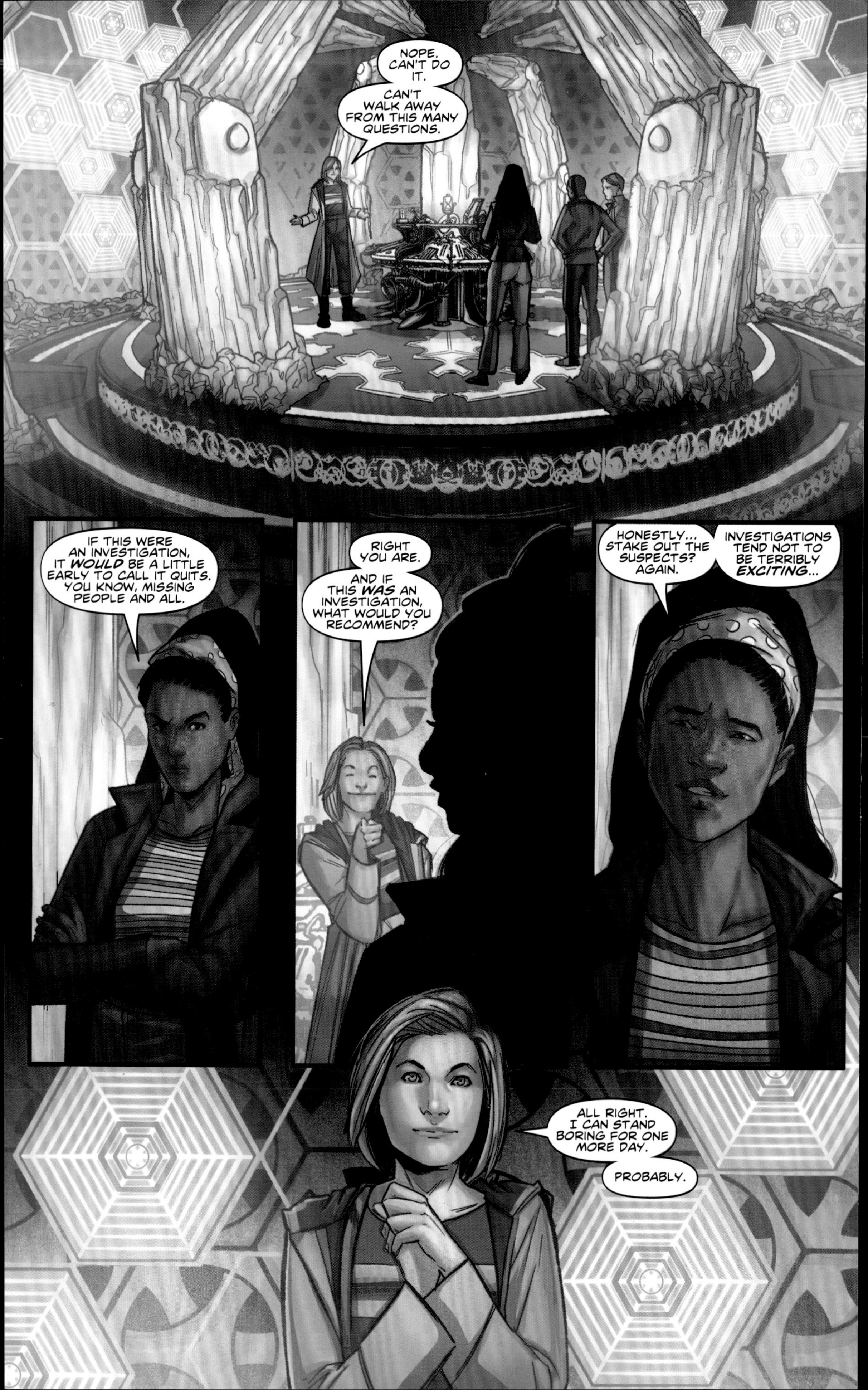
NOPE. CAN'T DO IT.
CAN'T WALK AWAY FROM THIS MANY QUESTIONS.
IF THIS WERE AN INVESTIGATION, IT WOULD BE A LITTLE EARLY TO CALL IT QUITS. YOU KNOW, MISSING PEOPLE AND ALL.
RIGHT YOU ARE.
AND IF THIS WAS AN INVESTIGATION, WHAT WOULD YOU RECOMMEND?
HONESTLY... STAKE OUT THE SUSPECTS? AGAIN.
INVESTIGATIONS TEND NOT TO BE TERRIBLY EXCITING...
ALL RIGHT. I CAN STAND BORING FOR ONE MORE DAY.
PROBABLY.

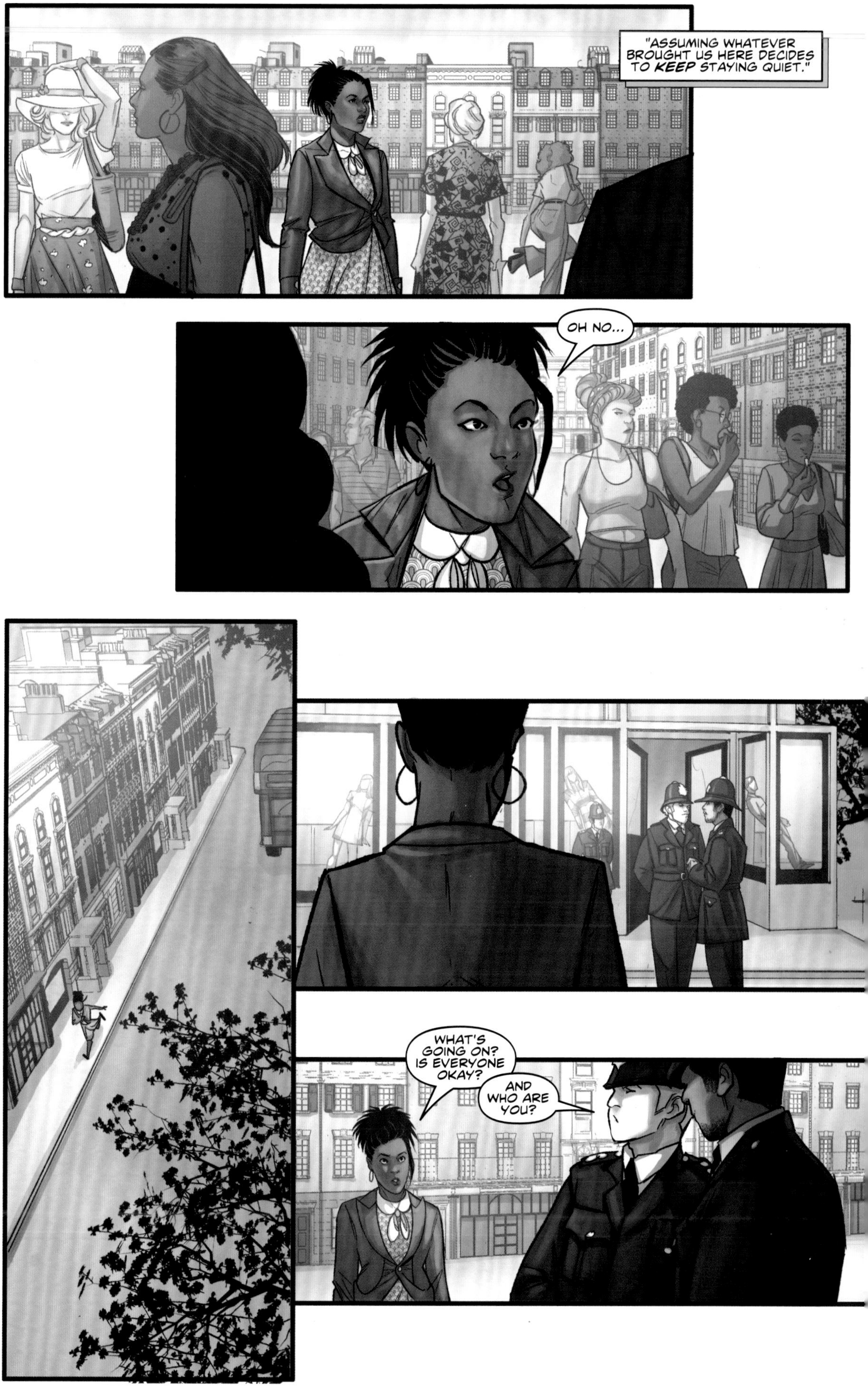
"ASSUMING WHATEVER BROUGHT US HERE DECIDES TO KEEP STAYING QUIET."
OH NO...
WHAT'S GOING ON? IS EVERYONE OKAY?
AND WHO ARE YOU?

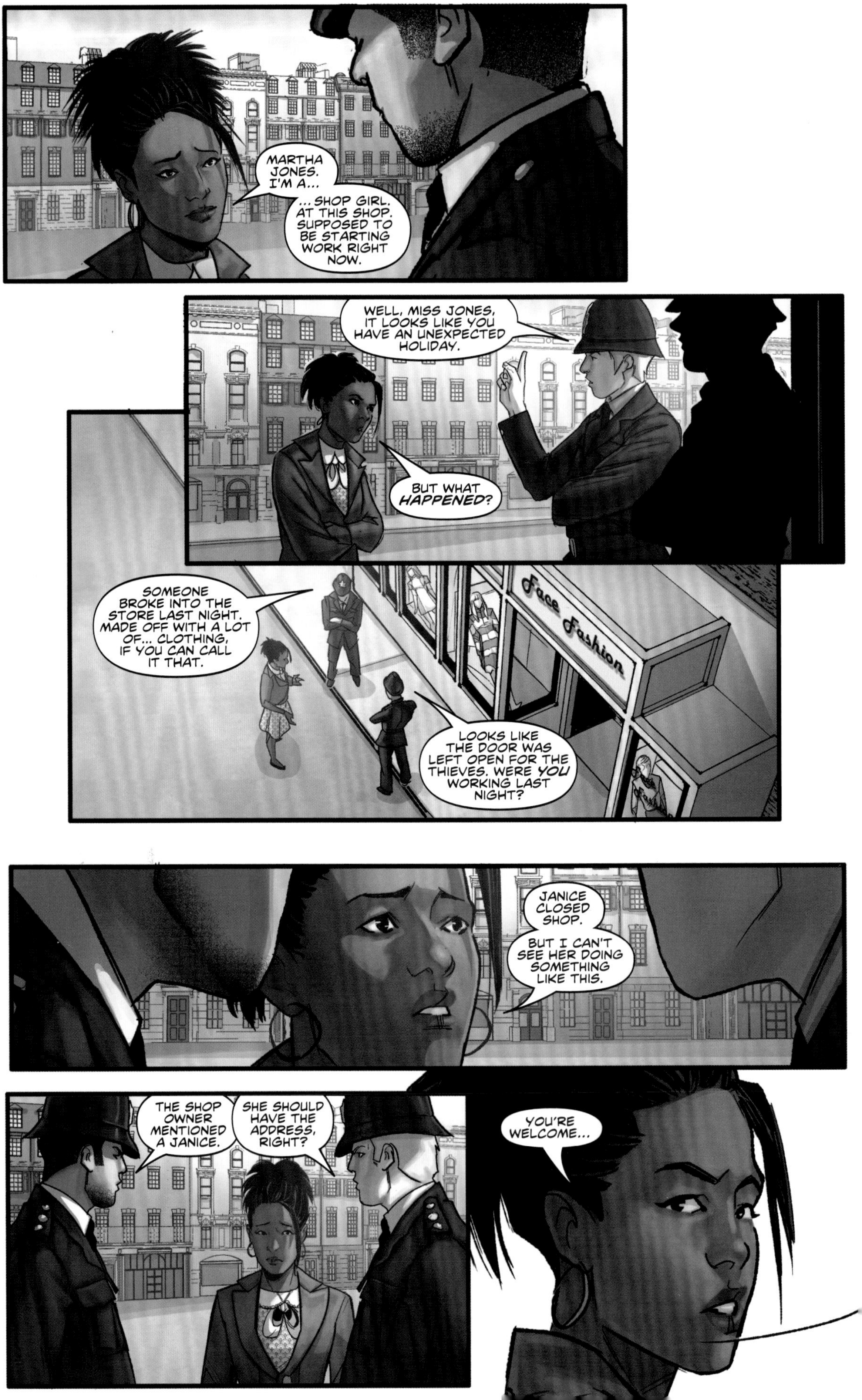
MARTHA JONES. I'M A...
...SHOP GIRL. AT THIS SHOP. SUPPOSED TO BE STARTING WORK RIGHT NOW.
WELL, MISS JONES, IT LOOKS LIKE YOU HAVE AN UNEXPECTED HOLIDAY.
BUT WHAT *HAPPENED*?
SOMEONE BROKE INTO THE STORE LAST NIGHT. MADE OFF WITH A LOT OF... CLOTHING, IF YOU CAN CALL IT THAT.
Face Fashion
LOOKS LIKE THE DOOR WAS LEFT OPEN FOR THE THIEVES. WERE *YOU* WORKING LAST NIGHT?
JANICE CLOSED SHOP.
BUT I CAN'T SEE HER DOING SOMETHING LIKE THIS.
THE SHOP OWNER MENTIONED A JANICE.
SHE SHOULD HAVE THE ADDRESS, RIGHT?
YOU'RE WELCOME...

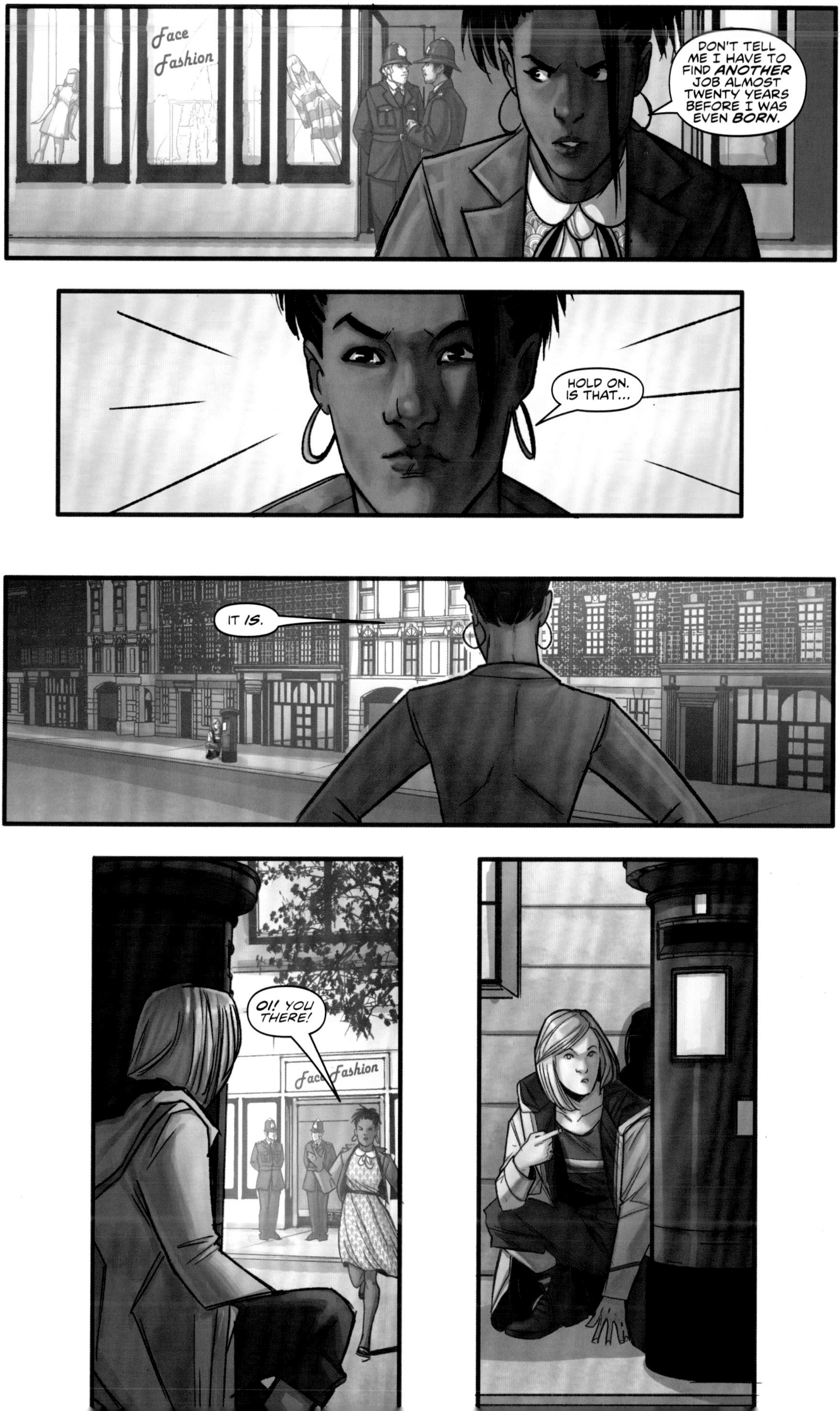
Face Fashion
DON'T TELL ME I HAVE TO FIND ANOTHER JOB ALMOST TWENTY YEARS BEFORE I WAS EVEN BORN.
HOLD ON. IS THAT...
IT IS.
OI! YOU THERE!
Face Fashion

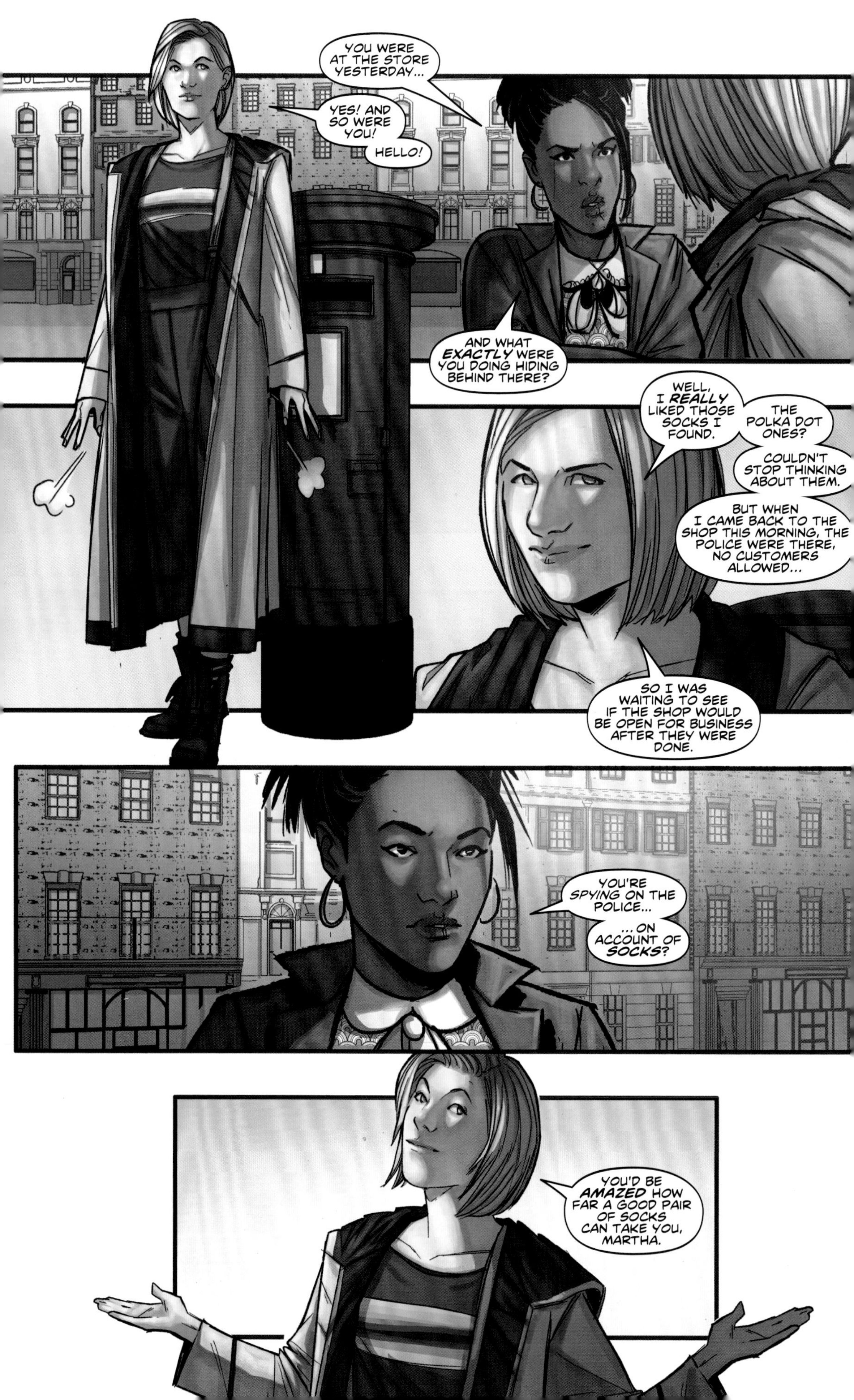
YOU WERE AT THE STORE YESTERDAY...
YES! AND SO WERE YOU!
HELLO!
AND WHAT EXACTLY WERE YOU DOING HIDING BEHIND THERE?
WELL, I REALLY LIKED THOSE SOCKS I FOUND.
THE POLKA DOT ONES?
COULDN'T STOP THINKING ABOUT THEM.
BUT WHEN I CAME BACK TO THE SHOP THIS MORNING, THE POLICE WERE THERE, NO CUSTOMERS ALLOWED...
SO I WAS WAITING TO SEE IF THE SHOP WOULD BE OPEN FOR BUSINESS AFTER THEY WERE DONE.
YOU'RE SPYING ON THE POLICE...
...ON ACCOUNT OF SOCKS?
YOU'D BE AMAZED HOW FAR A GOOD PAIR OF SOCKS CAN TAKE YOU, MARTHA.

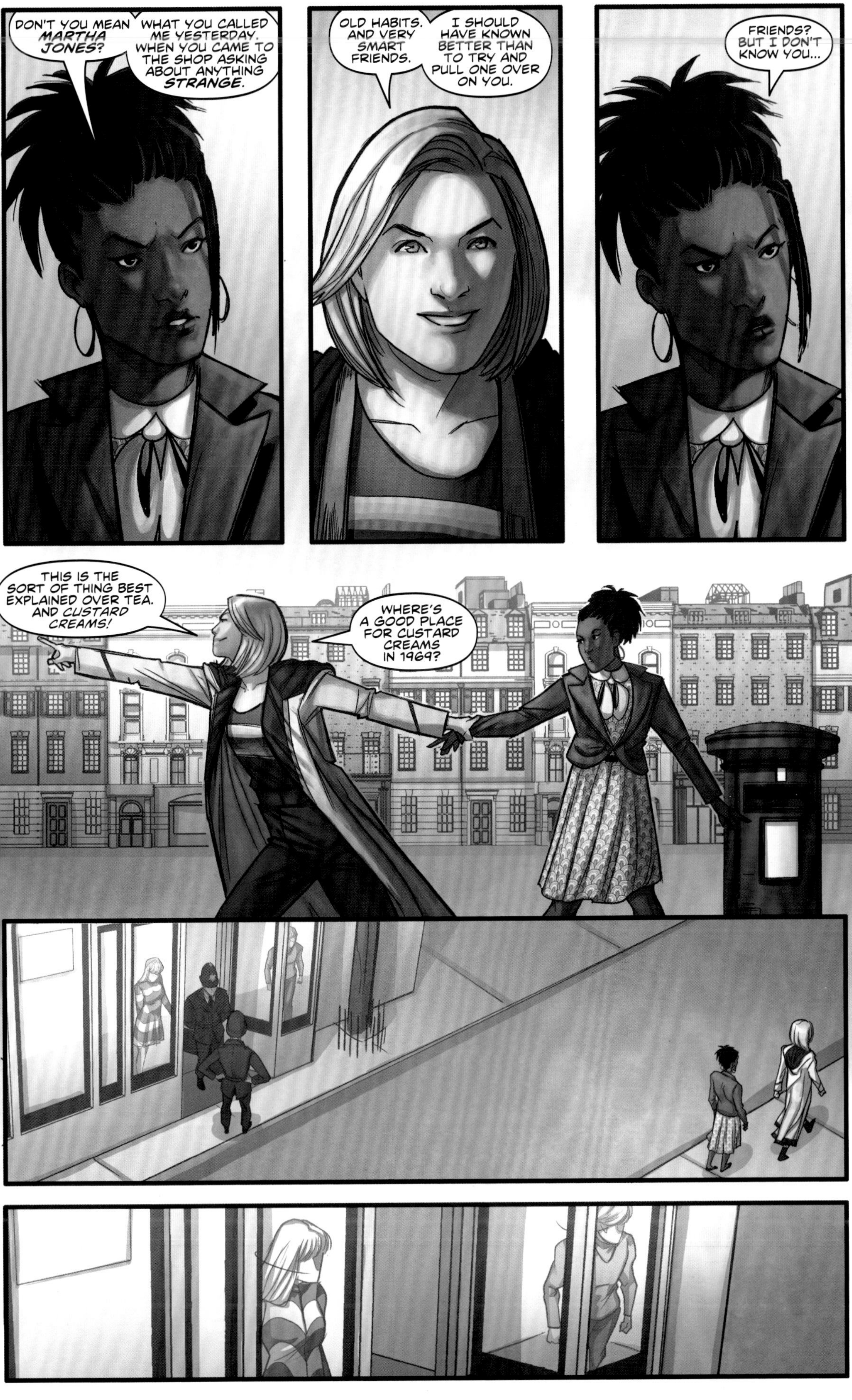
DON'T YOU MEAN MARTHA JONES?
WHAT YOU CALLED ME YESTERDAY. WHEN YOU CAME TO THE SHOP ASKING ABOUT ANYTHING STRANGE.
OLD HABITS. AND VERY SMART FRIENDS.
I SHOULD HAVE KNOWN BETTER THAN TO TRY AND PULL ONE OVER ON YOU.
FRIENDS? BUT I DON'T KNOW YOU...
THIS IS THE SORT OF THING BEST EXPLAINED OVER TEA. AND CUSTARD CREAMS!
WHERE'S A GOOD PLACE FOR CUSTARD CREAMS IN 1969?

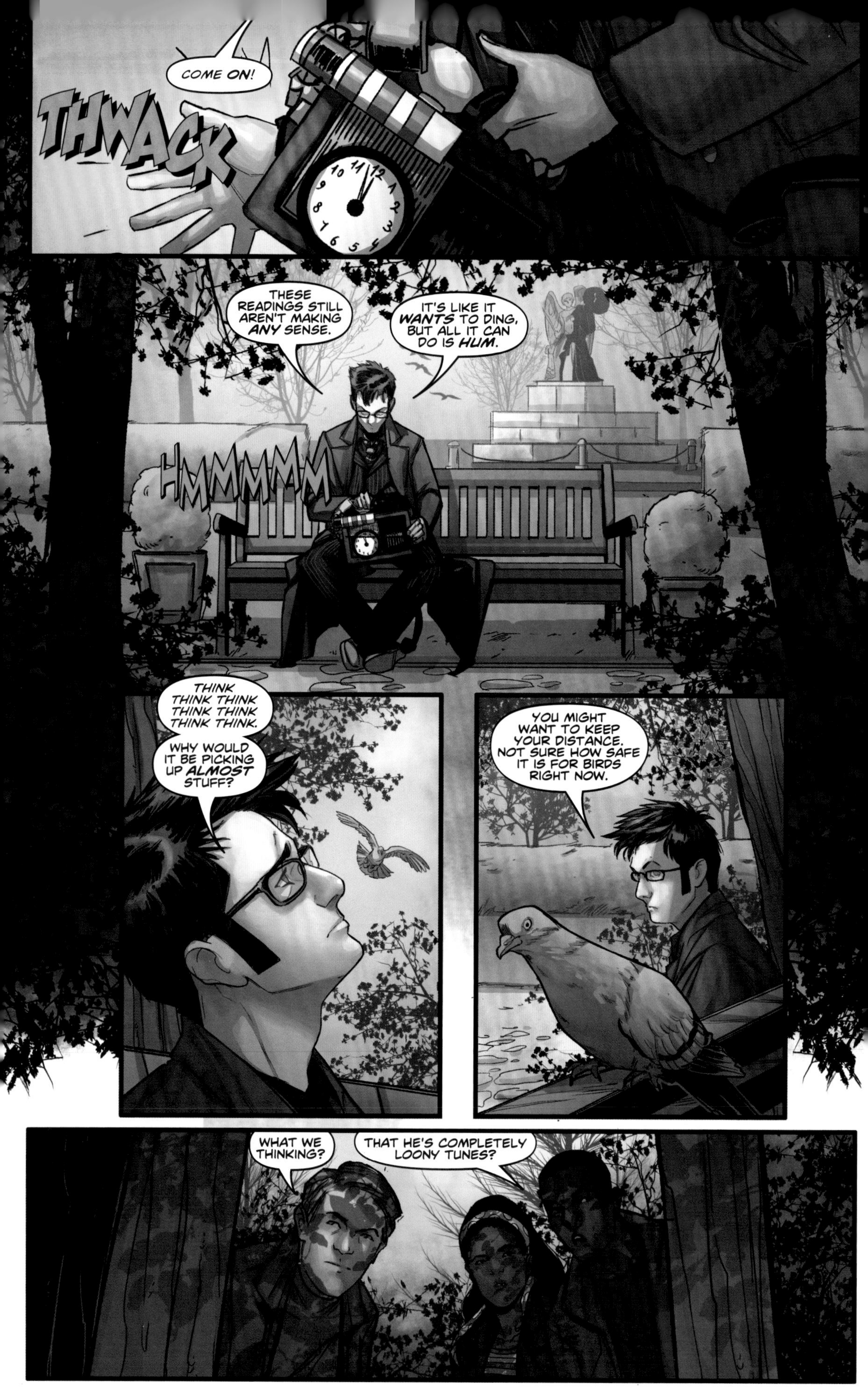
COME ON!
THWACK
THESE READINGS STILL AREN'T MAKING ANY SENSE.
IT'S LIKE IT WANTS TO DING, BUT ALL IT CAN DO IS HUM.
HMMMMM
THINK THINK THINK THINK THINK THINK THINK.
WHY WOULD IT BE PICKING UP ALMOST STUFF?
YOU MIGHT WANT TO KEEP YOUR DISTANCE. NOT SURE HOW SAFE IT IS FOR BIRDS RIGHT NOW.
WHAT WE THINKING?
THAT HE'S COMPLETELY LOONY TUNES?

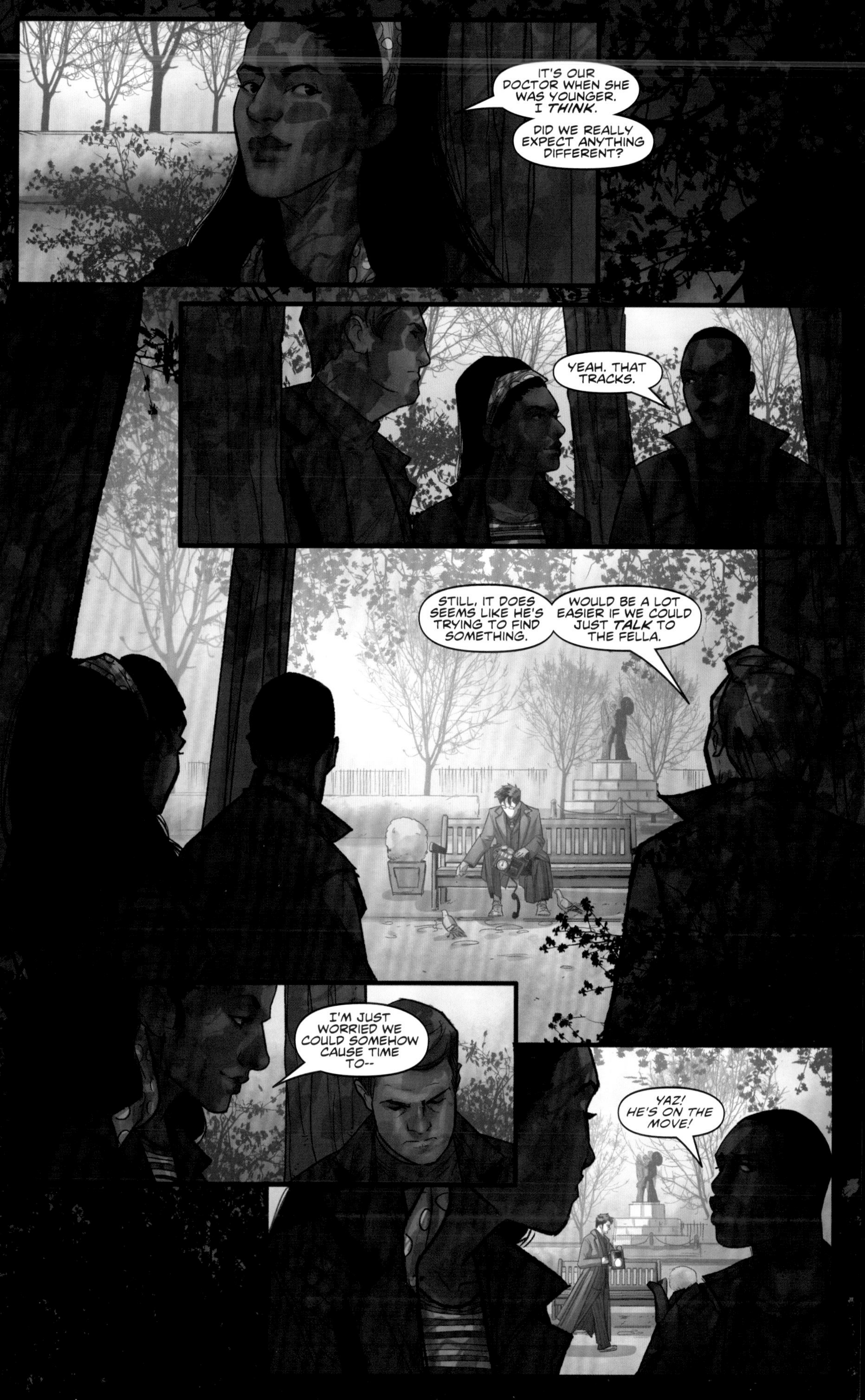
IT'S OUR DOCTOR WHEN SHE WAS YOUNGER. I *THINK*.
DID WE REALLY EXPECT ANYTHING DIFFERENT?
YEAH. THAT TRACKS.
STILL, IT DOES SEEMS LIKE HE'S TRYING TO FIND SOMETHING.
WOULD BE A LOT EASIER IF WE COULD JUST *TALK* TO THE FELLA.
I'M JUST WORRIED WE COULD SOMEHOW CAUSE TIME TO--
YAZ! HE'S ON THE MOVE!

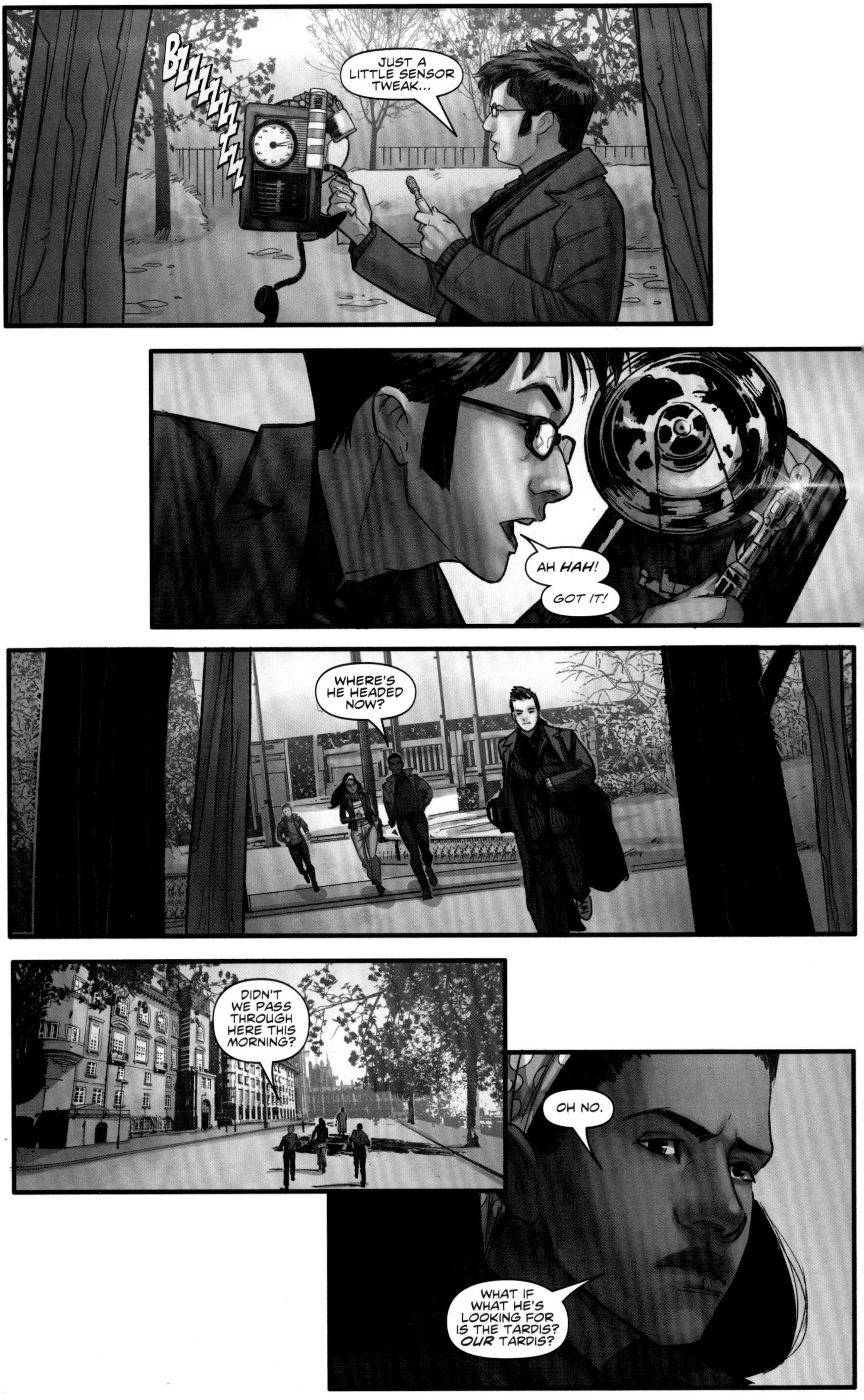
BZZZZZZZ
JUST A LITTLE SENSOR TWEAK...
AH *HAH*!
GOT IT!
WHERE'S HE HEADED NOW?
DIDN'T WE PASS THROUGH HERE THIS MORNING?
OH NO.
WHAT IF WHAT HE'S LOOKING FOR IS THE TARDIS? *OUR* TARDIS?

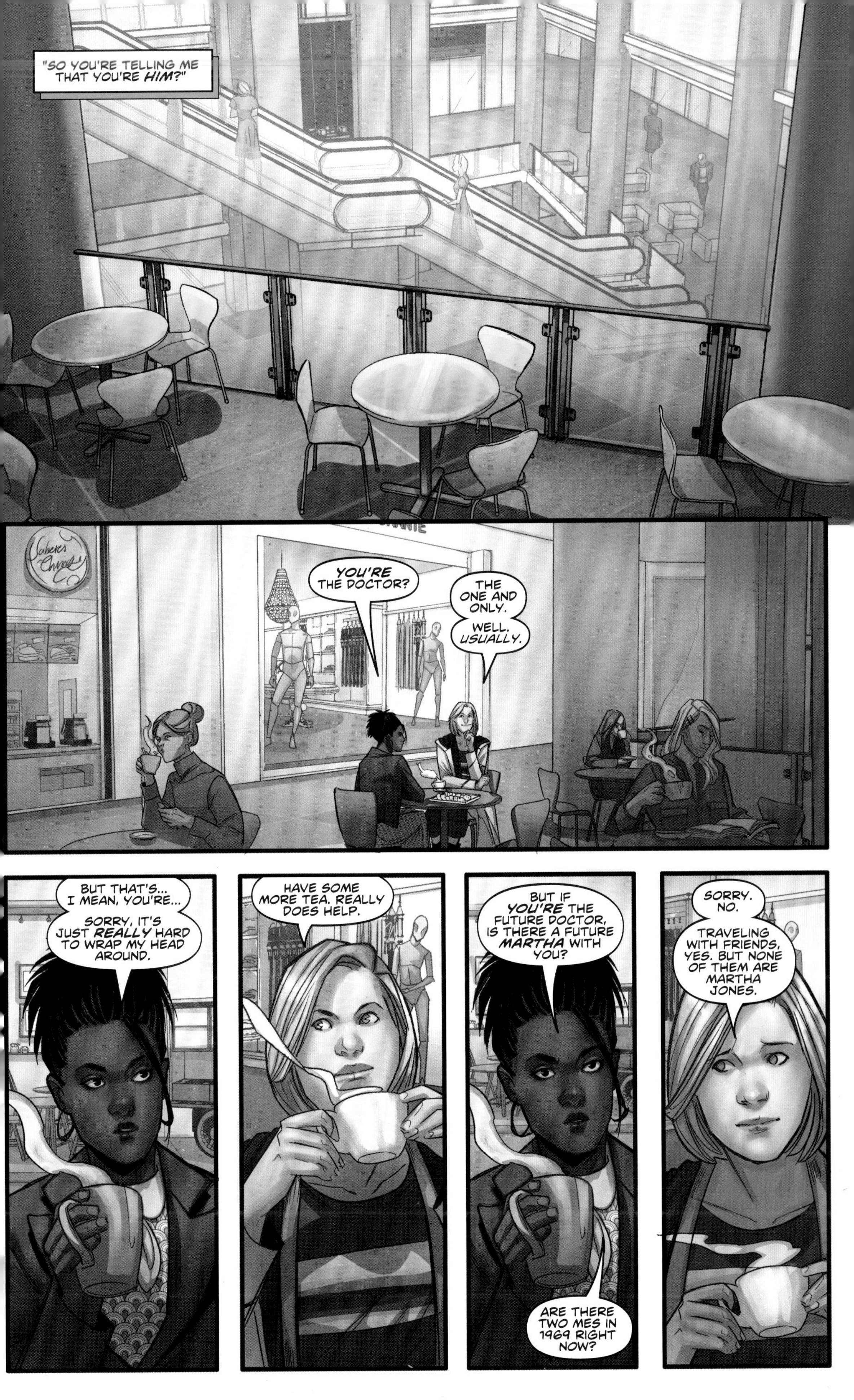
"SO YOU'RE TELLING ME THAT YOU'RE *HIM*?"
YOU'RE THE DOCTOR?
THE ONE AND ONLY.
WELL. *USUALLY.*
BUT THAT'S... I MEAN, YOU'RE...
SORRY, IT'S JUST *REALLY* HARD TO WRAP MY HEAD AROUND.
HAVE SOME MORE TEA. REALLY DOES HELP.
BUT IF *YOU'RE* THE FUTURE DOCTOR, IS THERE A FUTURE *MARTHA* WITH YOU?
ARE THERE TWO MES IN 1969 RIGHT NOW?
SORRY. NO.
TRAVELING WITH FRIENDS, YES. BUT NONE OF THEM ARE MARTHA JONES.

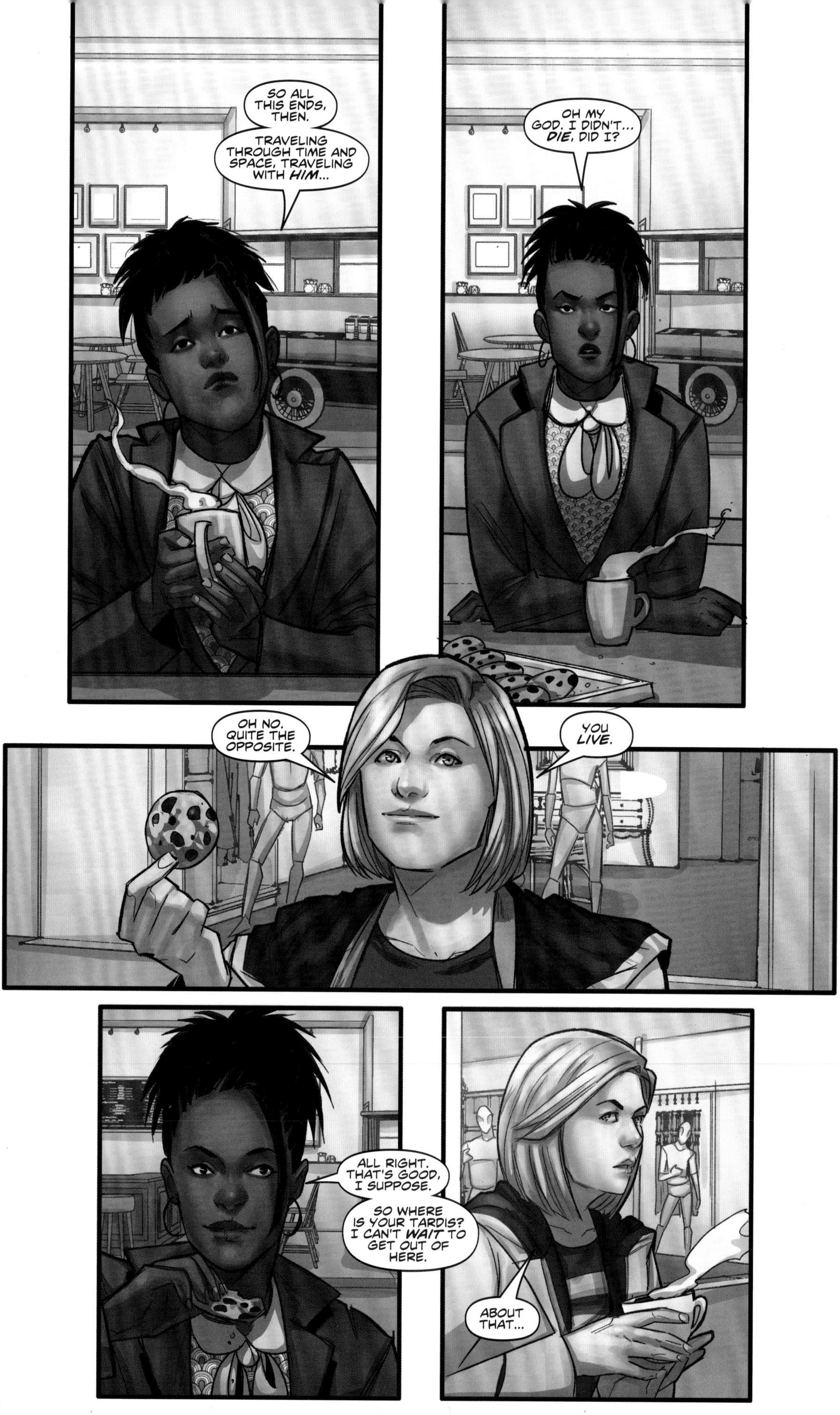
SO ALL THIS ENDS, THEN.
TRAVELING THROUGH TIME AND SPACE, TRAVELING WITH HIM...
OH MY GOD. I DIDN'T... DIE, DID I?
OH NO. QUITE THE OPPOSITE.
YOU LIVE.
ALL RIGHT. THAT'S GOOD, I SUPPOSE.
SO WHERE IS YOUR TARDIS? I CAN'T WAIT TO GET OUT OF HERE.
ABOUT THAT...

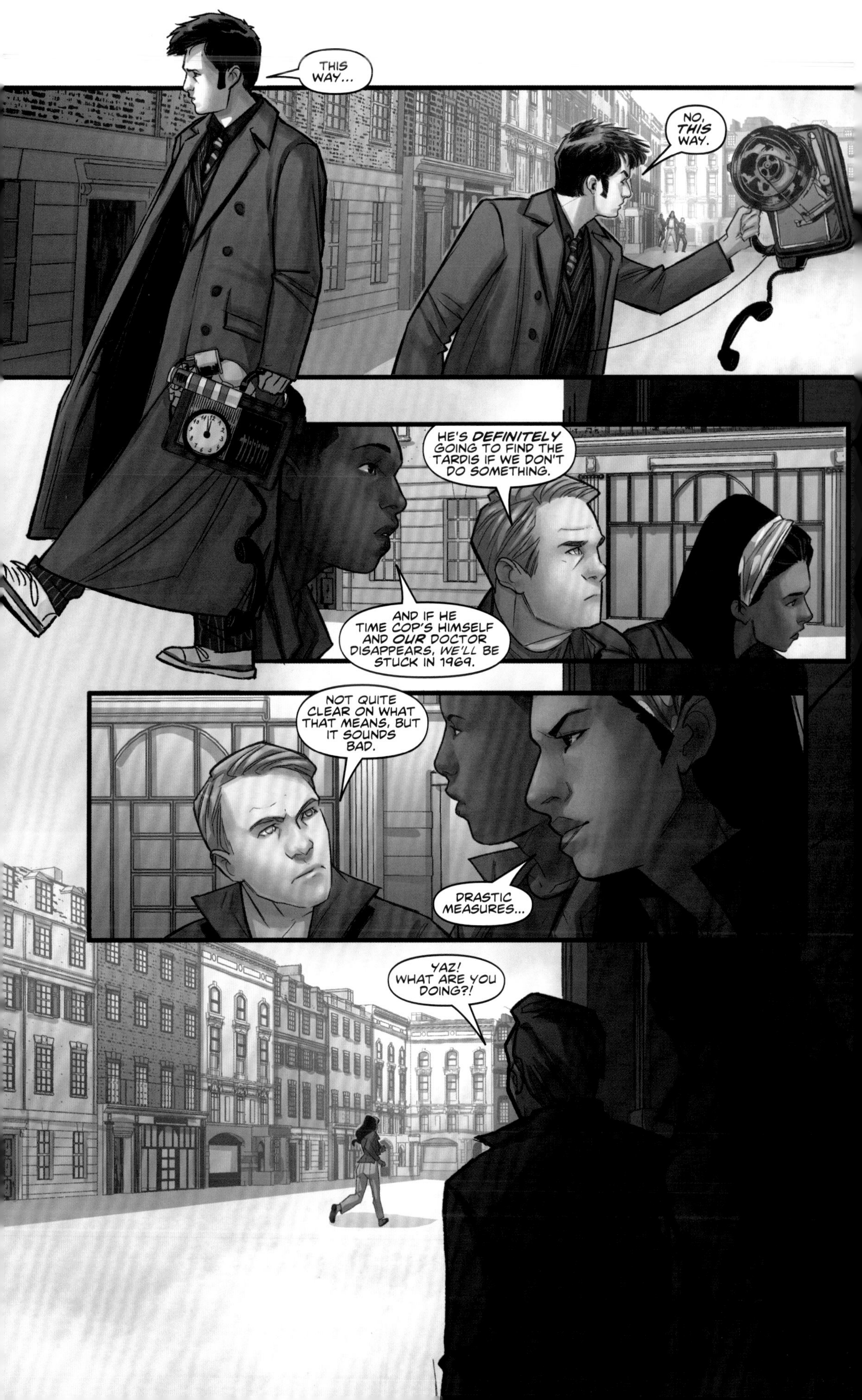
THIS WAY...
NO, THIS WAY.
HE'S DEFINITELY GOING TO FIND THE TARDIS IF WE DON'T DO SOMETHING.
AND IF HE TIME COP'S HIMSELF AND OUR DOCTOR DISAPPEARS, WE'LL BE STUCK IN 1969.
NOT QUITE CLEAR ON WHAT THAT MEANS, BUT IT SOUNDS BAD.
DRASTIC MEASURES...
YAZ! WHAT ARE YOU DOING?!

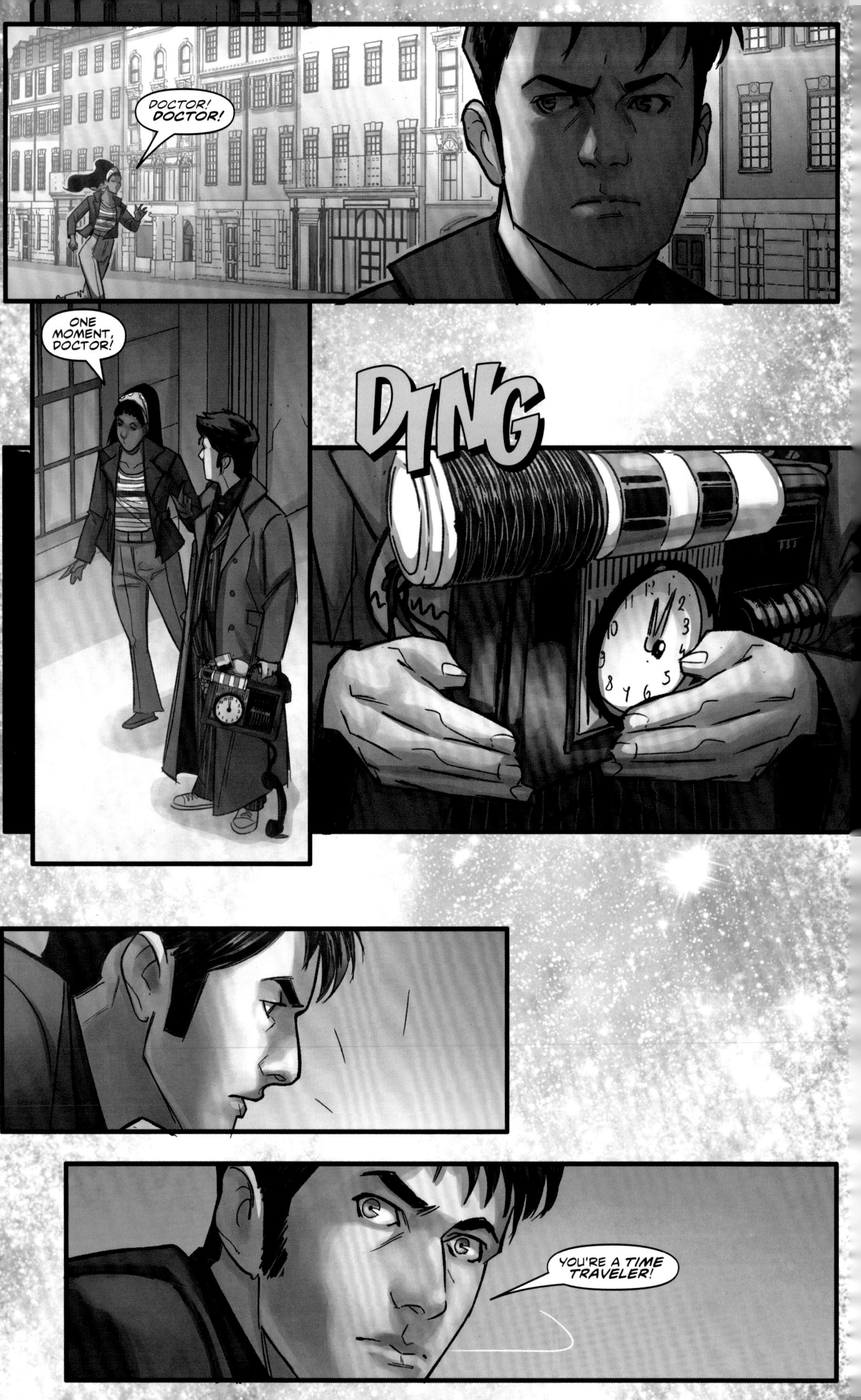
DOCTOR! DOCTOR!
ONE MOMENT, DOCTOR!
DING
YOU'RE A TIME TRAVELER!

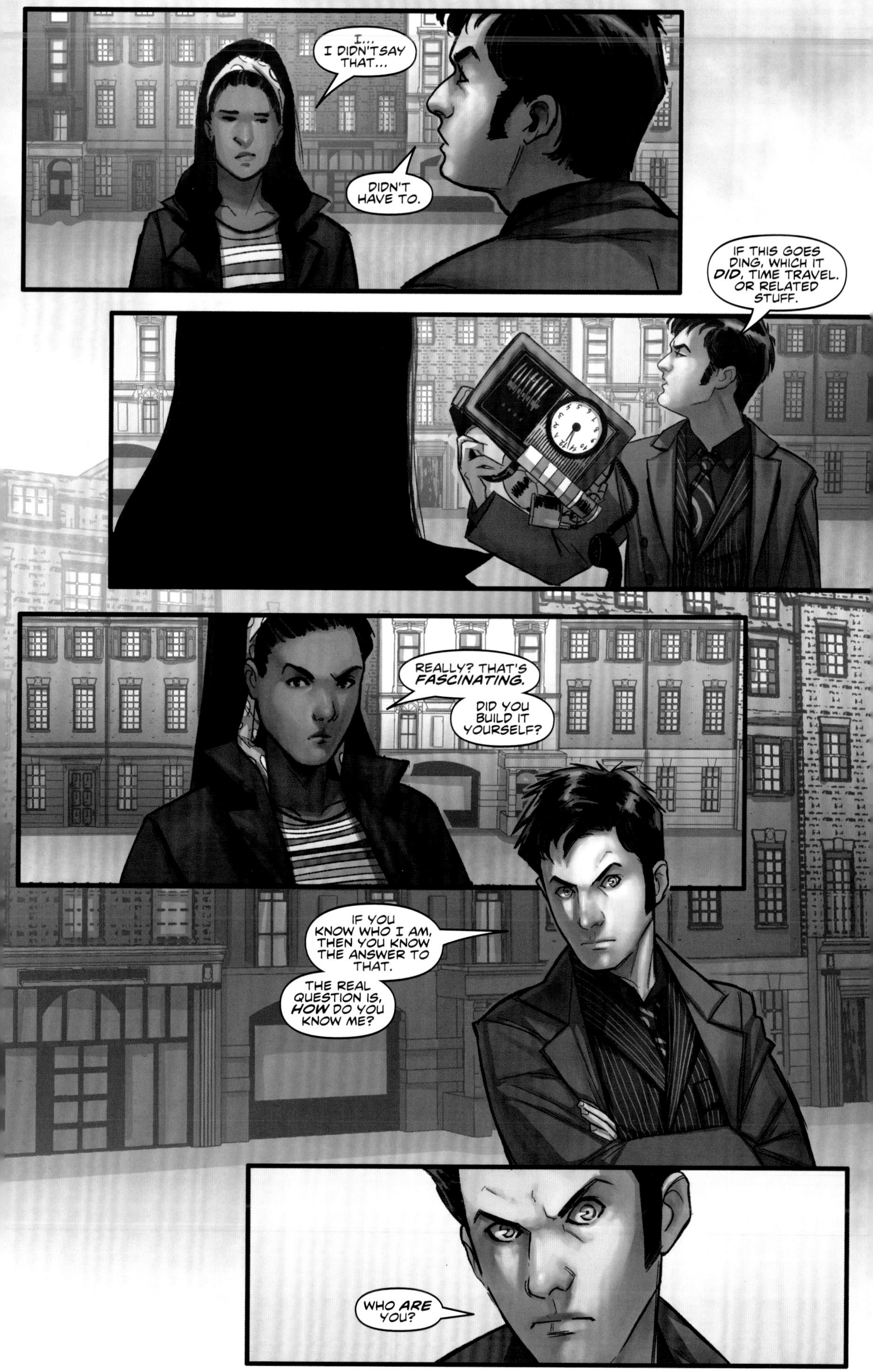
I... I DIDN'T SAY THAT...
DIDN'T HAVE TO.
IF THIS GOES DING, WHICH IT *DID*, TIME TRAVEL. OR RELATED STUFF.
REALLY? THAT'S *FASCINATING.*
DID YOU BUILD IT YOURSELF?
IF YOU KNOW WHO I AM, THEN YOU KNOW THE ANSWER TO THAT.
THE REAL QUESTION IS, *HOW* DO YOU KNOW ME?
WHO *ARE* YOU?

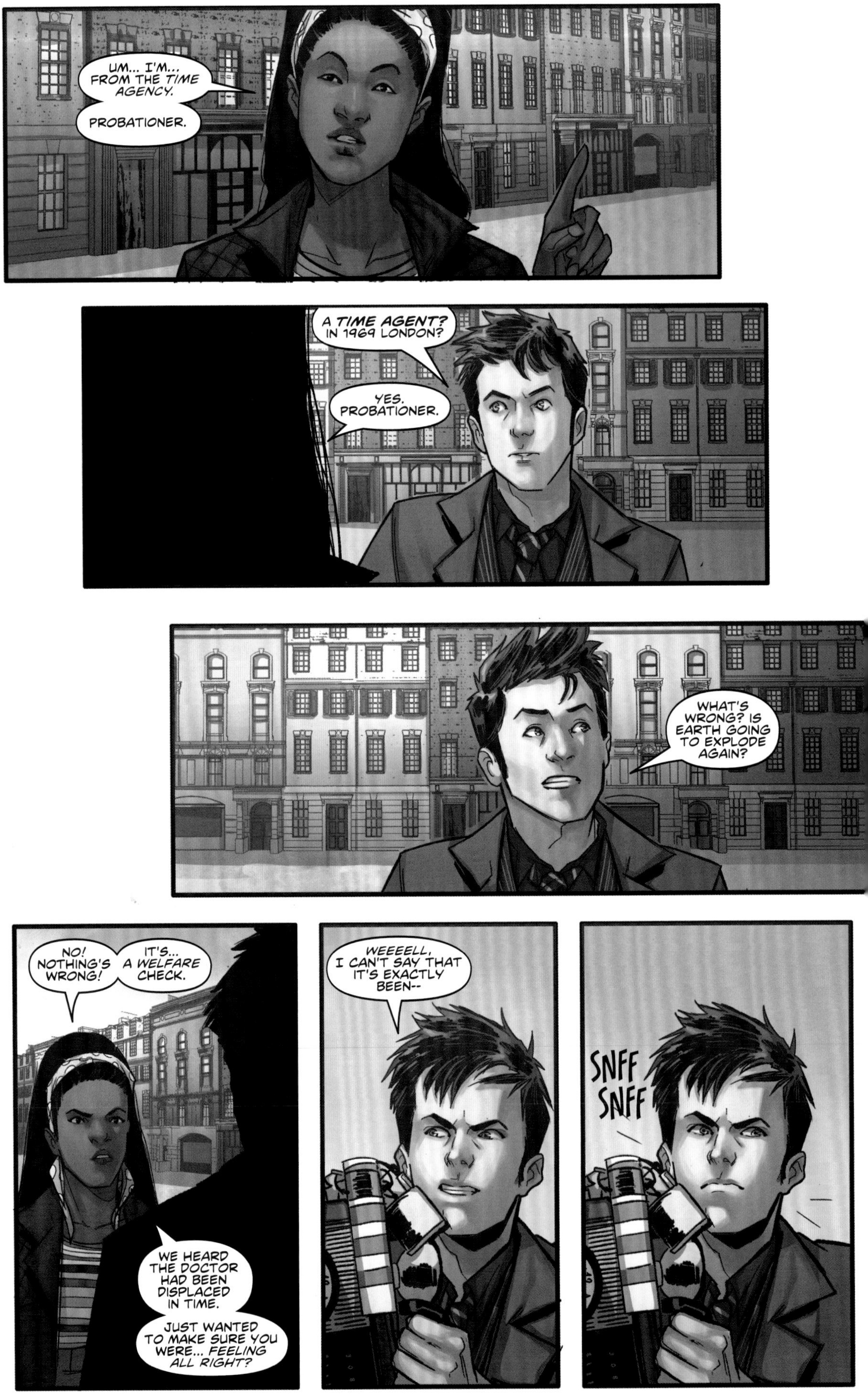
UM... I'M... FROM THE TIME AGENCY.
PROBATIONER.
A TIME AGENT? IN 1969 LONDON?
YES. PROBATIONER.
WHAT'S WRONG? IS EARTH GOING TO EXPLODE AGAIN?
NO! NOTHING'S WRONG!
IT'S... A WELFARE CHECK.
WE HEARD THE DOCTOR HAD BEEN DISPLACED IN TIME.
JUST WANTED TO MAKE SURE YOU WERE... FEELING ALL RIGHT?
WEEEELL, I CAN'T SAY THAT IT'S EXACTLY BEEN--
SNFF SNFF

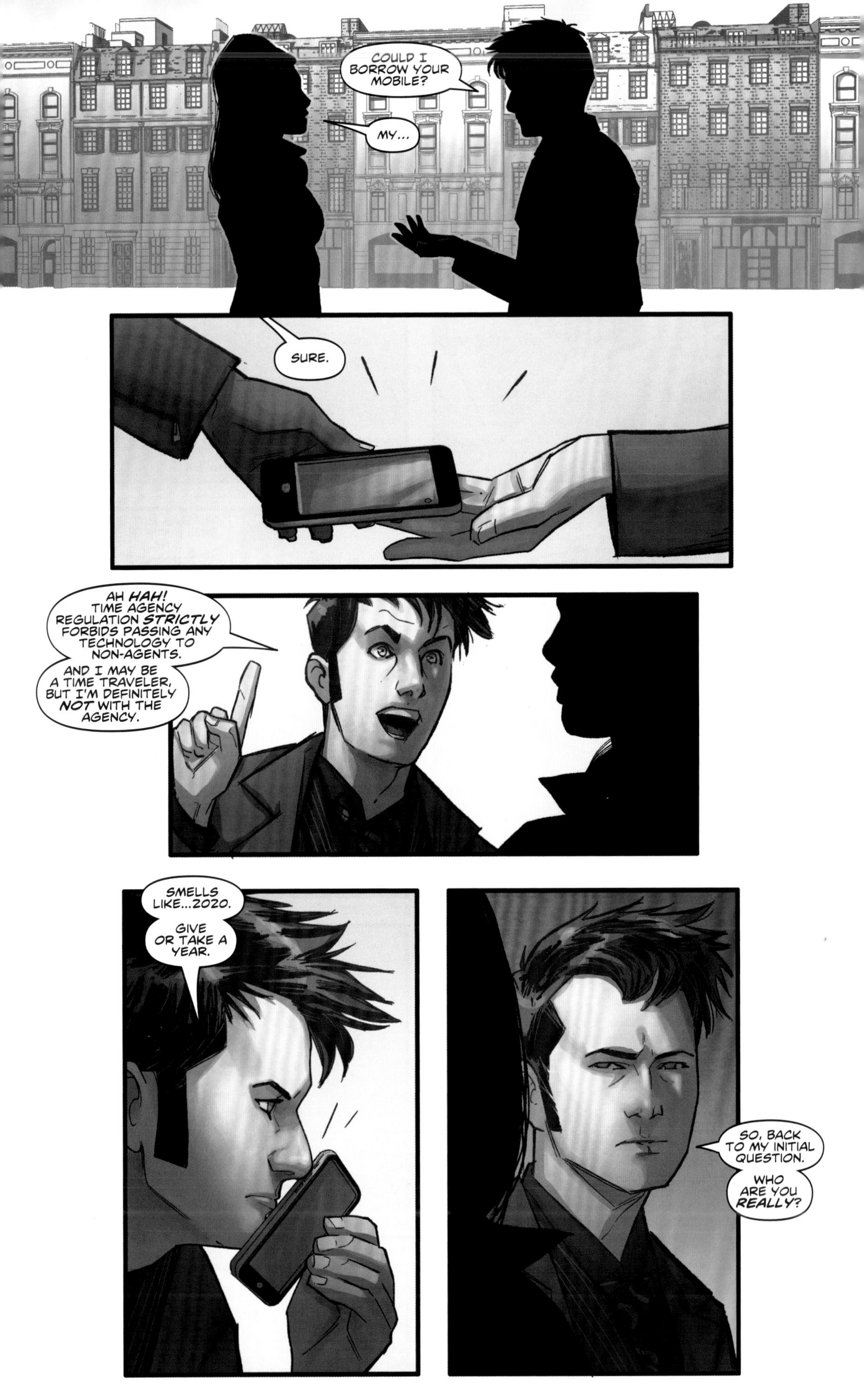
COULD I BORROW YOUR MOBILE?
MY...
SURE.
AH HAH! TIME AGENCY REGULATION STRICTLY FORBIDS PASSING ANY TECHNOLOGY TO NON-AGENTS.
AND I MAY BE A TIME TRAVELER, BUT I'M DEFINITELY NOT WITH THE AGENCY.
SMELLS LIKE...2020.
GIVE OR TAKE A YEAR.
SO, BACK TO MY INITIAL QUESTION.
WHO ARE YOU REALLY?

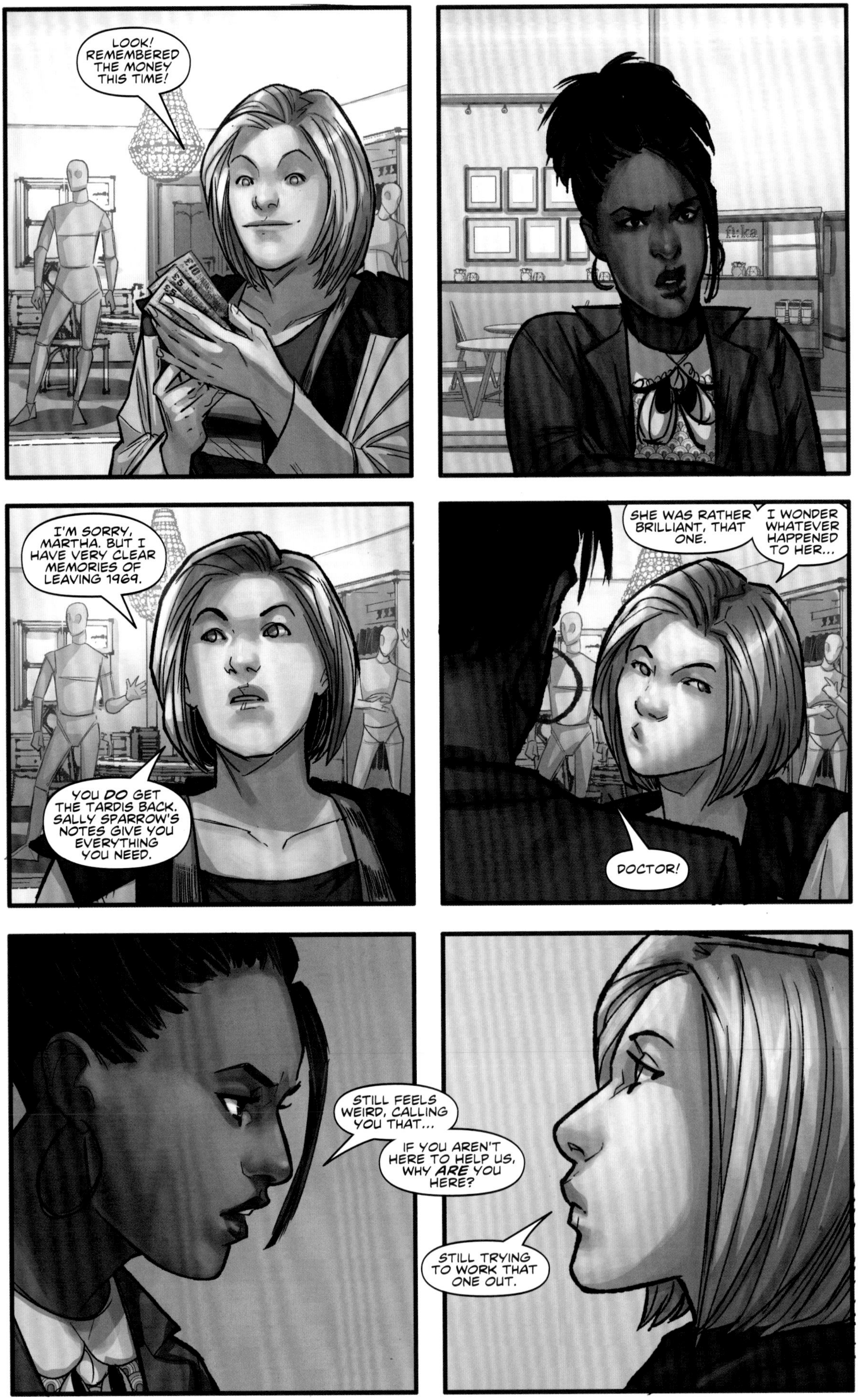
LOOK! REMEMBERED THE MONEY THIS TIME!
I'M SORRY, MARTHA. BUT I HAVE VERY CLEAR MEMORIES OF LEAVING 1969.
YOU DO GET THE TARDIS BACK. SALLY SPARROW'S NOTES GIVE YOU EVERYTHING YOU NEED.
SHE WAS RATHER BRILLIANT, THAT ONE.
I WONDER WHATEVER HAPPENED TO HER...
DOCTOR!
STILL FEELS WEIRD, CALLING YOU THAT...
IF YOU AREN'T HERE TO HELP US, WHY ARE YOU HERE?
STILL TRYING TO WORK THAT ONE OUT.

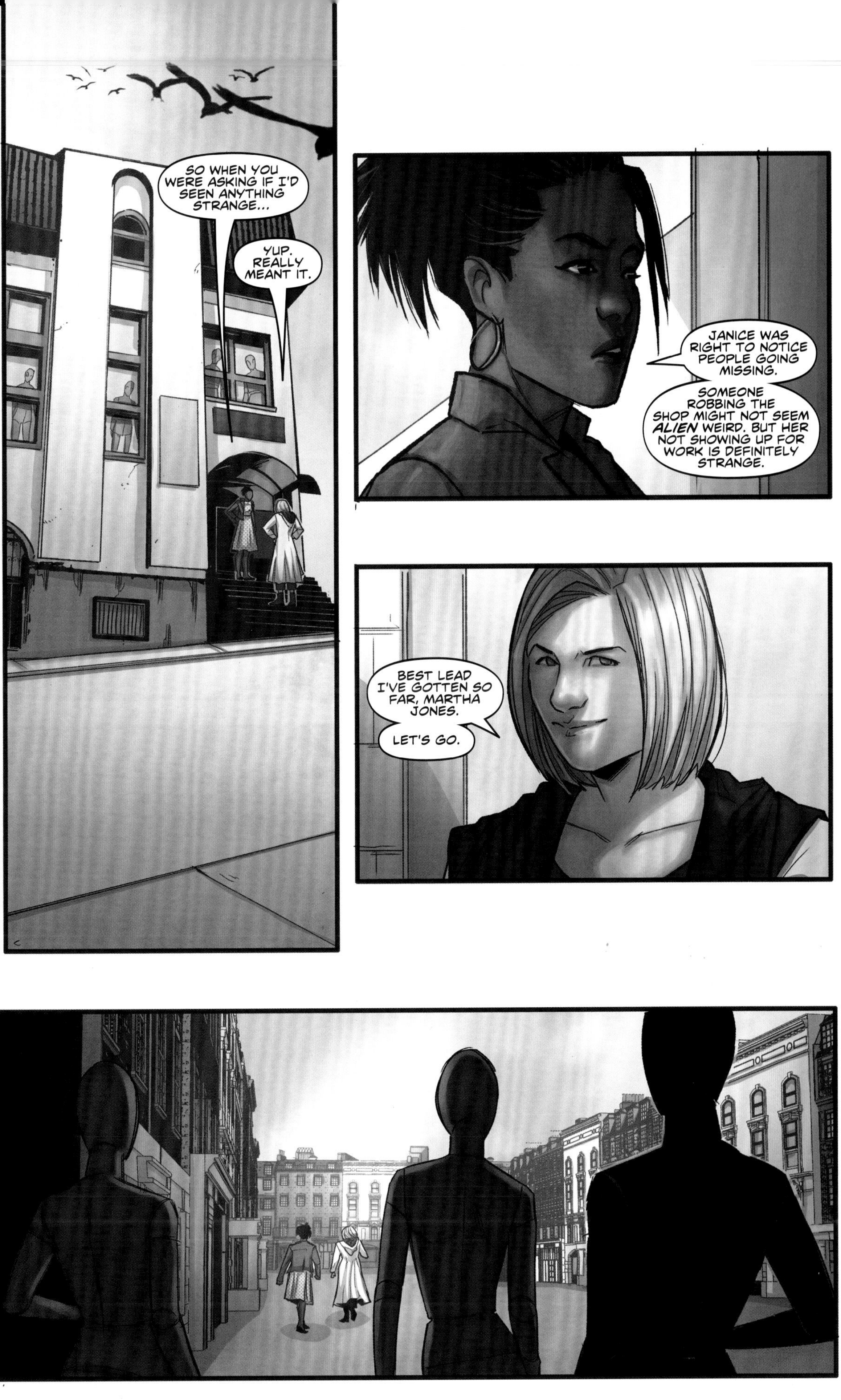

SO WHEN YOU WERE ASKING IF I'D SEEN ANYTHING STRANGE...
YUP. REALLY MEANT IT.
JANICE WAS RIGHT TO NOTICE PEOPLE GOING MISSING.
SOMEONE ROBBING THE SHOP MIGHT NOT SEEM ALIEN WEIRD. BUT HER NOT SHOWING UP FOR WORK IS DEFINITELY STRANGE.
BEST LEAD I'VE GOTTEN SO FAR, MARTHA JONES.
LET'S GO.

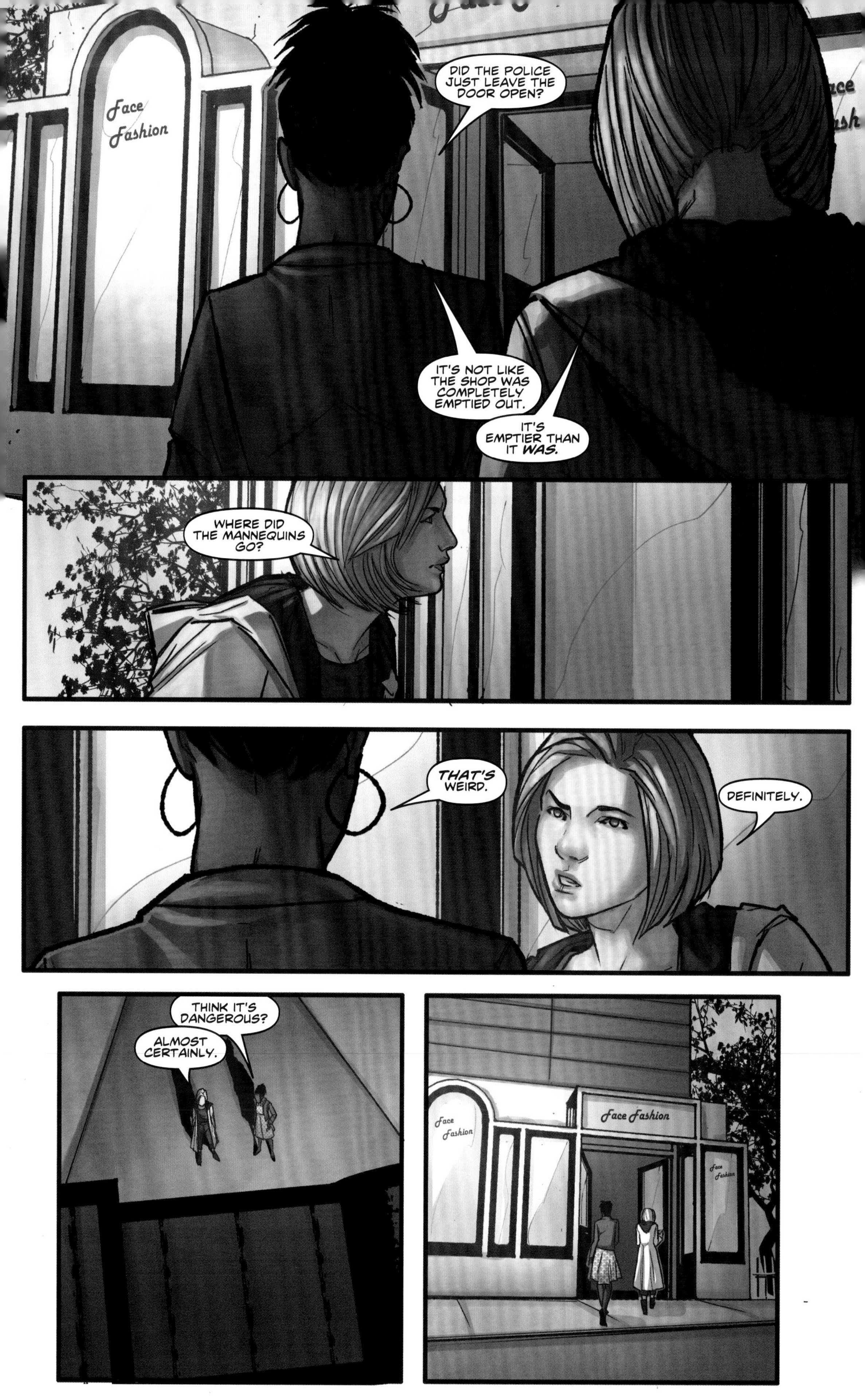
Face Fashion
DID THE POLICE JUST LEAVE THE DOOR OPEN?
IT'S NOT LIKE THE SHOP WAS COMPLETELY EMPTIED OUT.
IT'S EMPTIER THAN IT *WAS.*
WHERE DID THE MANNEQUINS GO?
THAT'S WEIRD.
DEFINITELY.
THINK IT'S DANGEROUS?
ALMOST CERTAINLY.
Face Fashion
Face Fashion
Face Fashion

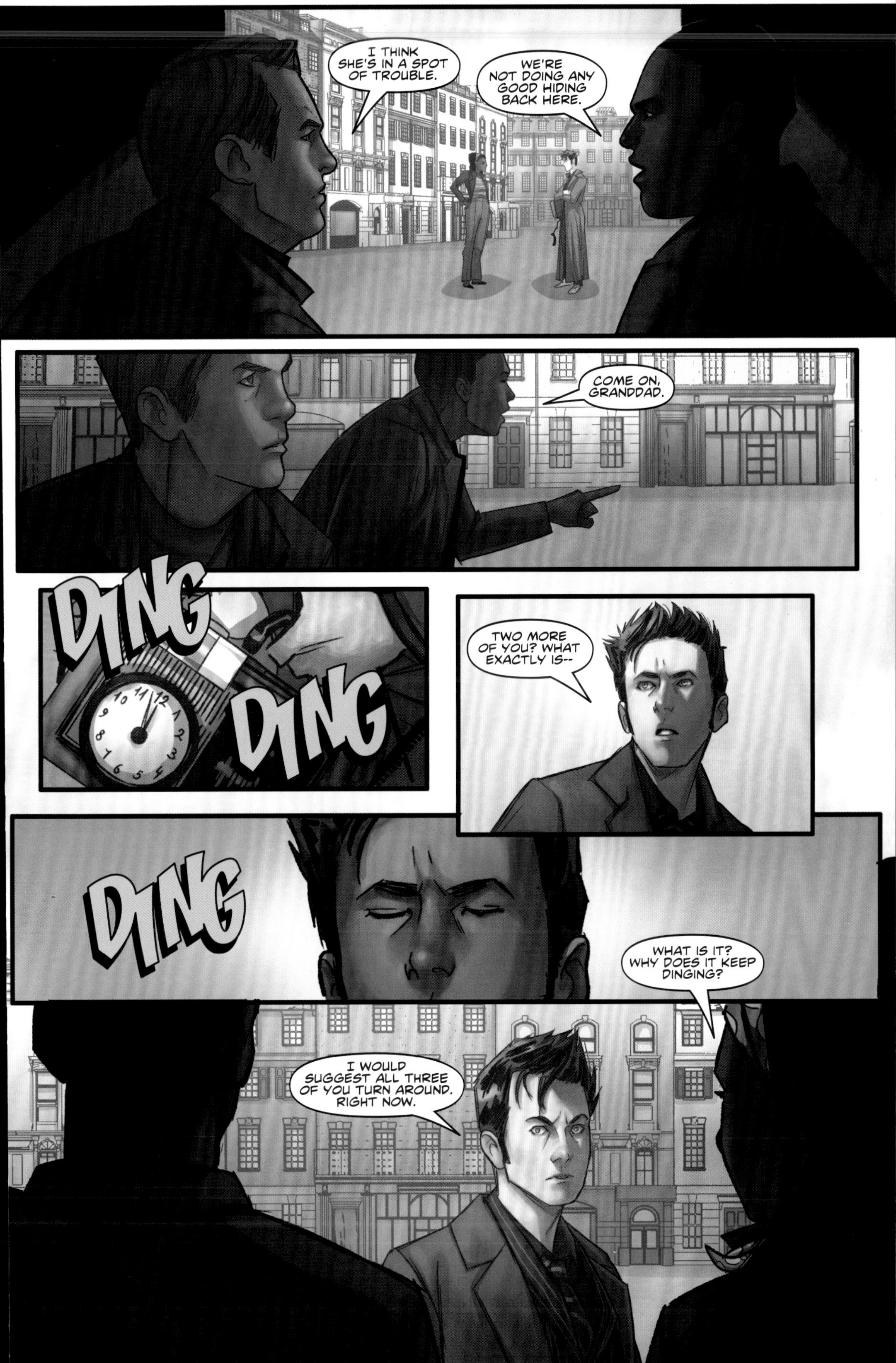
I THINK SHE'S IN A SPOT OF TROUBLE.
WE'RE NOT DOING ANY GOOD HIDING BACK HERE.
COME ON, GRANDDAD.
DING
DING
TWO MORE OF YOU? WHAT EXACTLY IS--
DING
WHAT IS IT? WHY DOES IT KEEP DINGING?
I WOULD SUGGEST ALL THREE OF YOU TURN AROUND. RIGHT NOW.

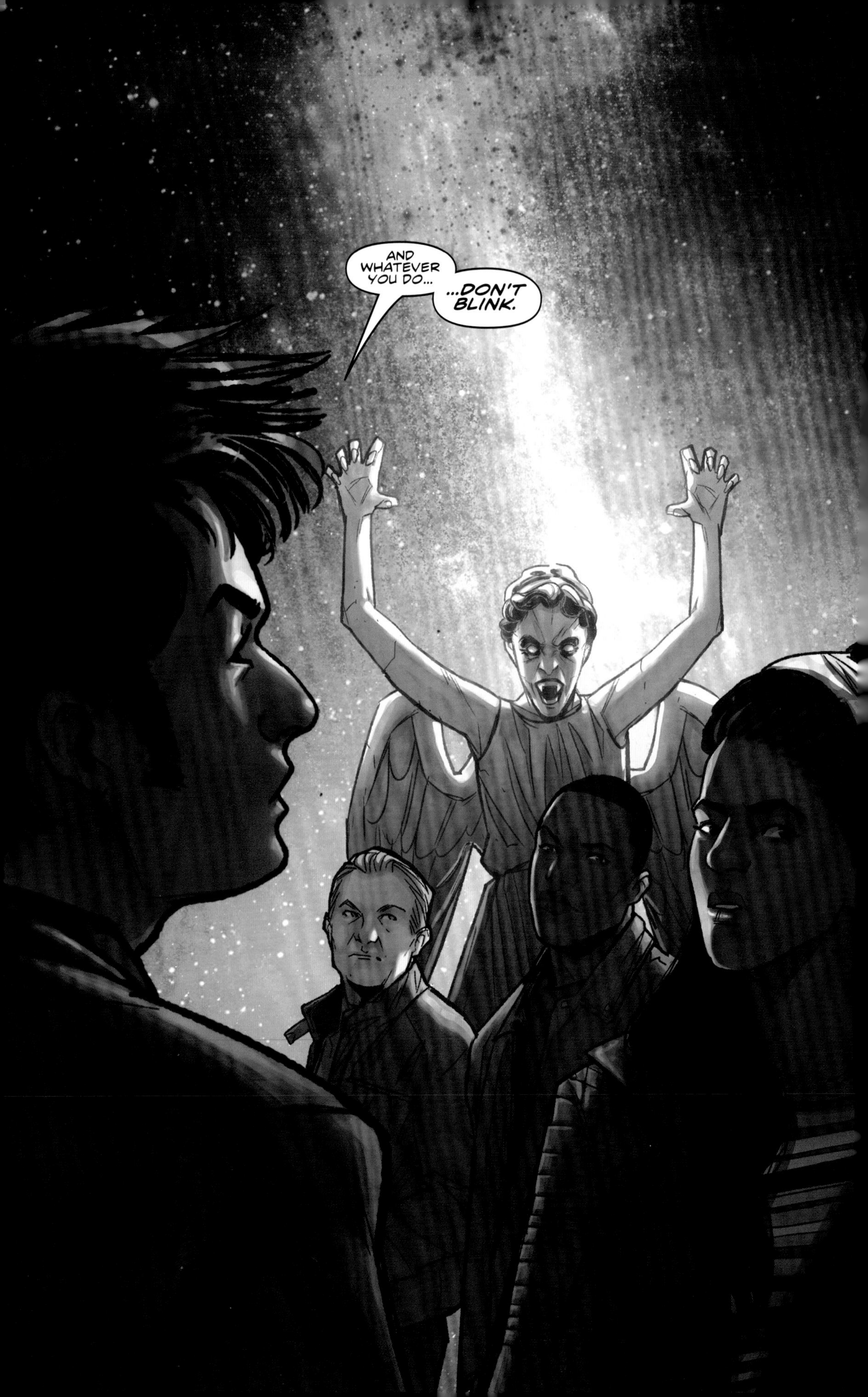
AND WHATEVER YOU DO...
...DON'T BLINK.

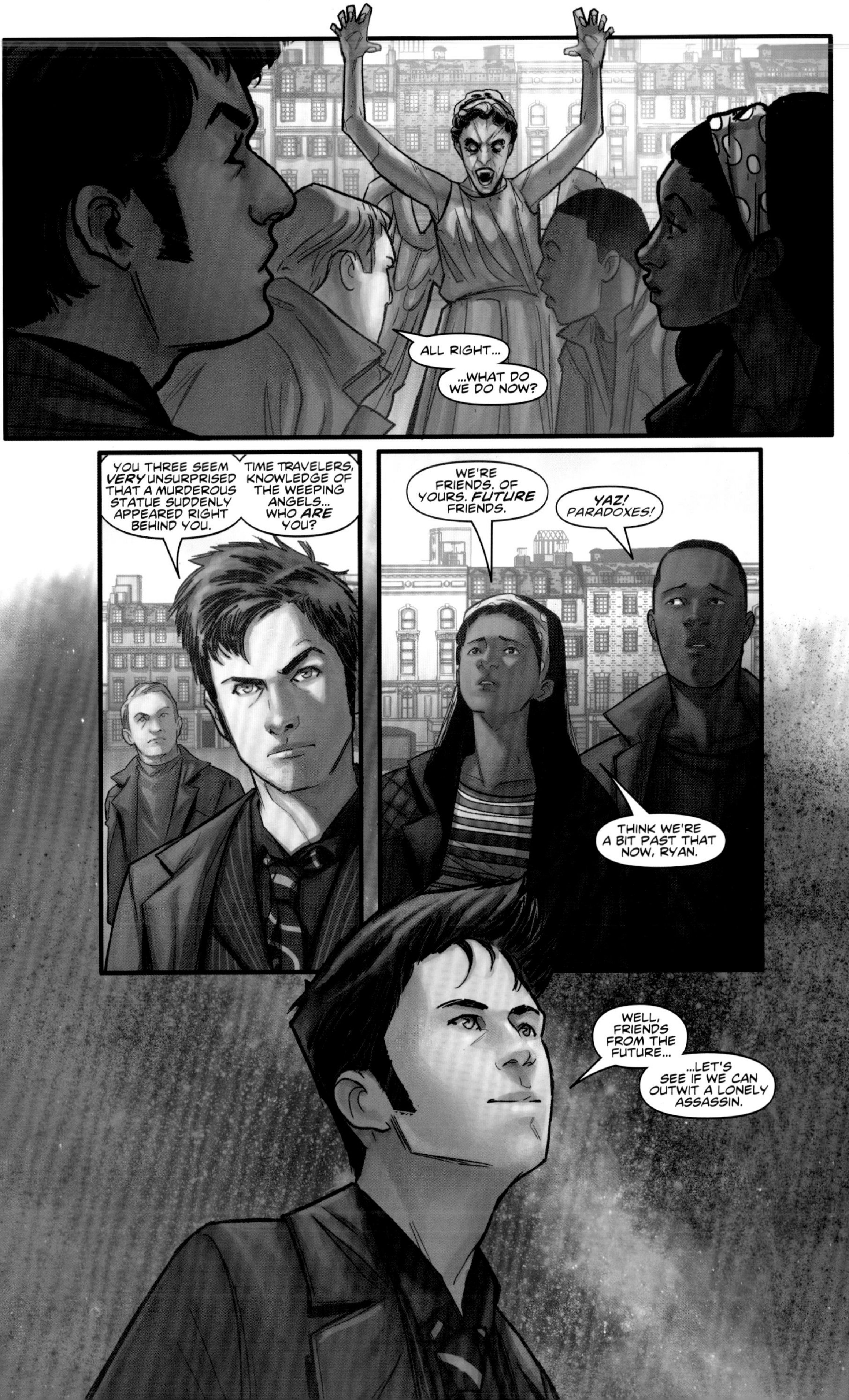
ALL RIGHT...
...WHAT DO WE DO NOW?
YOU THREE SEEM VERY UNSURPRISED THAT A MURDEROUS STATUE SUDDENLY APPEARED RIGHT BEHIND YOU.
TIME TRAVELERS, KNOWLEDGE OF THE WEEPING ANGELS... WHO ARE YOU?
WE'RE FRIENDS. OF YOURS. FUTURE FRIENDS.
YAZ! PARADOXES!
THINK WE'RE A BIT PAST THAT NOW, RYAN.
WELL, FRIENDS FROM THE FUTURE...
...LET'S SEE IF WE CAN OUTWIT A LONELY ASSASSIN.

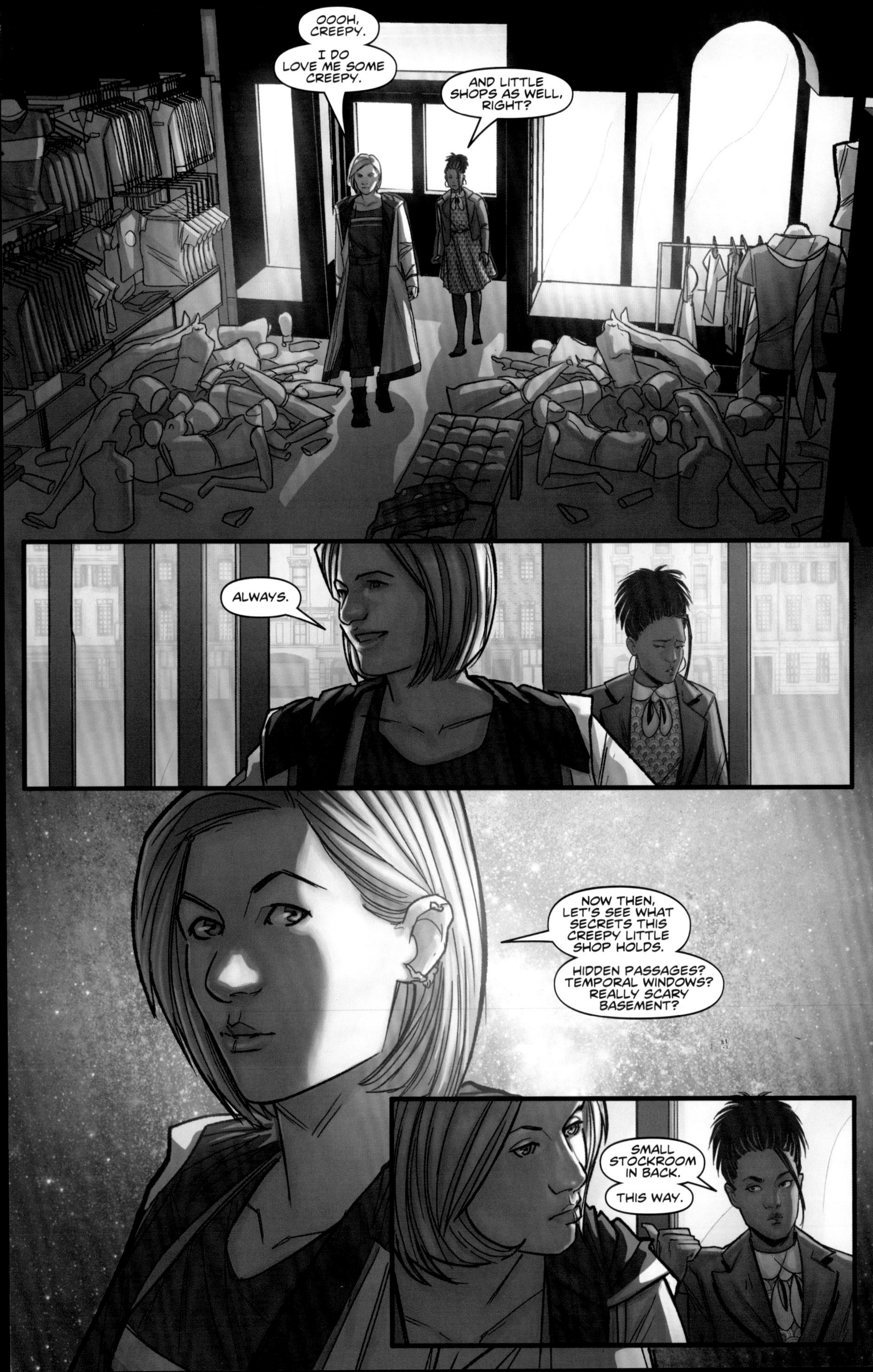
OOOH, CREEPY.
I DO LOVE ME SOME CREEPY.
AND LITTLE SHOPS AS WELL, RIGHT?
ALWAYS.
NOW THEN, LET'S SEE WHAT SECRETS THIS CREEPY LITTLE SHOP HOLDS.
HIDDEN PASSAGES? TEMPORAL WINDOWS? REALLY SCARY BASEMENT?
SMALL STOCKROOM IN BACK.
THIS WAY.

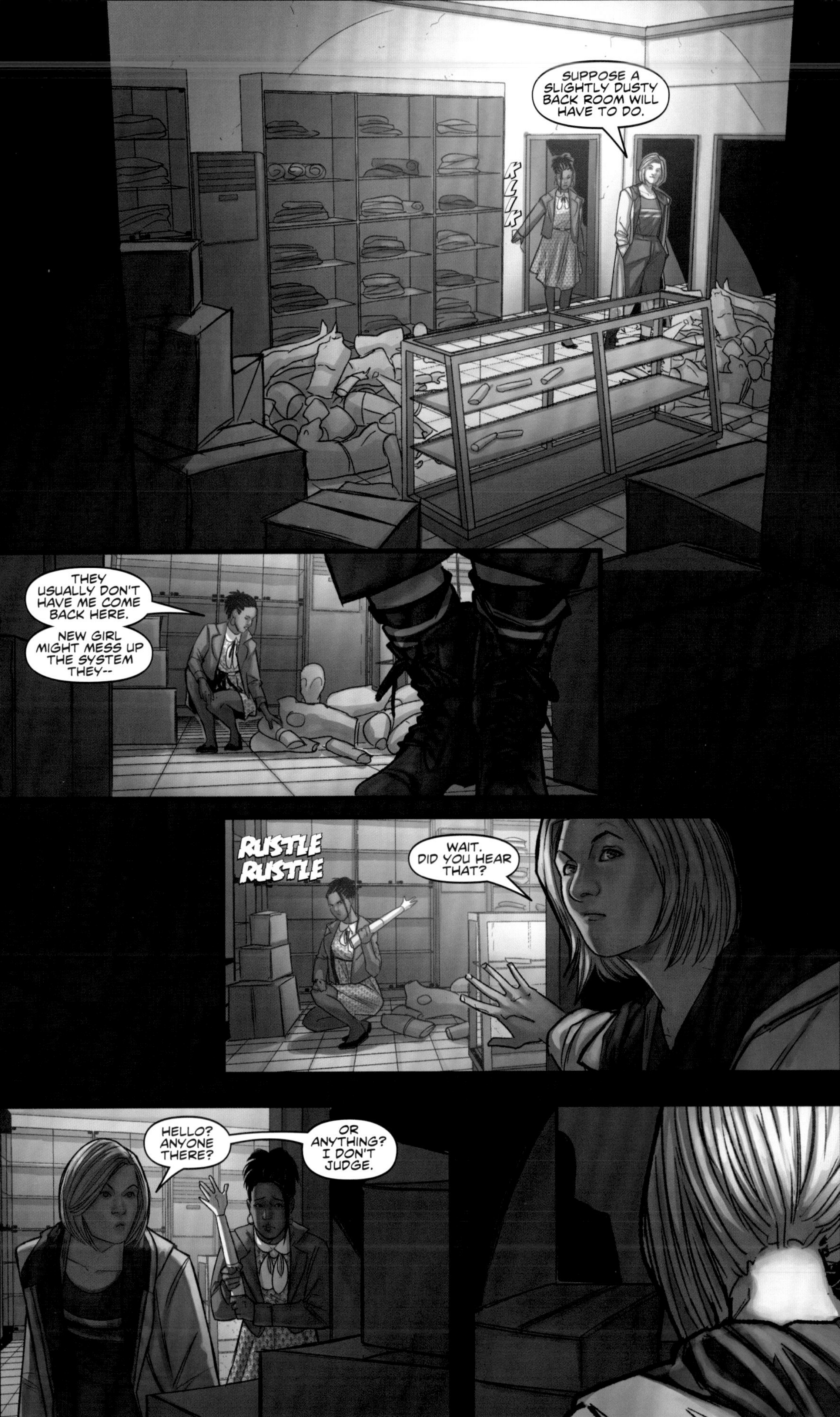
SUPPOSE A SLIGHTLY DUSTY BACK ROOM WILL HAVE TO DO.
KLIK!
THEY USUALLY DON'T HAVE ME COME BACK HERE.
NEW GIRL MIGHT MESS UP THE SYSTEM THEY--
RUSTLE RUSTLE
WAIT. DID YOU HEAR THAT?
HELLO? ANYONE THERE?
OR ANYTHING? I DON'T JUDGE.

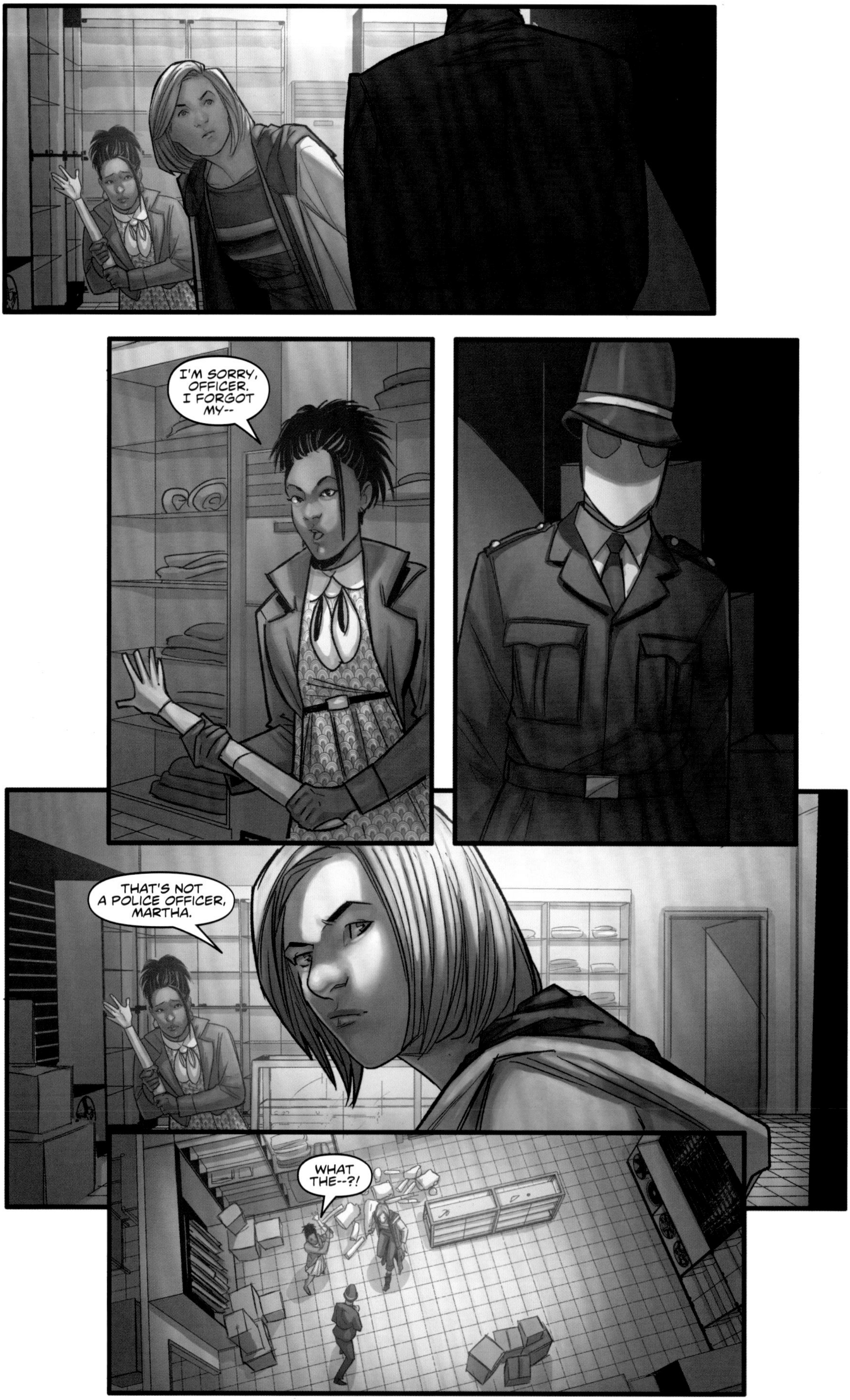
I'M SORRY, OFFICER. I FORGOT MY--
THAT'S NOT A POLICE OFFICER, MARTHA.
WHAT THE--?!

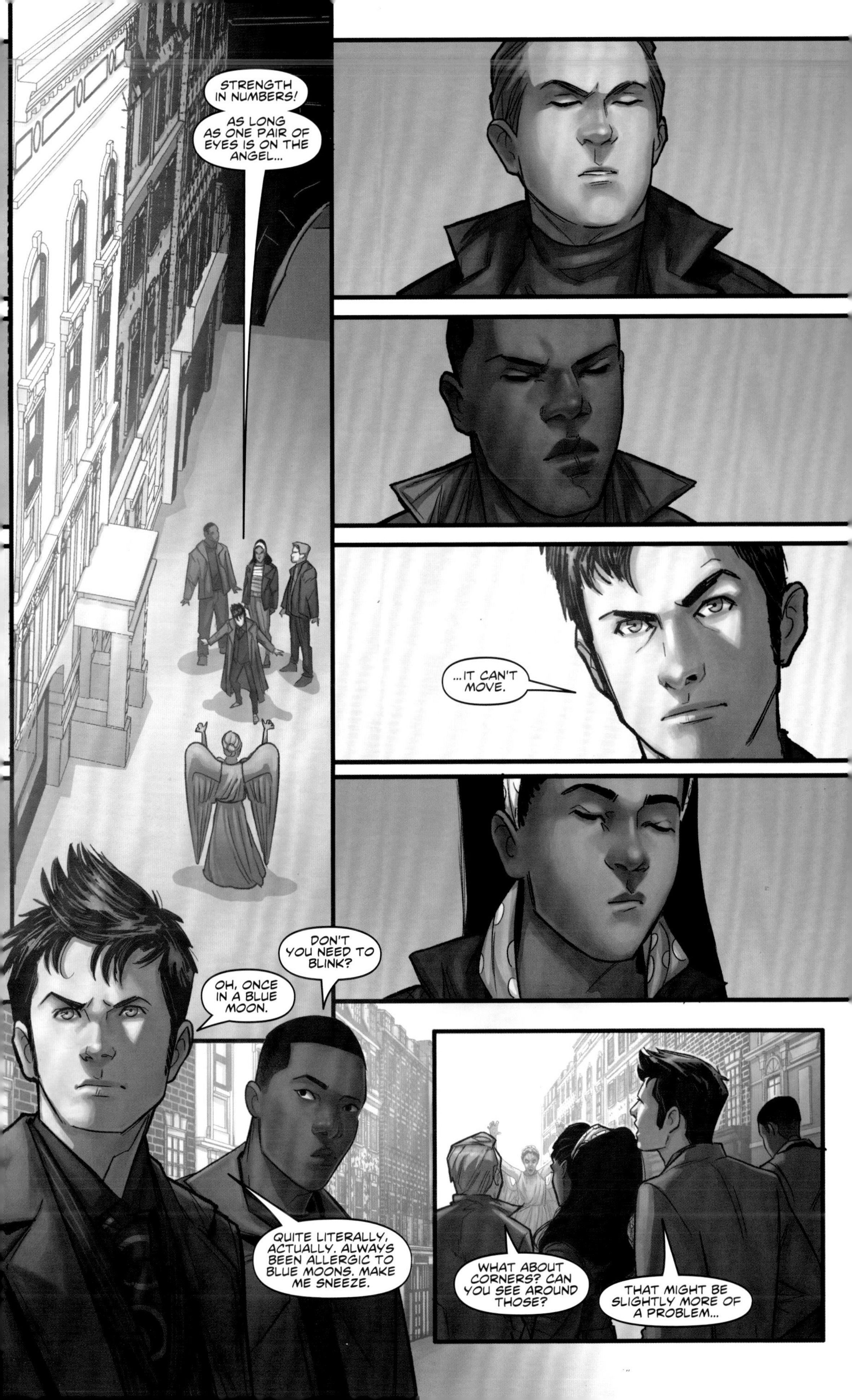
STRENGTH IN NUMBERS!
AS LONG AS ONE PAIR OF EYES IS ON THE ANGEL...
...IT CAN'T MOVE.
DON'T YOU NEED TO BLINK?
OH, ONCE IN A BLUE MOON.
QUITE LITERALLY, ACTUALLY. ALWAYS BEEN ALLERGIC TO BLUE MOONS. MAKE ME SNEEZE.
WHAT ABOUT CORNERS? CAN YOU SEE AROUND THOSE?
THAT MIGHT BE SLIGHTLY MORE OF A PROBLEM...

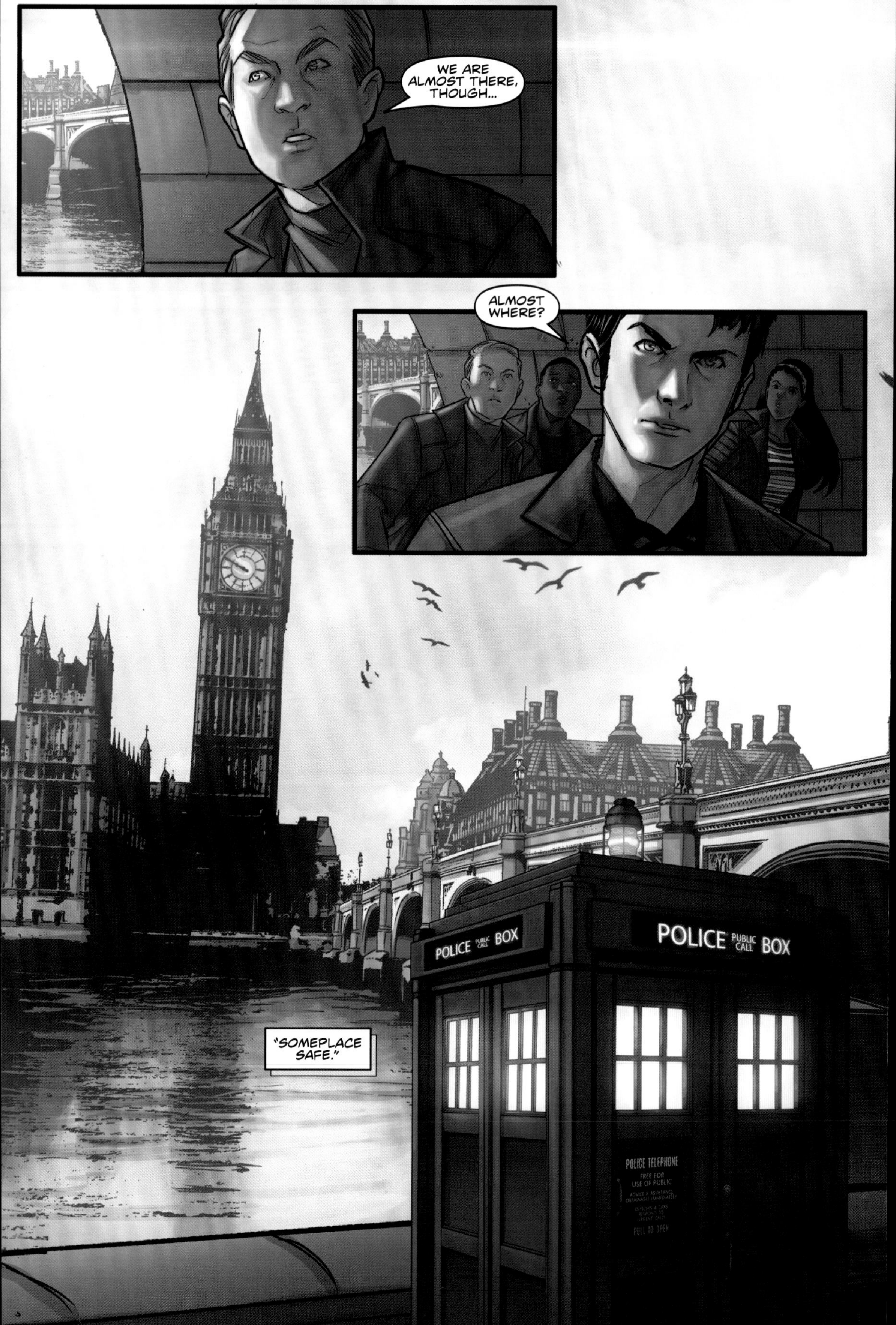
WE ARE ALMOST THERE, THOUGH...
ALMOST WHERE?
"SOMEPLACE SAFE."
POLICE PUBLIC CALL BOX
POLICE PUBLIC CALL BOX
POLICE TELEPHONE
FREE FOR USE OF PUBLIC
PULL TO OPEN

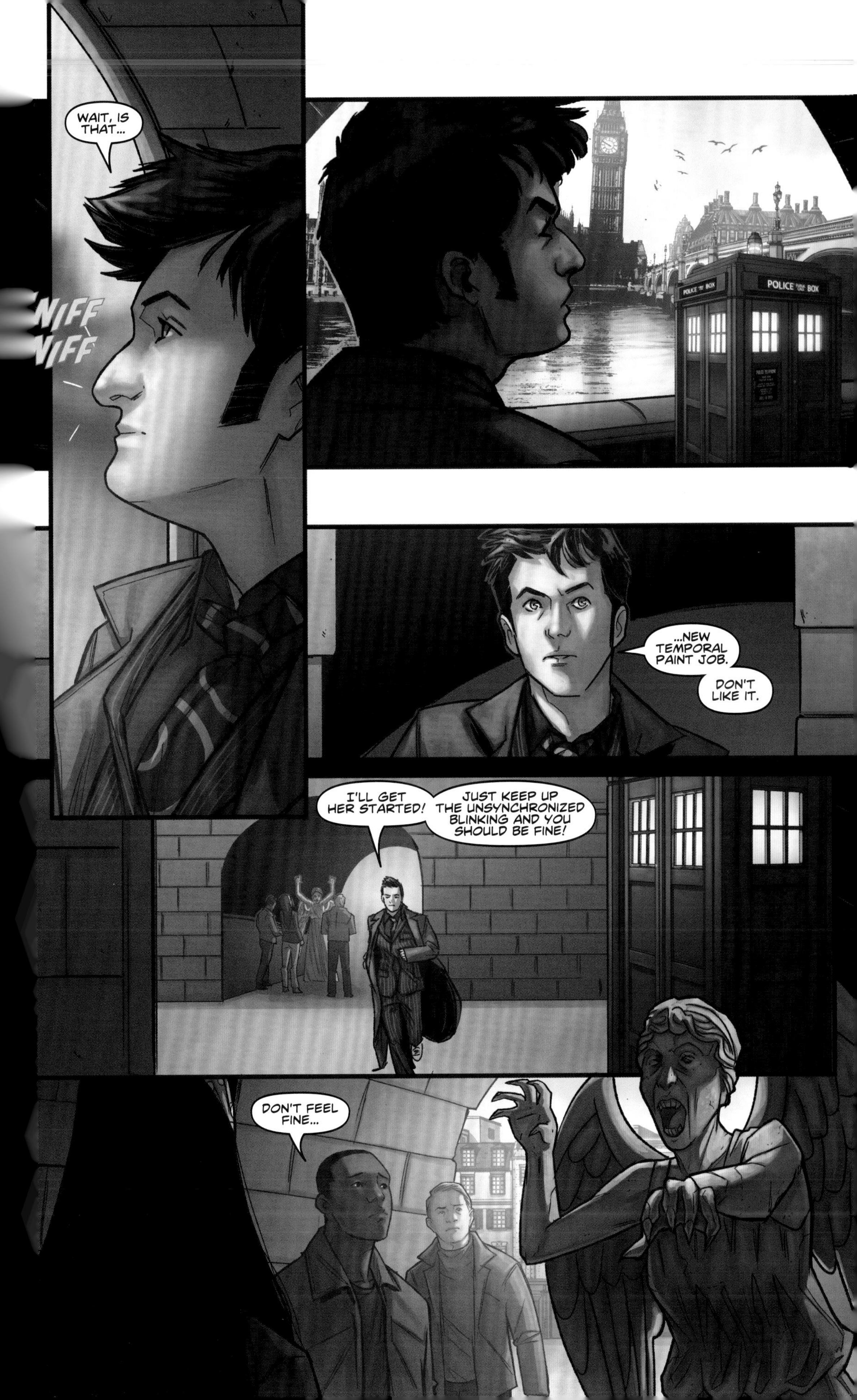
WAIT, IS THAT...
NIFF NIFF
POLICE BOX
...NEW TEMPORAL PAINT JOB.
DON'T LIKE IT.
I'LL GET HER STARTED!
JUST KEEP UP THE UNSYNCHRONIZED BLINKING AND YOU SHOULD BE FINE!
DON'T FEEL FINE...

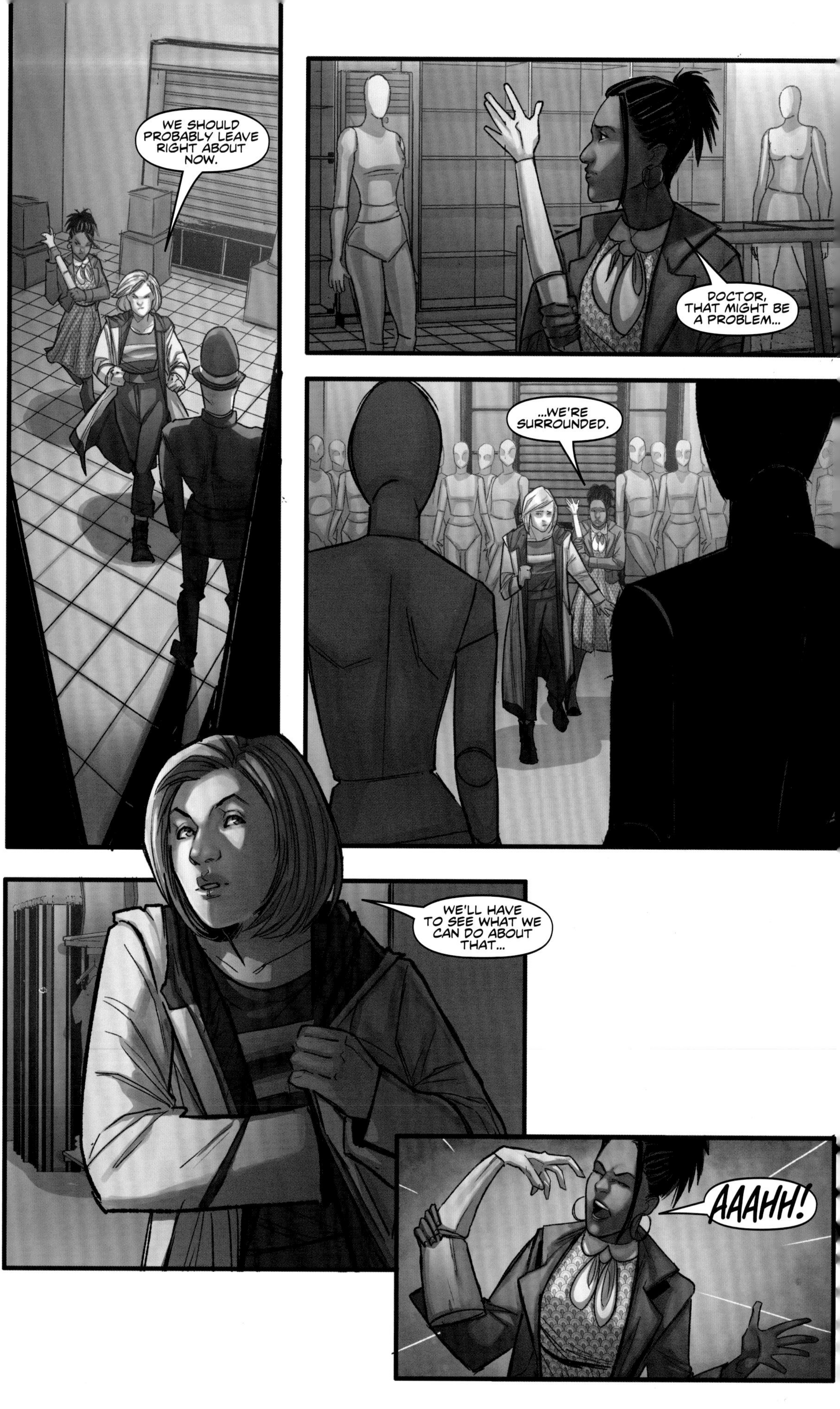
WE SHOULD PROBABLY LEAVE RIGHT ABOUT NOW.
DOCTOR, THAT MIGHT BE A PROBLEM...
...WE'RE SURROUNDED.
WE'LL HAVE TO SEE WHAT WE CAN DO ABOUT THAT...
AAAHH!

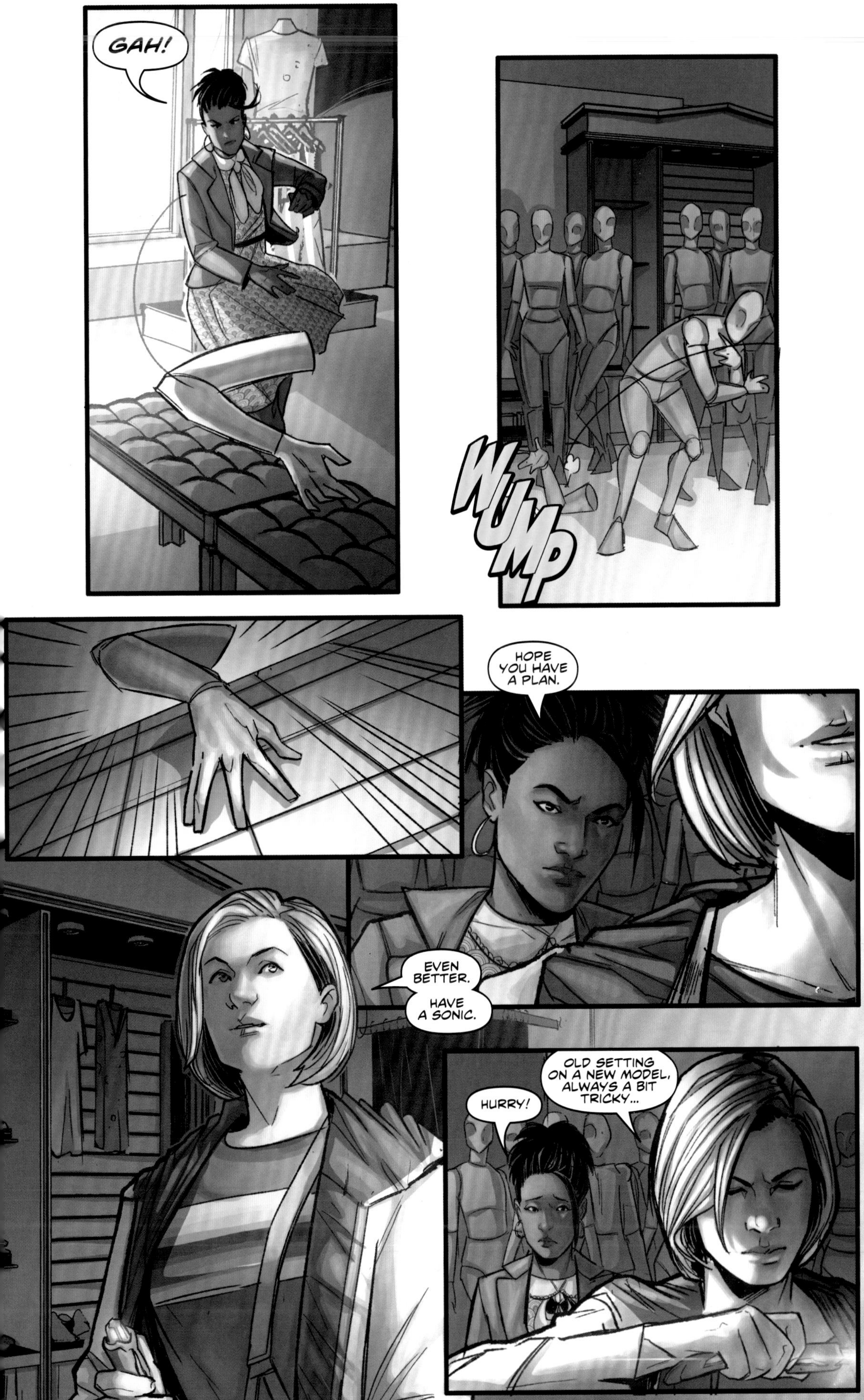
GAH!
WUMP
HOPE YOU HAVE A PLAN.
EVEN BETTER.
HAVE A SONIC.
OLD SETTING ON A NEW MODEL, ALWAYS A BIT TRICKY...
HURRY!

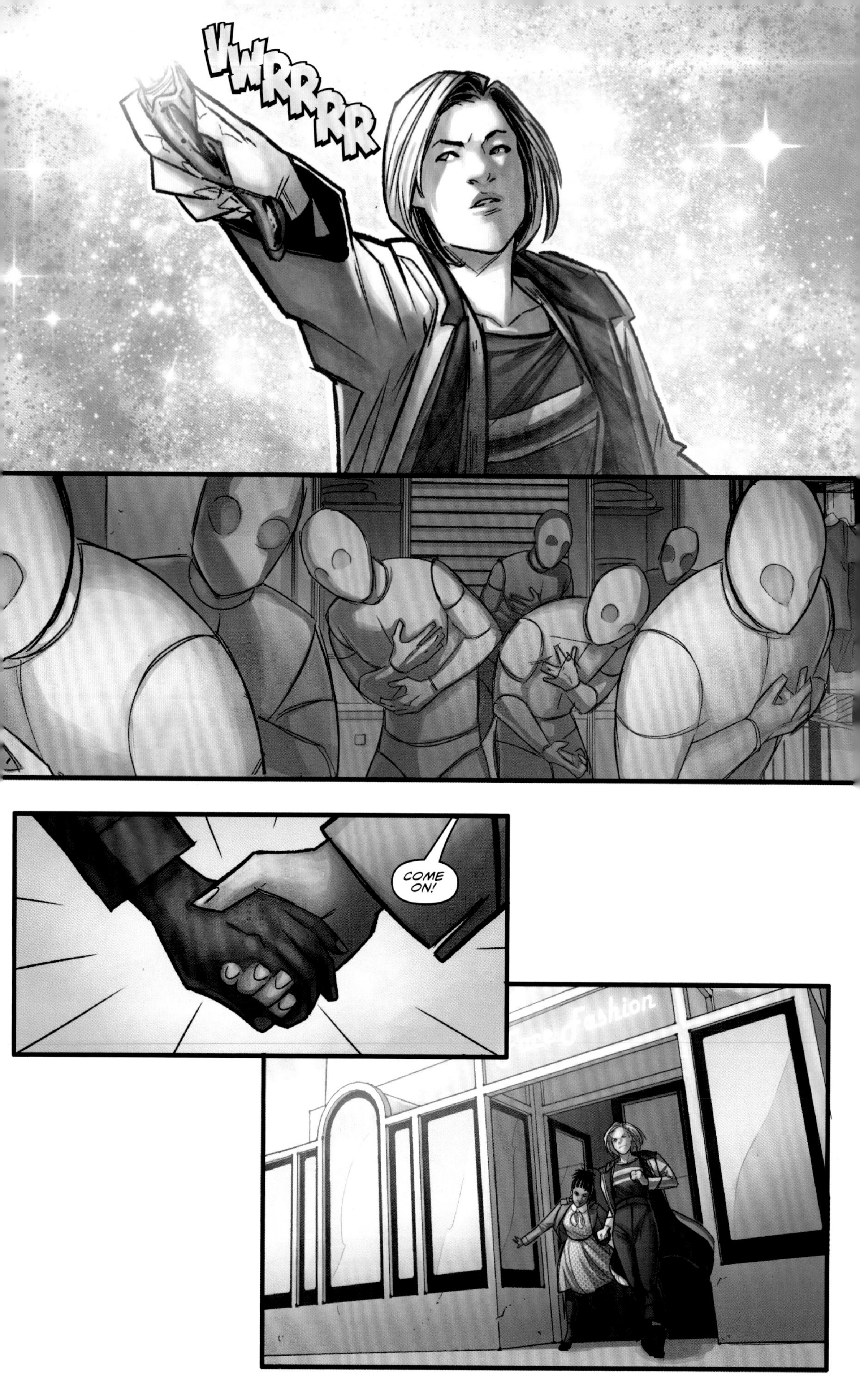
VWRRRRR
COME ON!
Fashion

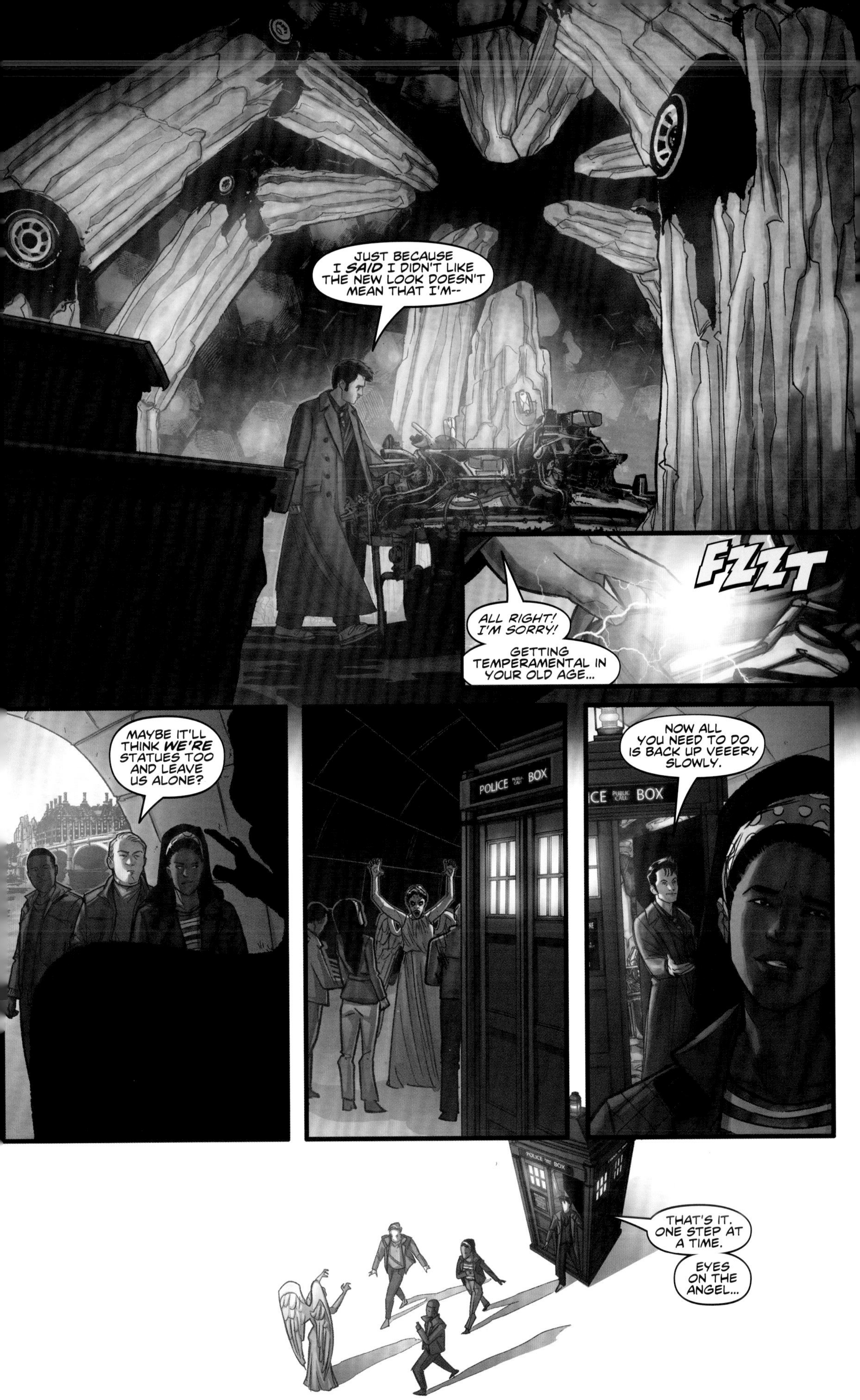
JUST BECAUSE I SAID I DIDN'T LIKE THE NEW LOOK DOESN'T MEAN THAT I'M--
FZZT
ALL RIGHT! I'M SORRY!
GETTING TEMPERAMENTAL IN YOUR OLD AGE...
MAYBE IT'LL THINK WE'RE STATUES TOO AND LEAVE US ALONE?
POLICE PUBLIC CALL BOX
NOW ALL YOU NEED TO DO IS BACK UP VEEERY SLOWLY.
THAT'S IT. ONE STEP AT A TIME.
EYES ON THE ANGEL...

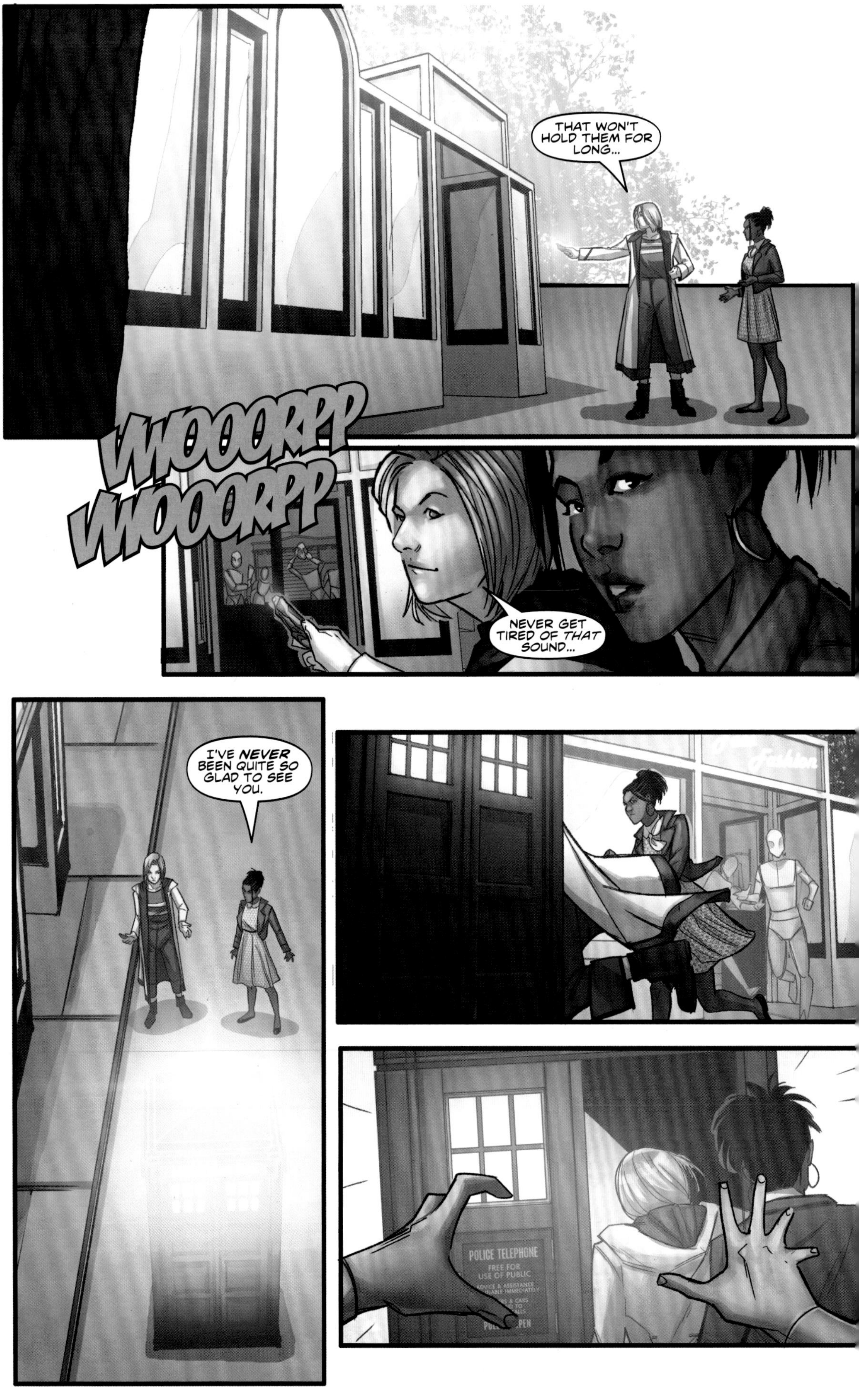
THAT WON'T HOLD THEM FOR LONG...
VWOOORPP VWOOORPP
NEVER GET TIRED OF *THAT* SOUND...
I'VE ***NEVER*** BEEN QUITE SO GLAD TO SEE YOU.
POLICE TELEPHONE
FREE FOR USE OF PUBLIC

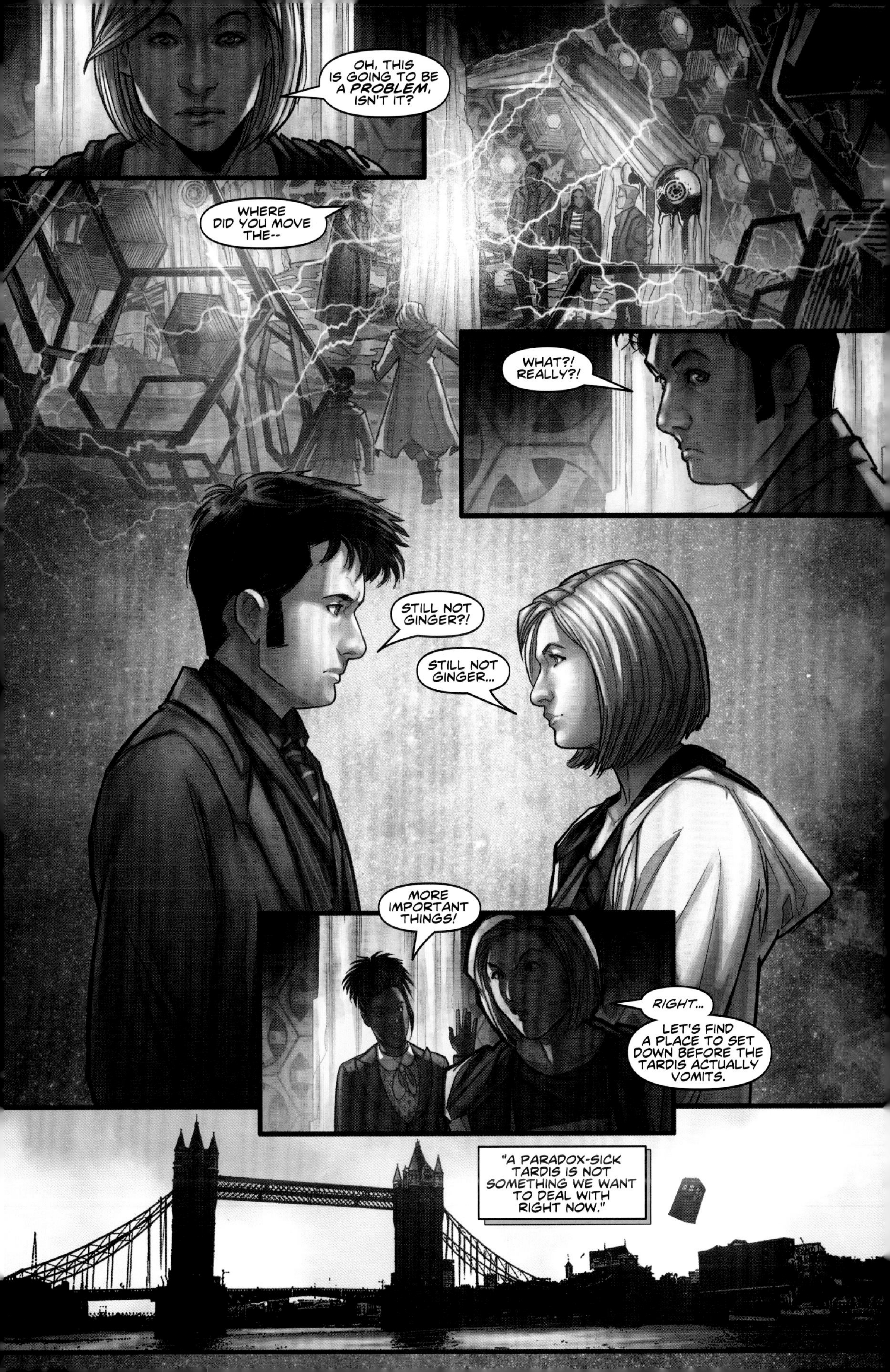
OH, THIS IS GOING TO BE A *PROBLEM*, ISN'T IT?
WHERE DID YOU MOVE THE--
WHAT?! REALLY?!
STILL NOT GINGER?!
STILL NOT GINGER...
MORE IMPORTANT THINGS!
RIGHT...
LET'S FIND A PLACE TO SET DOWN BEFORE THE TARDIS ACTUALLY VOMITS.
"A PARADOX-SICK TARDIS IS NOT SOMETHING WE WANT TO DEAL WITH RIGHT NOW."

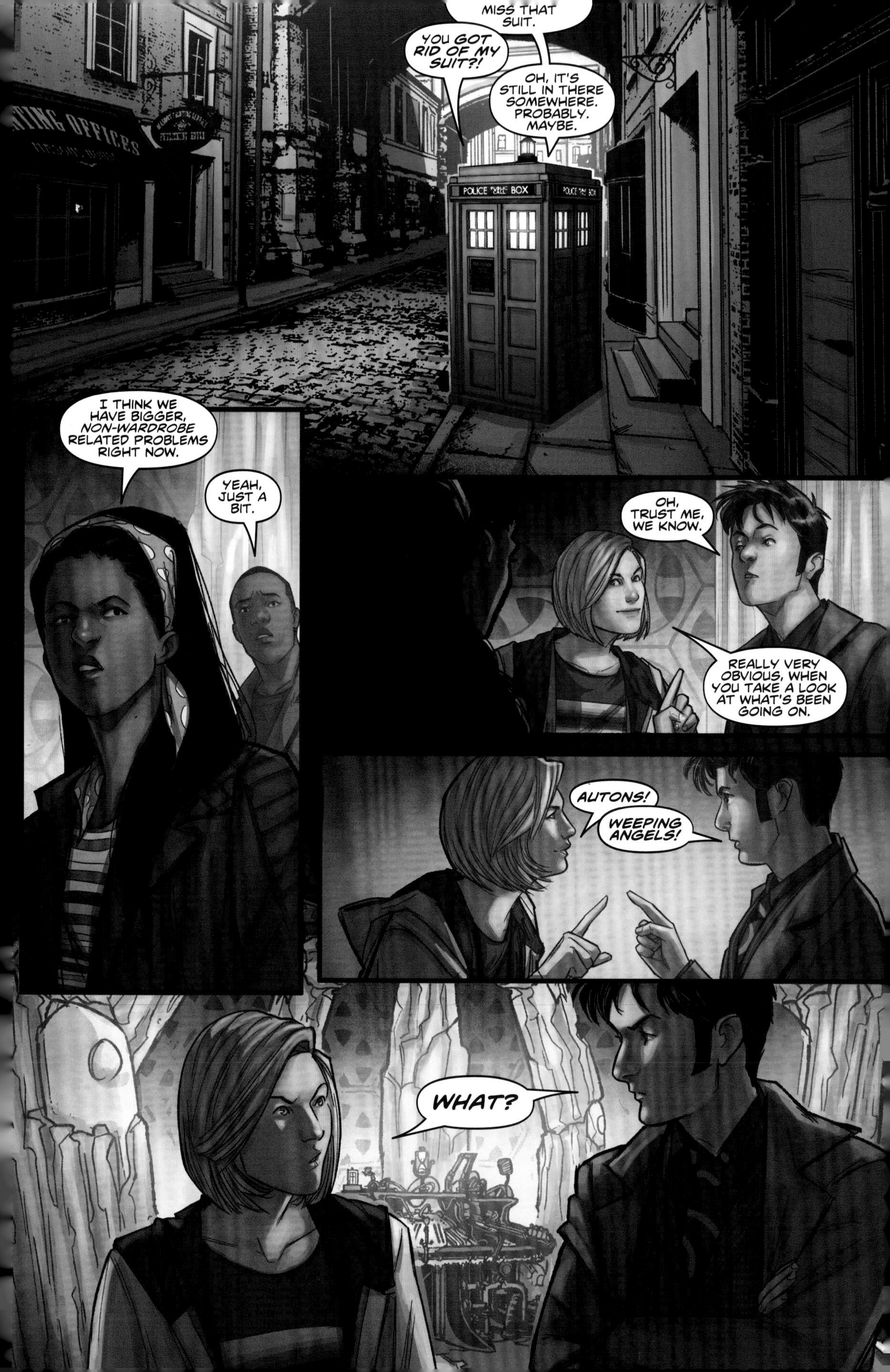
MISS THAT SUIT.
YOU GOT RID OF MY SUIT?!
OH, IT'S STILL IN THERE SOMEWHERE. PROBABLY. MAYBE.
POLICE PUBLIC CALL BOX
I THINK WE HAVE BIGGER, NON-WARDROBE RELATED PROBLEMS RIGHT NOW.
YEAH, JUST A BIT.
OH, TRUST ME, WE KNOW.
REALLY VERY OBVIOUS, WHEN YOU TAKE A LOOK AT WHAT'S BEEN GOING ON.
AUTONS!
WEEPING ANGELS!
WHAT?

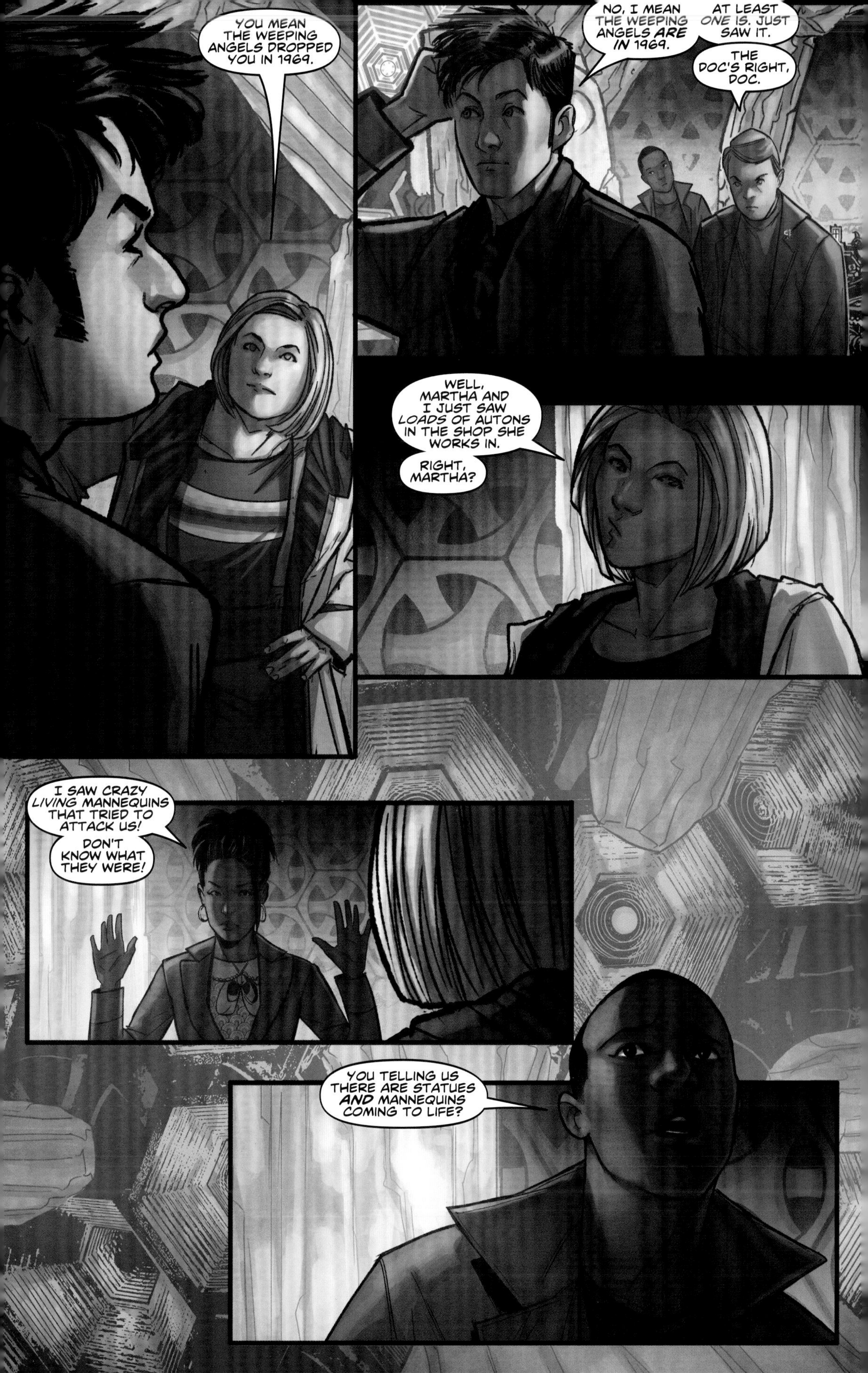
YOU MEAN THE WEEPING ANGELS DROPPED YOU IN 1969.
NO, I MEAN THE WEEPING ANGELS **ARE IN** 1969.
AT LEAST *ONE* IS. JUST SAW IT.
THE DOC'S RIGHT, DOC.
WELL, MARTHA AND I JUST SAW *LOADS OF AUTONS* IN THE SHOP SHE WORKS IN.
RIGHT, MARTHA?
I SAW CRAZY *LIVING* MANNEQUINS THAT TRIED TO ATTACK US!
DON'T KNOW WHAT THEY WERE!
YOU TELLING US THERE ARE STATUES **AND** MANNEQUINS COMING TO LIFE?

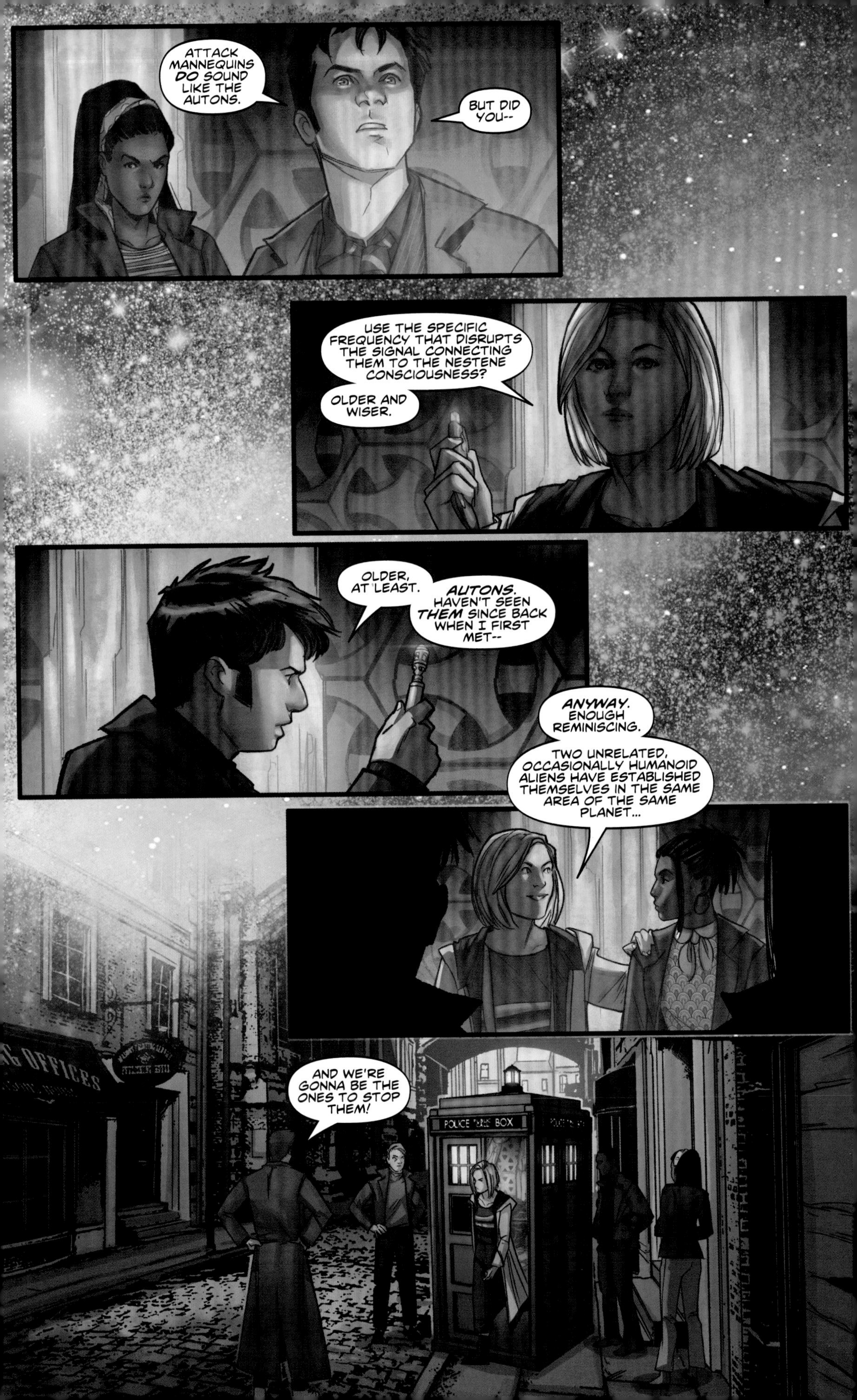
ATTACK MANNEQUINS *DO* SOUND LIKE THE AUTONS.
BUT DID YOU--
USE THE SPECIFIC FREQUENCY THAT DISRUPTS THE SIGNAL CONNECTING THEM TO THE NESTENE CONSCIOUSNESS?
OLDER AND WISER.
OLDER, AT LEAST.
AUTONS. HAVEN'T SEEN ***THEM*** SINCE BACK WHEN I FIRST MET--
ANYWAY. ENOUGH REMINISCING.
TWO UNRELATED, OCCASIONALLY HUMANOID ALIENS HAVE ESTABLISHED THEMSELVES IN THE SAME AREA OF THE SAME PLANET...
AND WE'RE GONNA BE THE ONES TO STOP THEM!

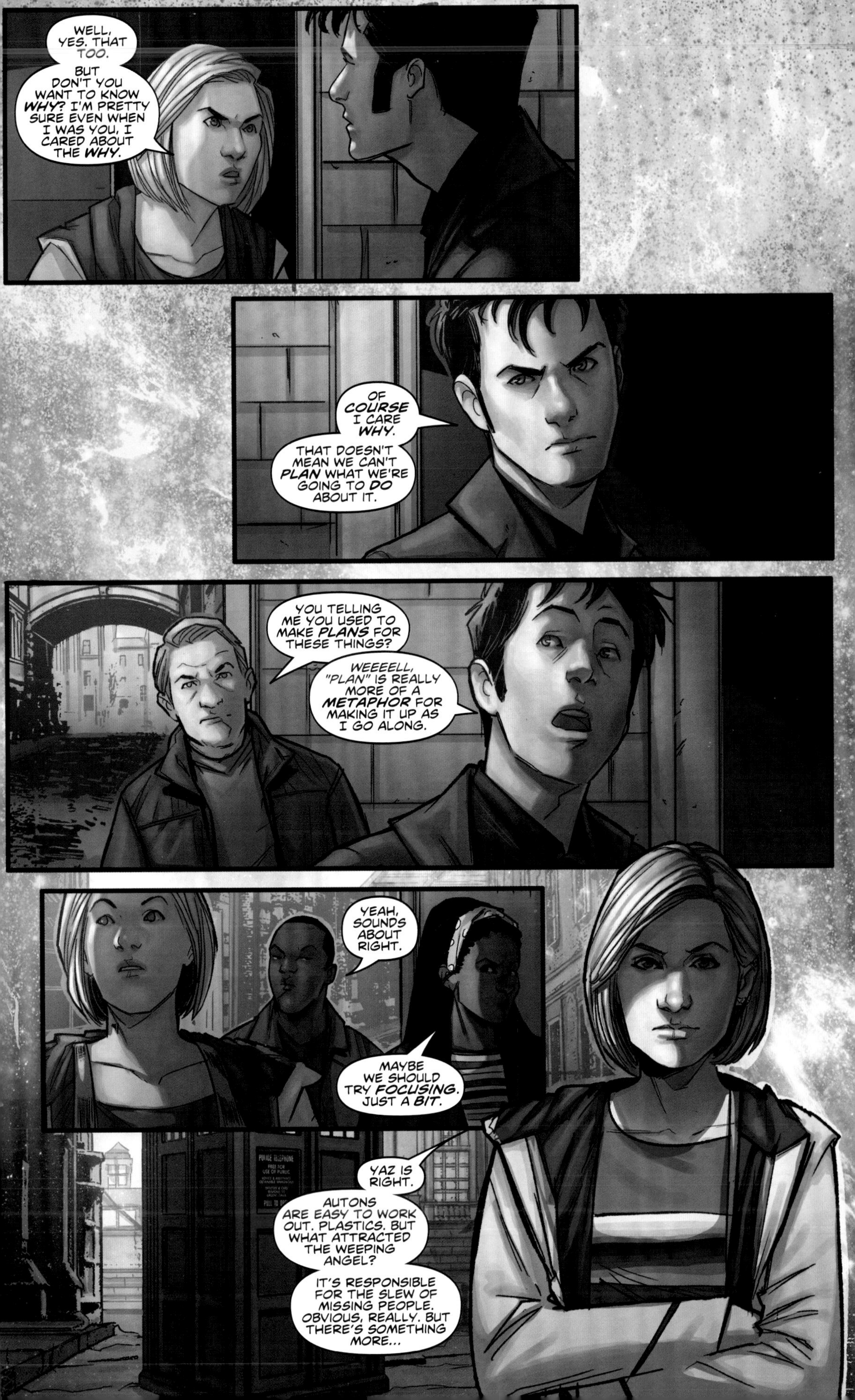
WELL, YES. THAT TOO.
BUT DON'T YOU WANT TO KNOW WHY? I'M PRETTY SURE EVEN WHEN I WAS YOU, I CARED ABOUT THE WHY.
OF COURSE I CARE WHY.
THAT DOESN'T MEAN WE CAN'T PLAN WHAT WE'RE GOING TO DO ABOUT IT.
YOU TELLING ME YOU USED TO MAKE PLANS FOR THESE THINGS?
WEEEELL, "PLAN" IS REALLY MORE OF A METAPHOR FOR MAKING IT UP AS I GO ALONG.
YEAH, SOUNDS ABOUT RIGHT.
MAYBE WE SHOULD TRY FOCUSING. JUST A BIT.
POLICE TELEPHONE
FREE FOR USE OF PUBLIC
PULL TO OPEN
YAZ IS RIGHT.
AUTONS ARE EASY TO WORK OUT. PLASTICS. BUT WHAT ATTRACTED THE WEEPING ANGEL?
IT'S RESPONSIBLE FOR THE SLEW OF MISSING PEOPLE. OBVIOUS, REALLY. BUT THERE'S SOMETHING MORE...

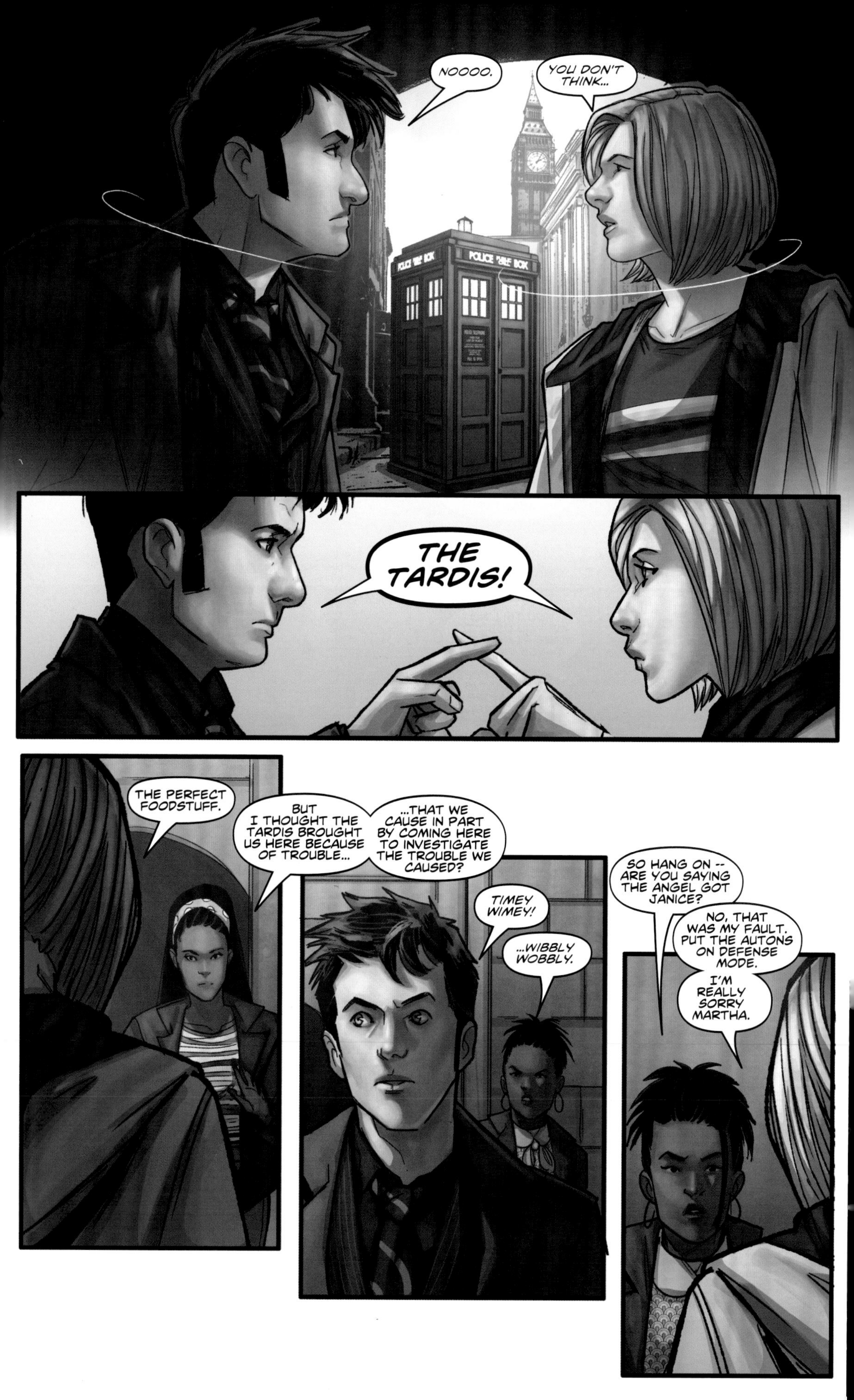
NOOOO.
YOU DON'T THINK...
POLICE PUBLIC CALL BOX
THE TARDIS!
THE PERFECT FOODSTUFF.
BUT I THOUGHT THE TARDIS BROUGHT US HERE BECAUSE OF TROUBLE...
...THAT WE CAUSE IN PART BY COMING HERE TO INVESTIGATE THE TROUBLE WE CAUSED?
TIMEY WIMEY!
...WIBBLY WOBBLY.
SO HANG ON -- ARE YOU SAYING THE ANGEL GOT JANICE?
NO, THAT WAS MY FAULT. PUT THE AUTONS ON DEFENSE MODE.
I'M REALLY SORRY MARTHA.

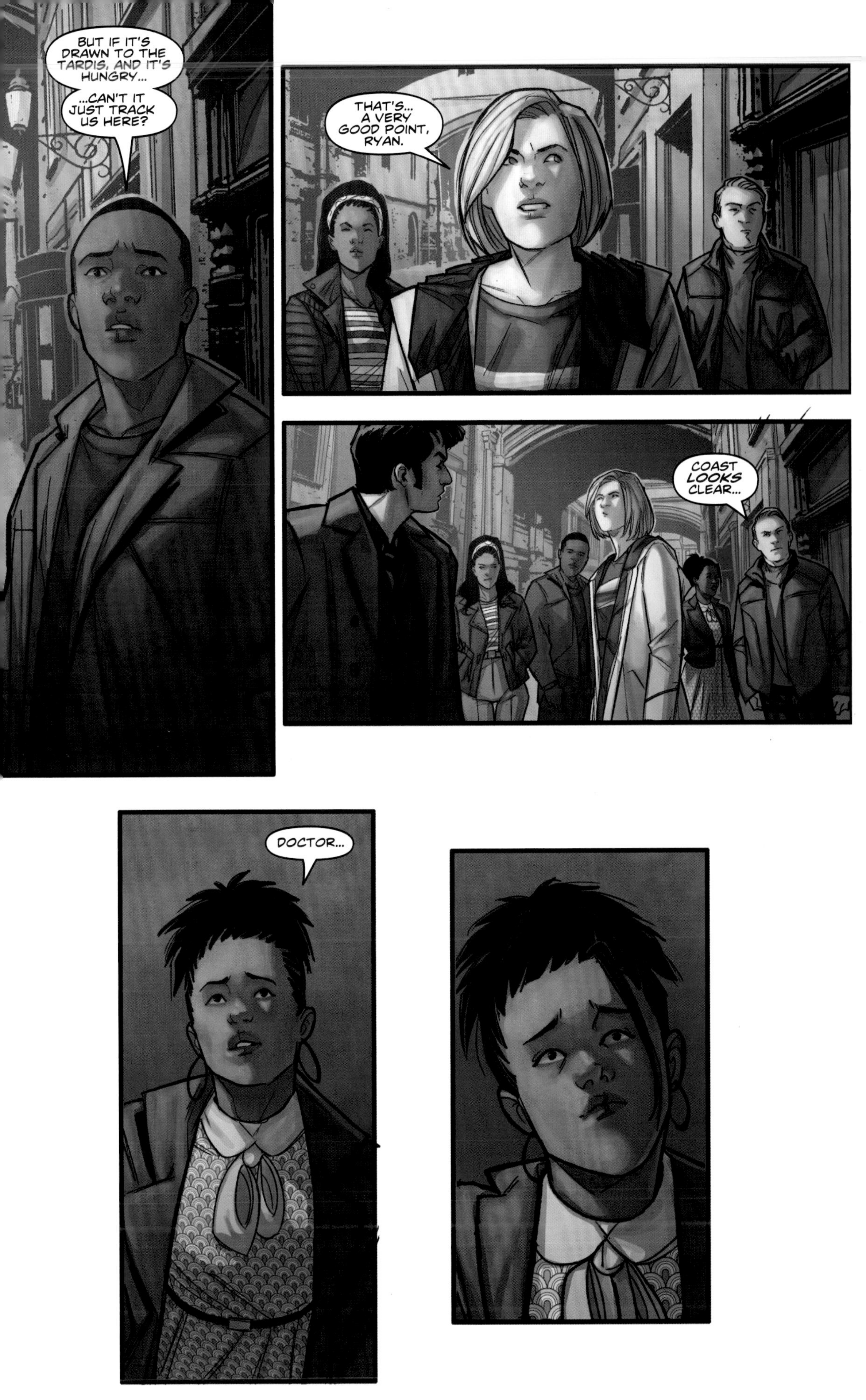
BUT IF IT'S DRAWN TO THE TARDIS, AND IT'S HUNGRY...
...CAN'T IT JUST TRACK US HERE?
THAT'S... A VERY GOOD POINT, RYAN.
COAST LOOKS CLEAR...
DOCTOR...

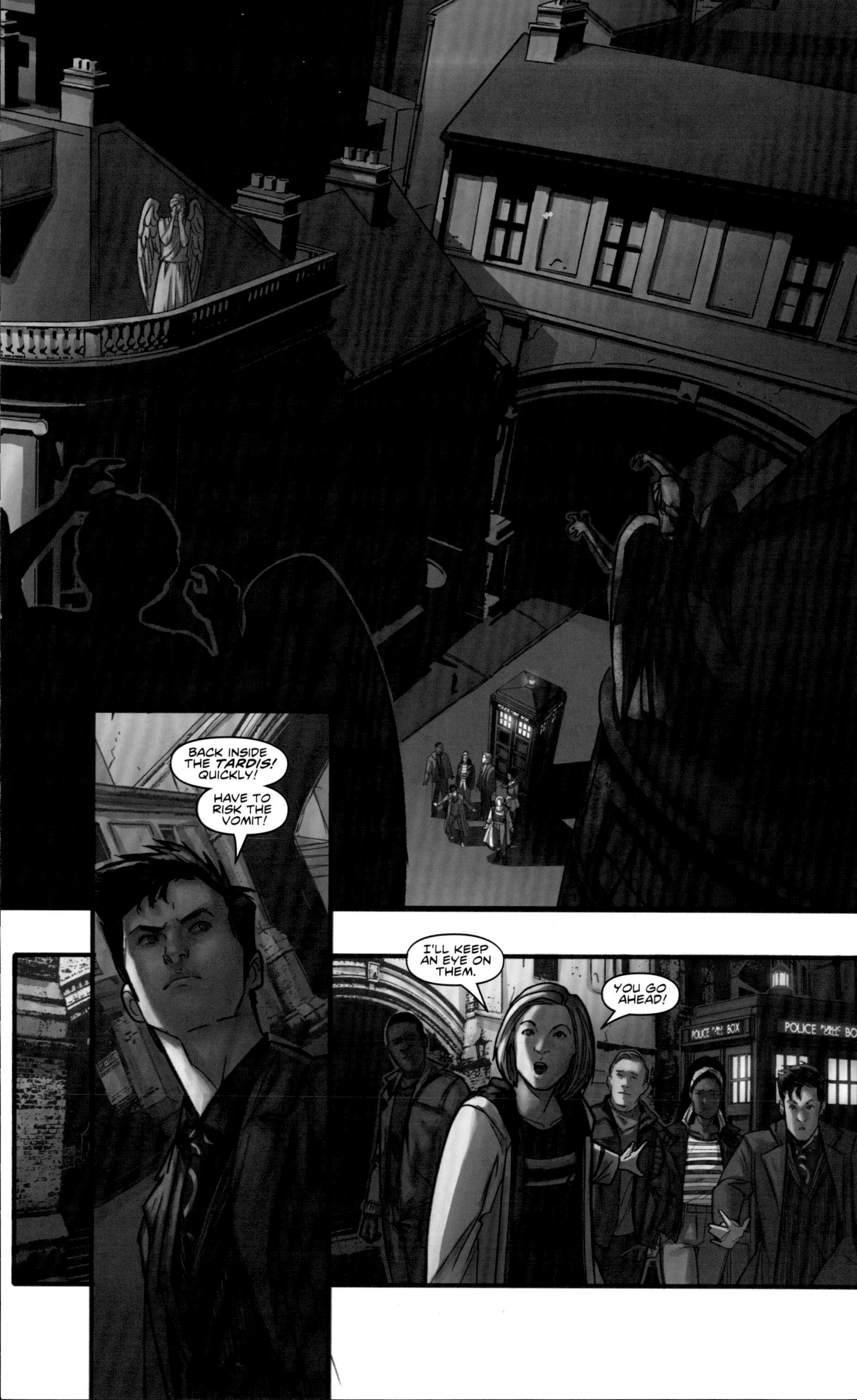
BACK INSIDE THE *TARDIS!* QUICKLY!
HAVE TO RISK THE VOMIT!
I'LL KEEP AN EYE ON THEM.
YOU GO AHEAD!
POLICE BOX
POLICE BOX

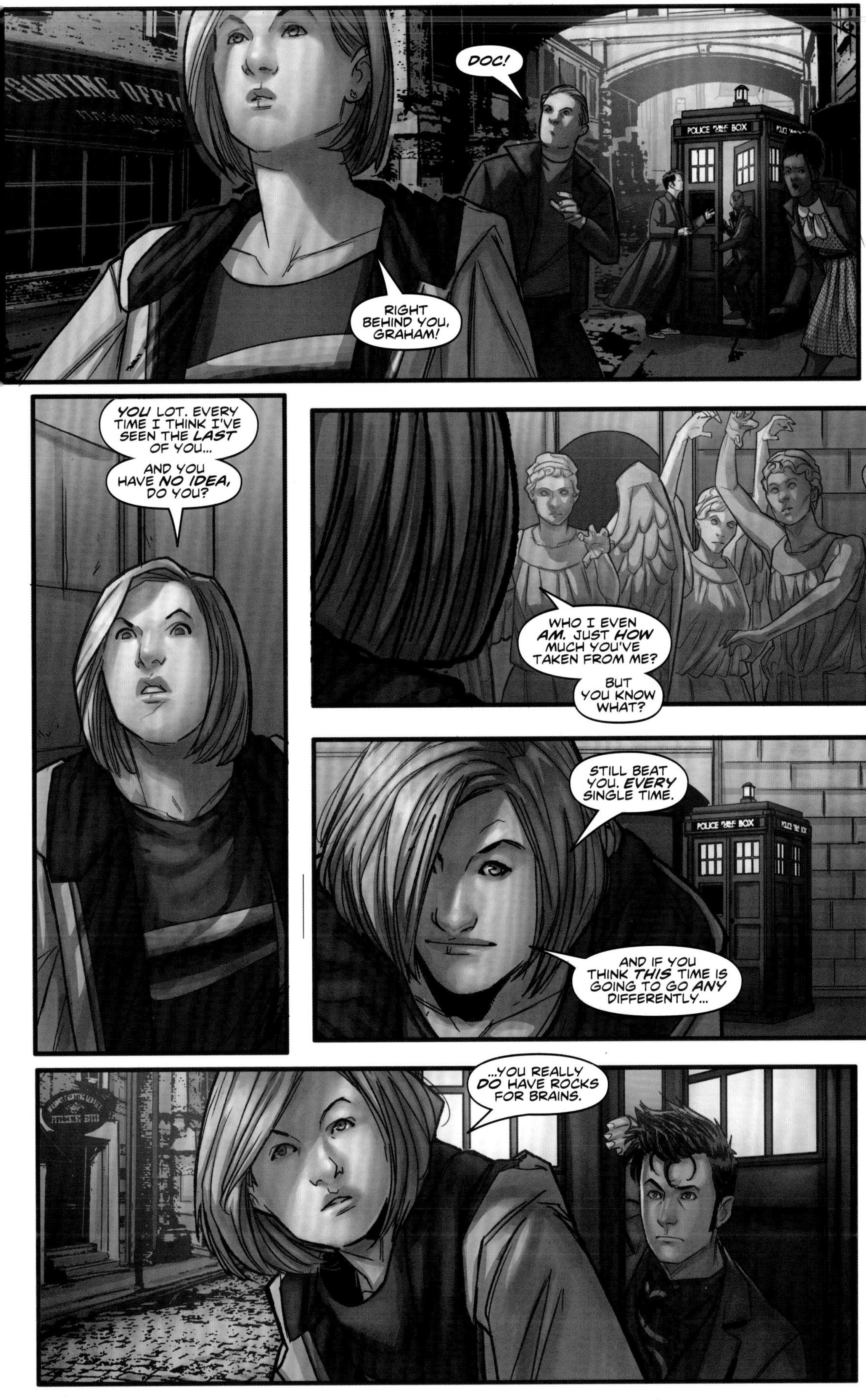
PRINTING OFFI
POLICE PUBLIC CALL BOX
DOC!
RIGHT BEHIND YOU, GRAHAM!
YOU LOT. EVERY TIME I THINK I'VE SEEN THE LAST OF YOU...
AND YOU HAVE NO IDEA, DO YOU?
WHO I EVEN AM. JUST HOW MUCH YOU'VE TAKEN FROM ME?
BUT YOU KNOW WHAT?
STILL BEAT YOU. EVERY SINGLE TIME.
POLICE PUBLIC CALL BOX
AND IF YOU THINK THIS TIME IS GOING TO GO ANY DIFFERENTLY...
...YOU REALLY DO HAVE ROCKS FOR BRAINS.

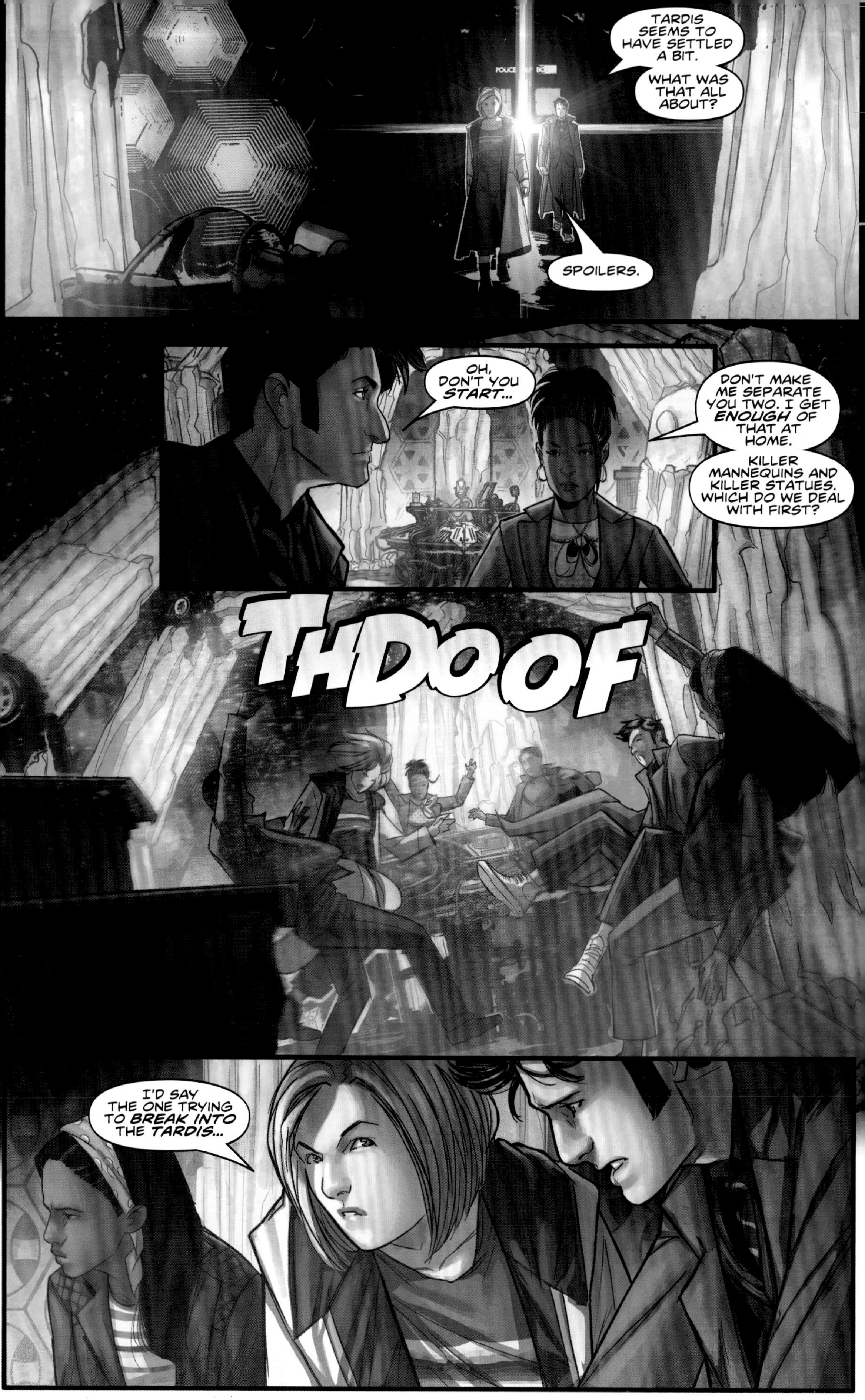
TARDIS SEEMS TO HAVE SETTLED A BIT.
WHAT WAS THAT ALL ABOUT?
SPOILERS.
OH, DON'T YOU *START*...
DON'T MAKE ME SEPARATE YOU TWO. I GET *ENOUGH* OF THAT AT HOME.
KILLER MANNEQUINS AND KILLER STATUES. WHICH DO WE DEAL WITH FIRST?
THDOOF
I'D SAY THE ONE TRYING TO *BREAK INTO* THE *TARDIS*...

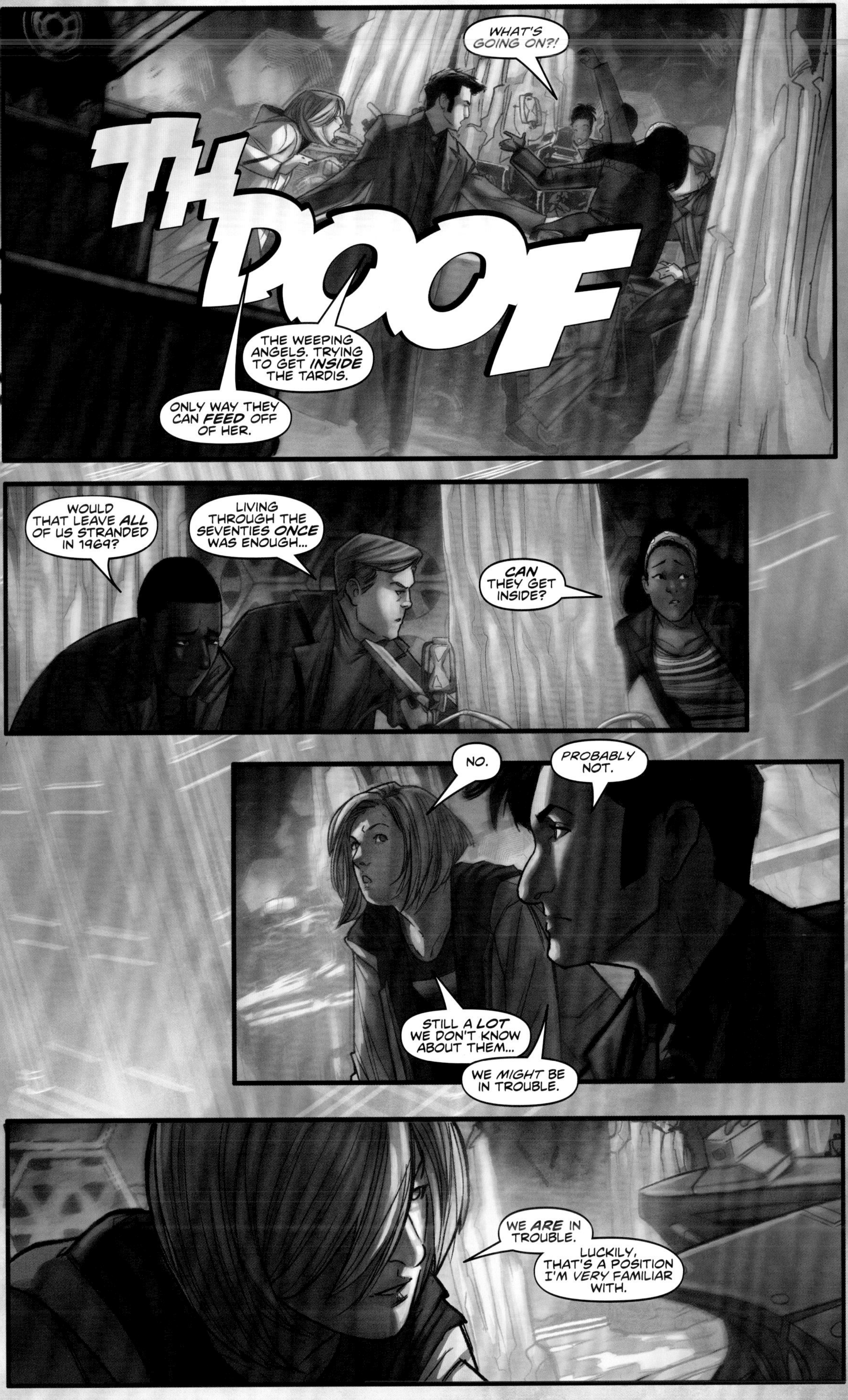
WHAT'S GOING ON?!
THOOF
THE WEEPING ANGELS. TRYING TO GET INSIDE THE TARDIS.
ONLY WAY THEY CAN FEED OFF OF HER.
WOULD THAT LEAVE ALL OF US STRANDED IN 1969?
LIVING THROUGH THE SEVENTIES ONCE WAS ENOUGH...
CAN THEY GET INSIDE?
NO.
PROBABLY NOT.
STILL A LOT WE DON'T KNOW ABOUT THEM...
WE MIGHT BE IN TROUBLE.
WE ARE IN TROUBLE.
LUCKILY, THAT'S A POSITION I'M VERY FAMILIAR WITH.

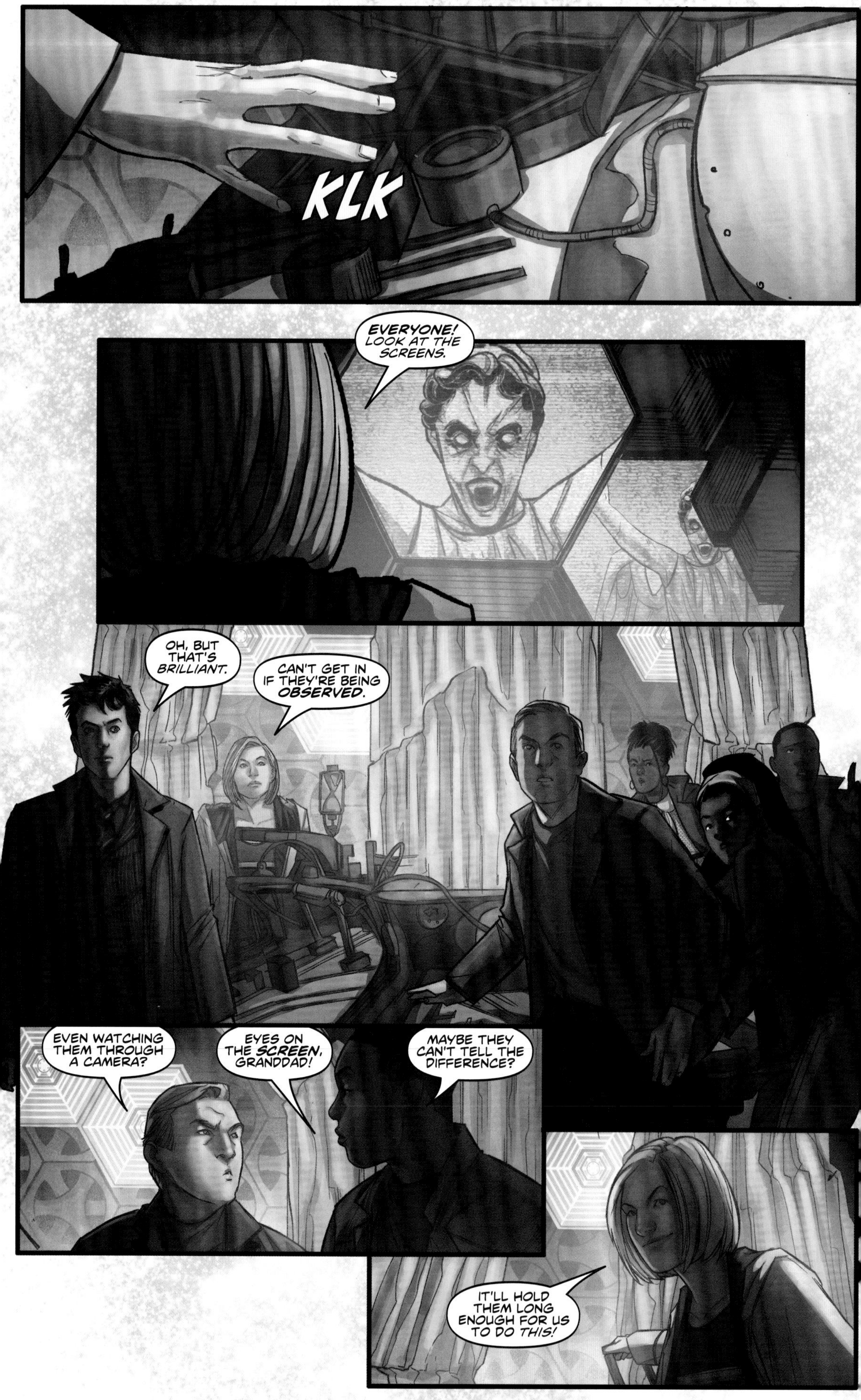
KLK
EVERYONE! LOOK AT THE SCREENS.
OH, BUT THAT'S BRILLIANT.
CAN'T GET IN IF THEY'RE BEING OBSERVED.
EVEN WATCHING THEM THROUGH A CAMERA?
EYES ON THE SCREEN, GRANDDAD!
MAYBE THEY CAN'T TELL THE DIFFERENCE?
IT'LL HOLD THEM LONG ENOUGH FOR US TO DO THIS!

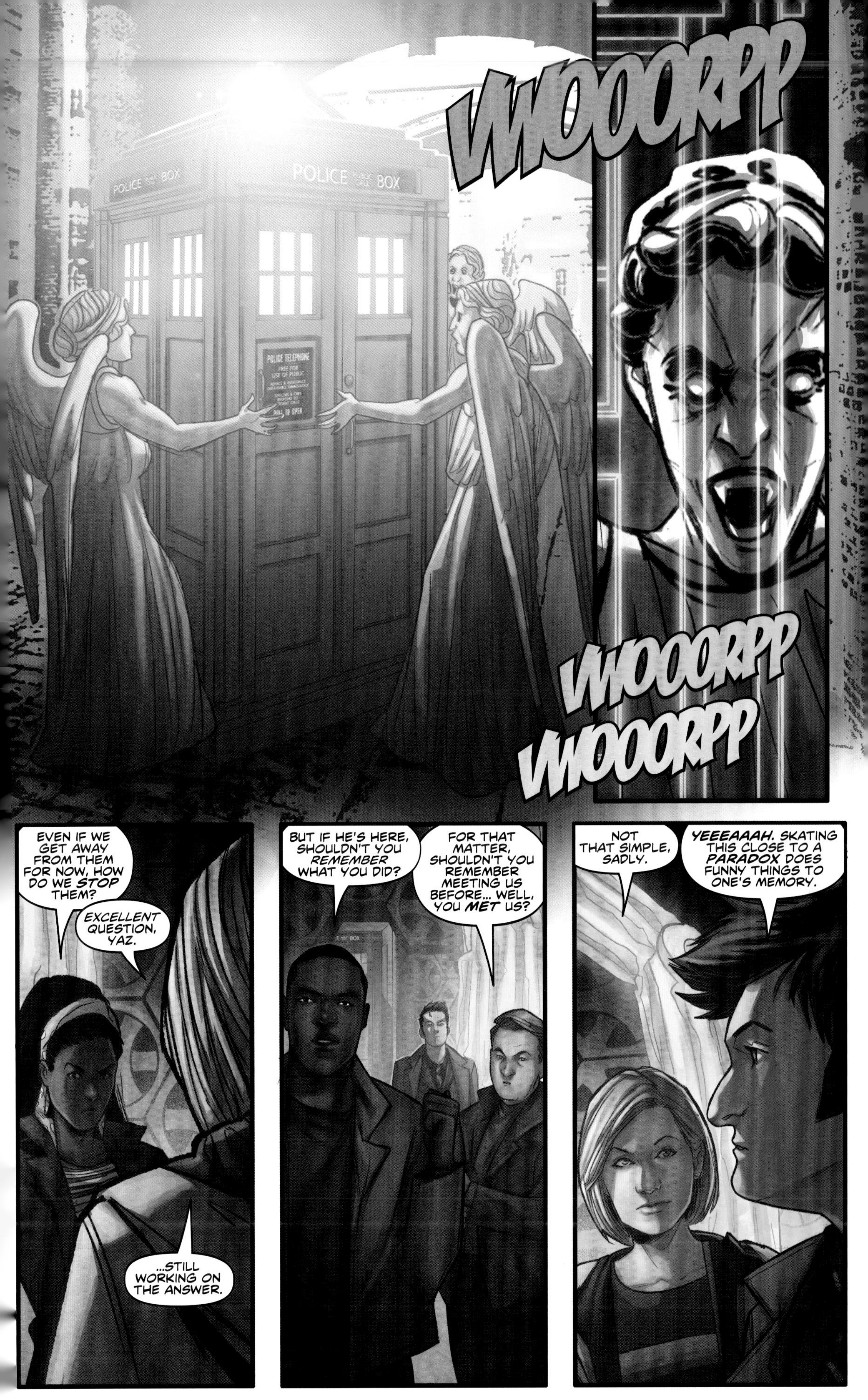
VWOOORPP
VWOOORPP
VWOOORPP
EVEN IF WE GET AWAY FROM THEM FOR NOW, HOW DO WE *STOP* THEM?
EXCELLENT QUESTION, YAZ.
...STILL WORKING ON THE ANSWER.
BUT IF HE'S HERE, SHOULDN'T YOU *REMEMBER* WHAT YOU DID?
FOR THAT MATTER, SHOULDN'T YOU REMEMBER MEETING US BEFORE... WELL, YOU *MET* US?
NOT THAT SIMPLE, SADLY.
YEEEAAAH. SKATING THIS CLOSE TO A ***PARADOX*** DOES FUNNY THINGS TO ONE'S MEMORY.

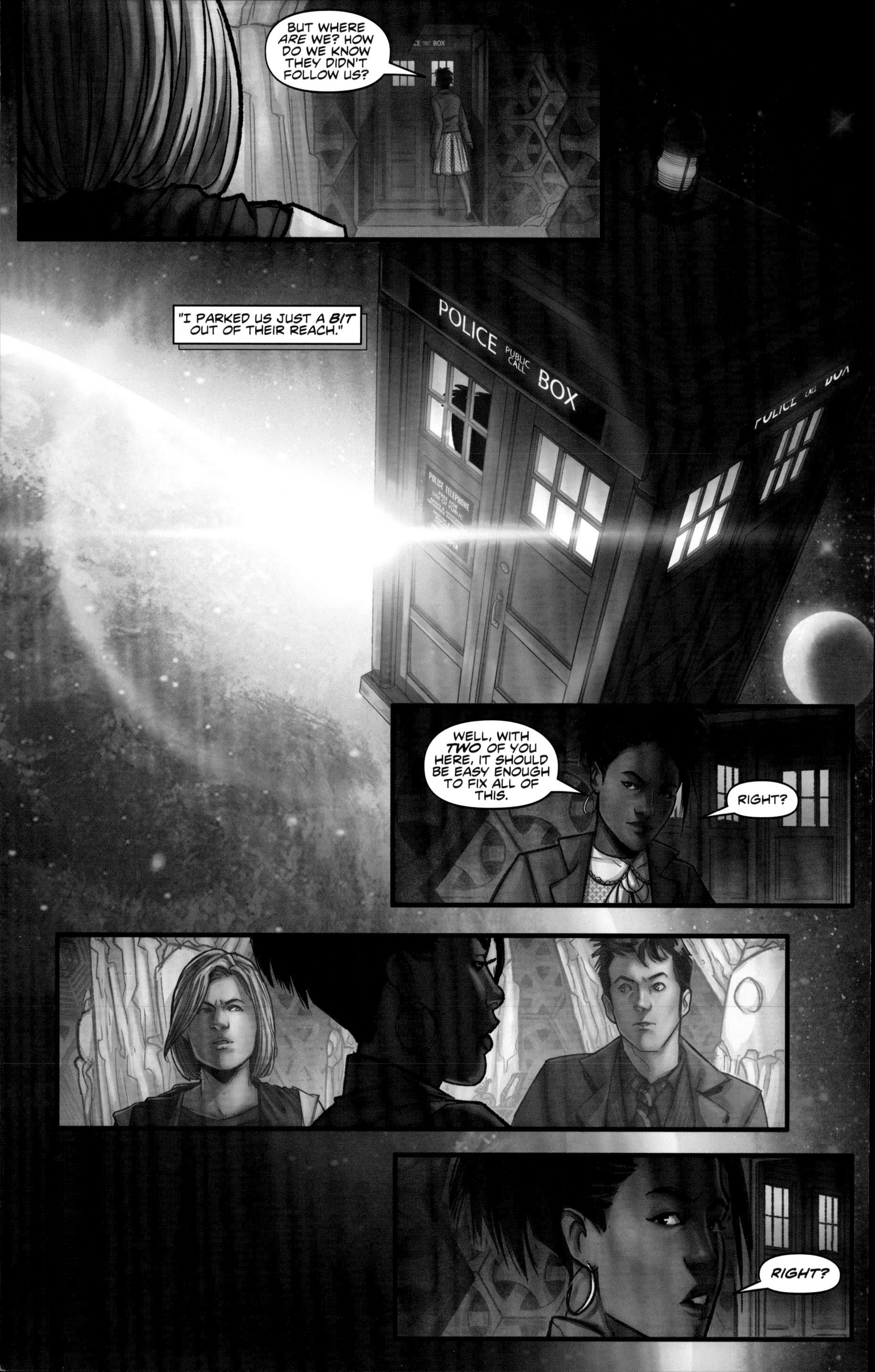

BUT WHERE *ARE* WE? HOW DO WE KNOW THEY DIDN'T FOLLOW US?
"I PARKED US JUST A *BIT* OUT OF THEIR REACH."
POLICE PUBLIC CALL BOX
WELL, WITH *TWO* OF YOU HERE, IT SHOULD BE EASY ENOUGH TO FIX ALL OF THIS.
RIGHT?
RIGHT?

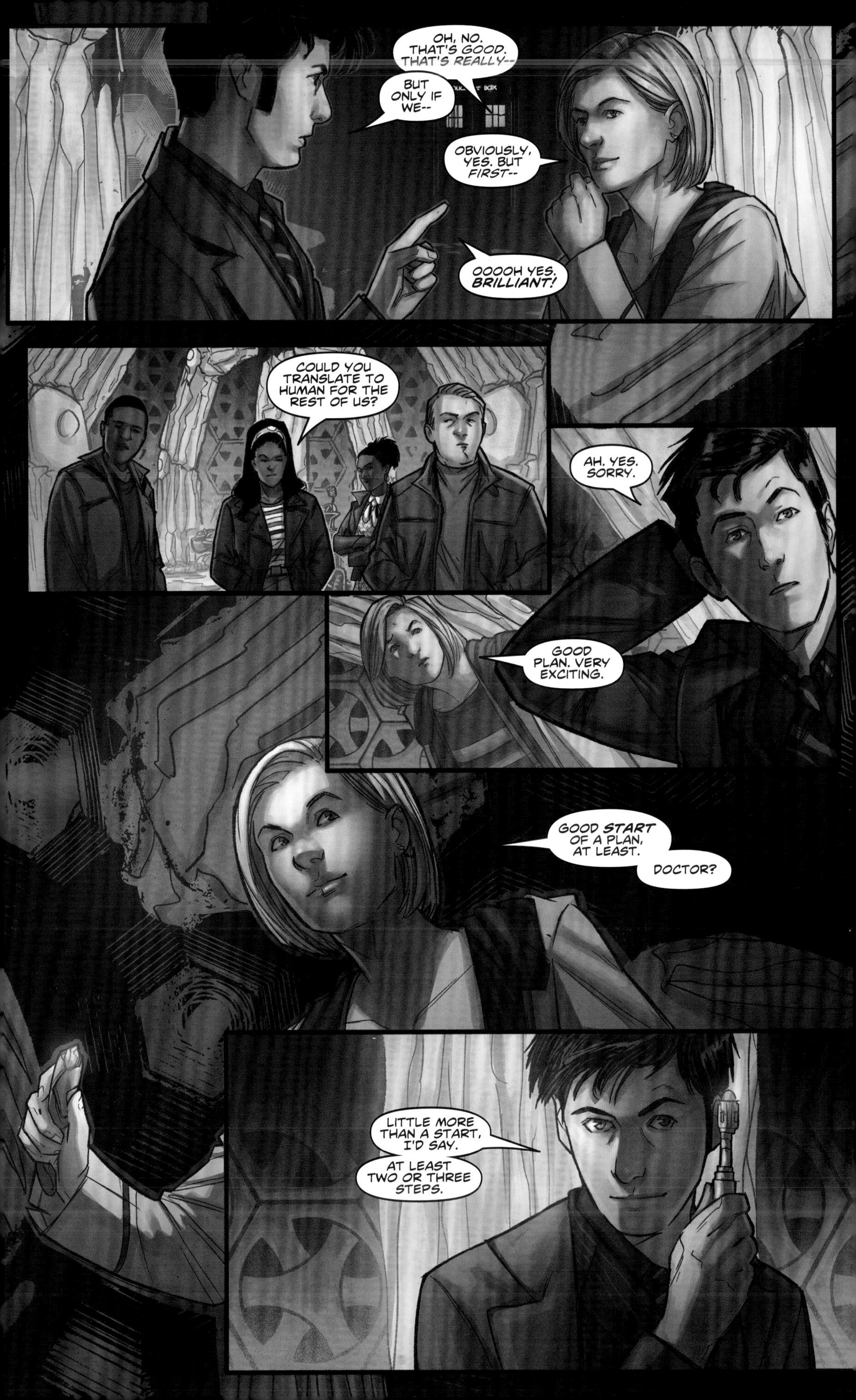
OH, NO. THAT'S GOOD. THAT'S REALLY--
BUT ONLY IF WE--
OBVIOUSLY, YES. BUT FIRST--
OOOOH YES. BRILLIANT!
COULD YOU TRANSLATE TO HUMAN FOR THE REST OF US?
AH. YES. SORRY.
GOOD PLAN. VERY EXCITING.
GOOD START OF A PLAN, AT LEAST.
DOCTOR?
LITTLE MORE THAN A START, I'D SAY.
AT LEAST TWO OR THREE STEPS.

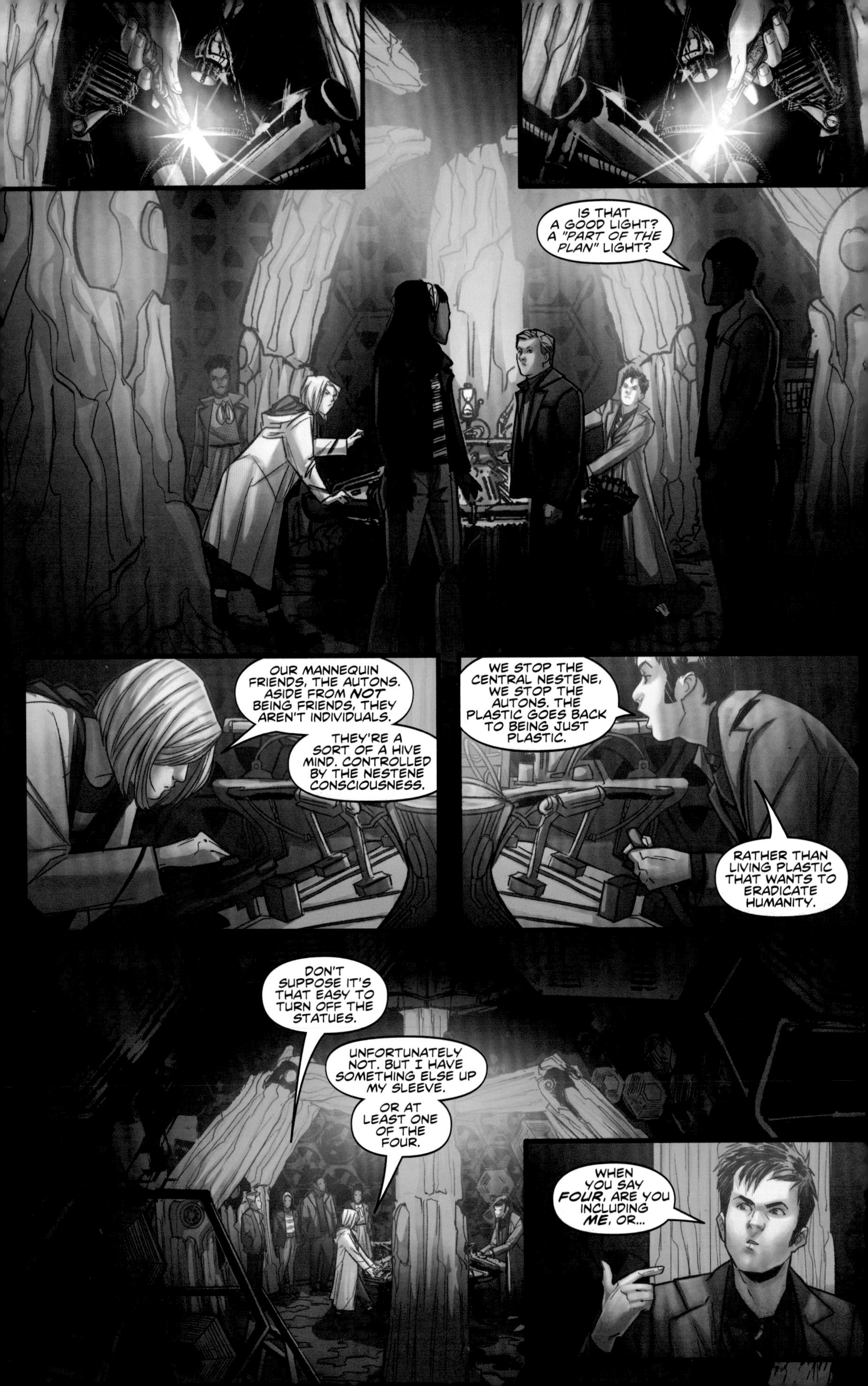
IS THAT A GOOD LIGHT? A "PART OF THE PLAN" LIGHT?
OUR MANNEQUIN FRIENDS, THE AUTONS. ASIDE FROM NOT BEING FRIENDS, THEY AREN'T INDIVIDUALS.
THEY'RE A SORT OF A HIVE MIND. CONTROLLED BY THE NESTENE CONSCIOUSNESS.
WE STOP THE CENTRAL NESTENE, WE STOP THE AUTONS. THE PLASTIC GOES BACK TO BEING JUST PLASTIC.
RATHER THAN LIVING PLASTIC THAT WANTS TO ERADICATE HUMANITY.
DON'T SUPPOSE IT'S THAT EASY TO TURN OFF THE STATUES.
UNFORTUNATELY NOT. BUT I HAVE SOMETHING ELSE UP MY SLEEVE.
OR AT LEAST ONE OF THE FOUR.
WHEN YOU SAY FOUR, ARE YOU INCLUDING ME, OR...

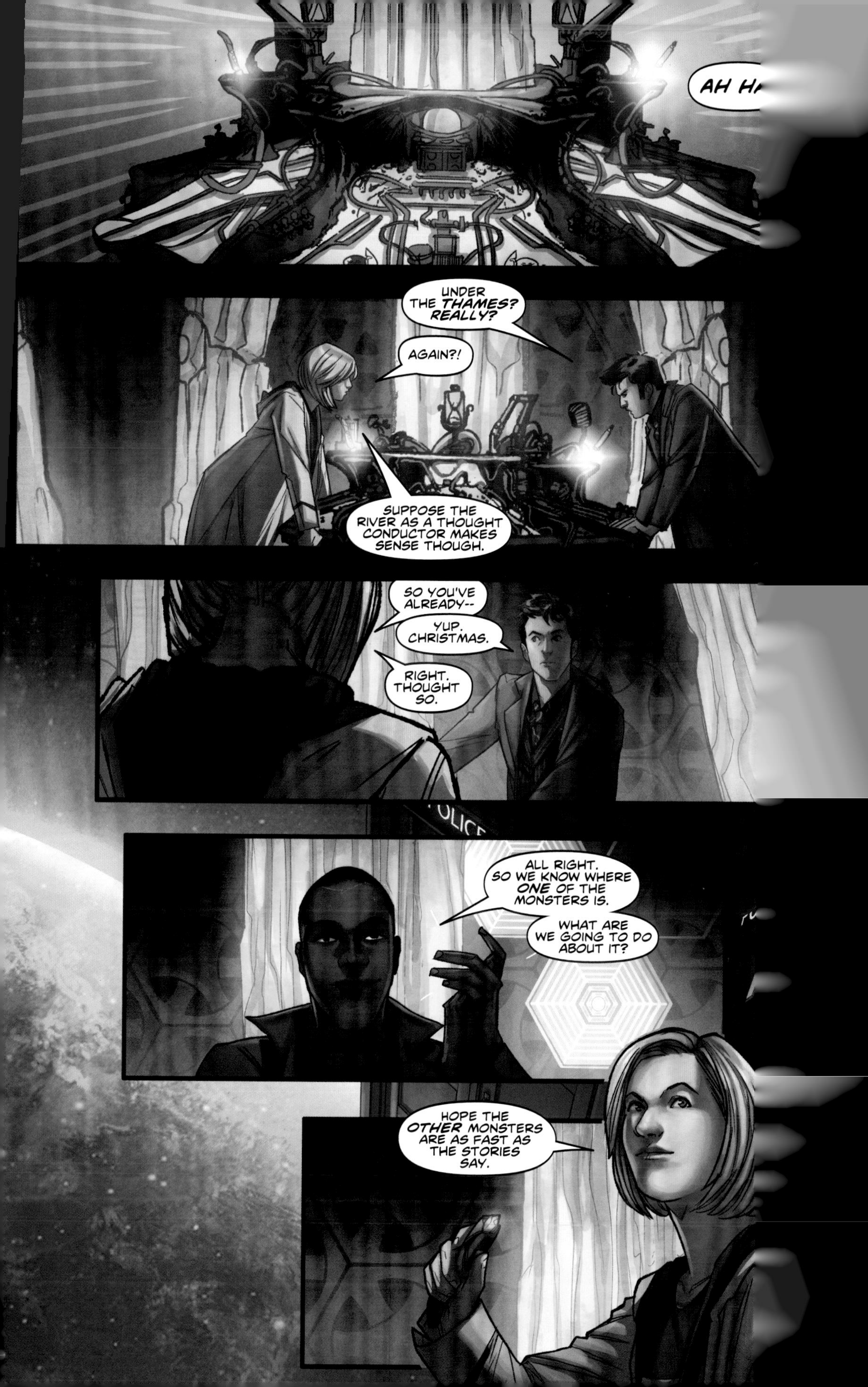

AH HA
UNDER THE THAMES? REALLY?
AGAIN?!
SUPPOSE THE RIVER AS A THOUGHT CONDUCTOR MAKES SENSE THOUGH.
SO YOU'VE ALREADY--
YUP. CHRISTMAS.
RIGHT. THOUGHT SO.
POLICE
ALL RIGHT. SO WE KNOW WHERE ONE OF THE MONSTERS IS.
WHAT ARE WE GOING TO DO ABOUT IT?
HOPE THE OTHER MONSTERS ARE AS FAST AS THE STORIES SAY.

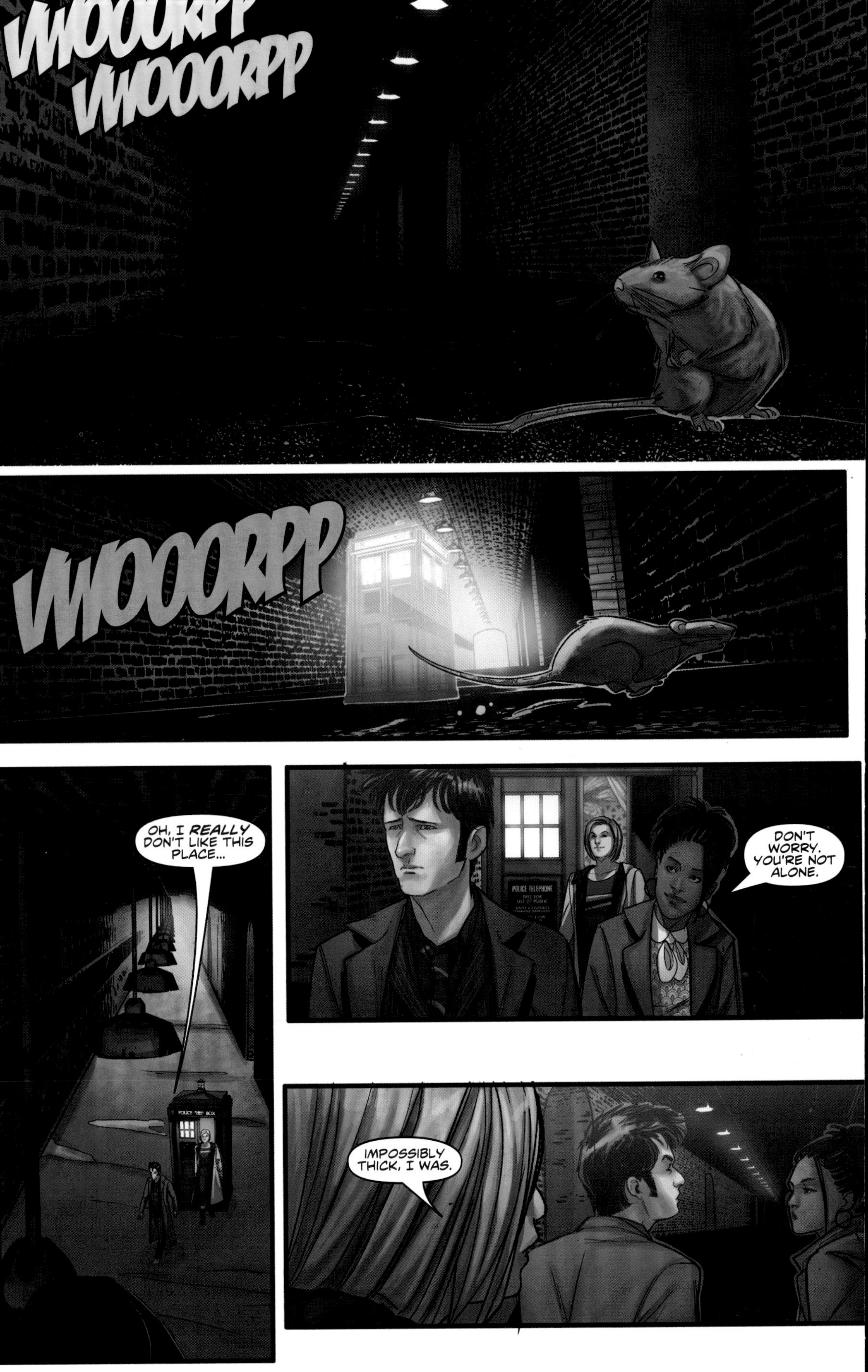
VWOORPP
VWOOORPP
VWOOORPP
OH, I REALLY DON'T LIKE THIS PLACE...
DON'T WORRY. YOU'RE NOT ALONE.
IMPOSSIBLY THICK, I WAS.

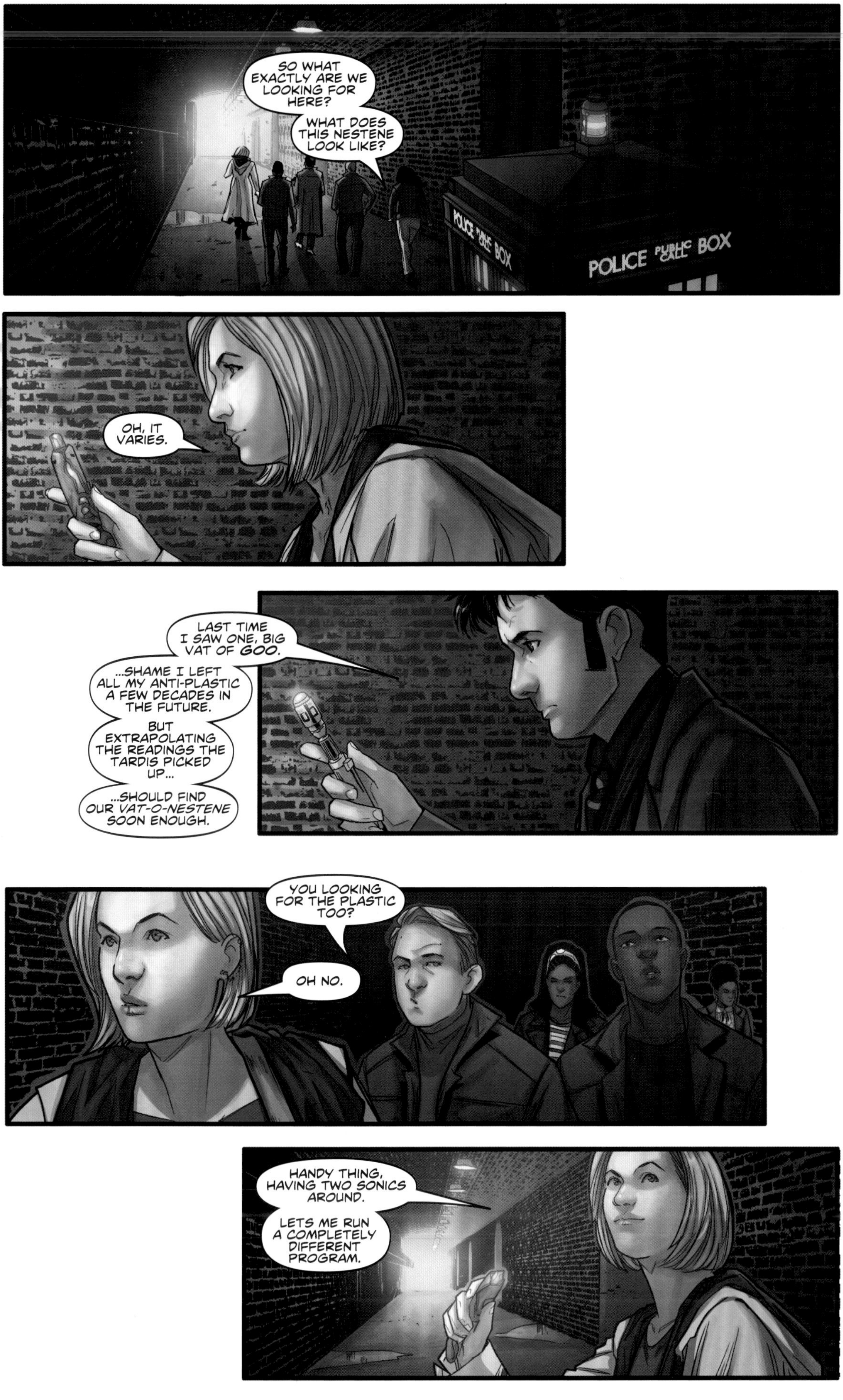
SO WHAT EXACTLY ARE WE LOOKING FOR HERE?
WHAT DOES THIS NESTENE LOOK LIKE?
POLICE PUBLIC CALL BOX
POLICE PUBLIC CALL BOX
OH, IT VARIES.
LAST TIME I SAW ONE, BIG VAT OF GOO.
...SHAME I LEFT ALL MY ANTI-PLASTIC A FEW DECADES IN THE FUTURE.
BUT EXTRAPOLATING THE READINGS THE TARDIS PICKED UP...
...SHOULD FIND OUR VAT-O-NESTENE SOON ENOUGH.
YOU LOOKING FOR THE PLASTIC TOO?
OH NO.
HANDY THING, HAVING TWO SONICS AROUND.
LETS ME RUN A COMPLETELY DIFFERENT PROGRAM.

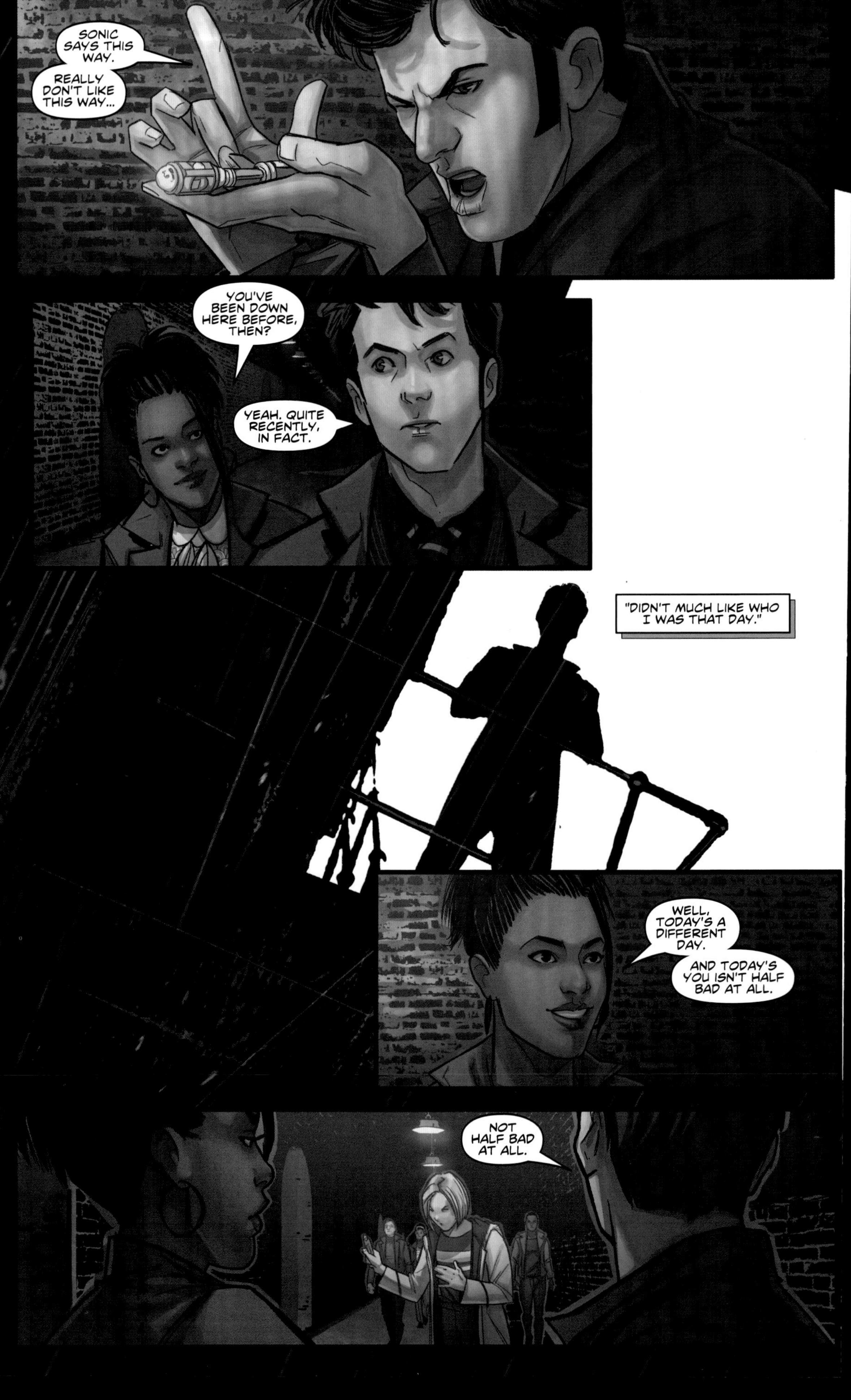
SONIC SAYS THIS WAY.
REALLY DON'T LIKE THIS WAY...
YOU'VE BEEN DOWN HERE BEFORE, THEN?
YEAH. QUITE RECENTLY, IN FACT.
"DIDN'T MUCH LIKE WHO I WAS THAT DAY."
WELL, TODAY'S A DIFFERENT DAY.
AND TODAY'S YOU ISN'T HALF BAD AT ALL.
NOT HALF BAD AT ALL.

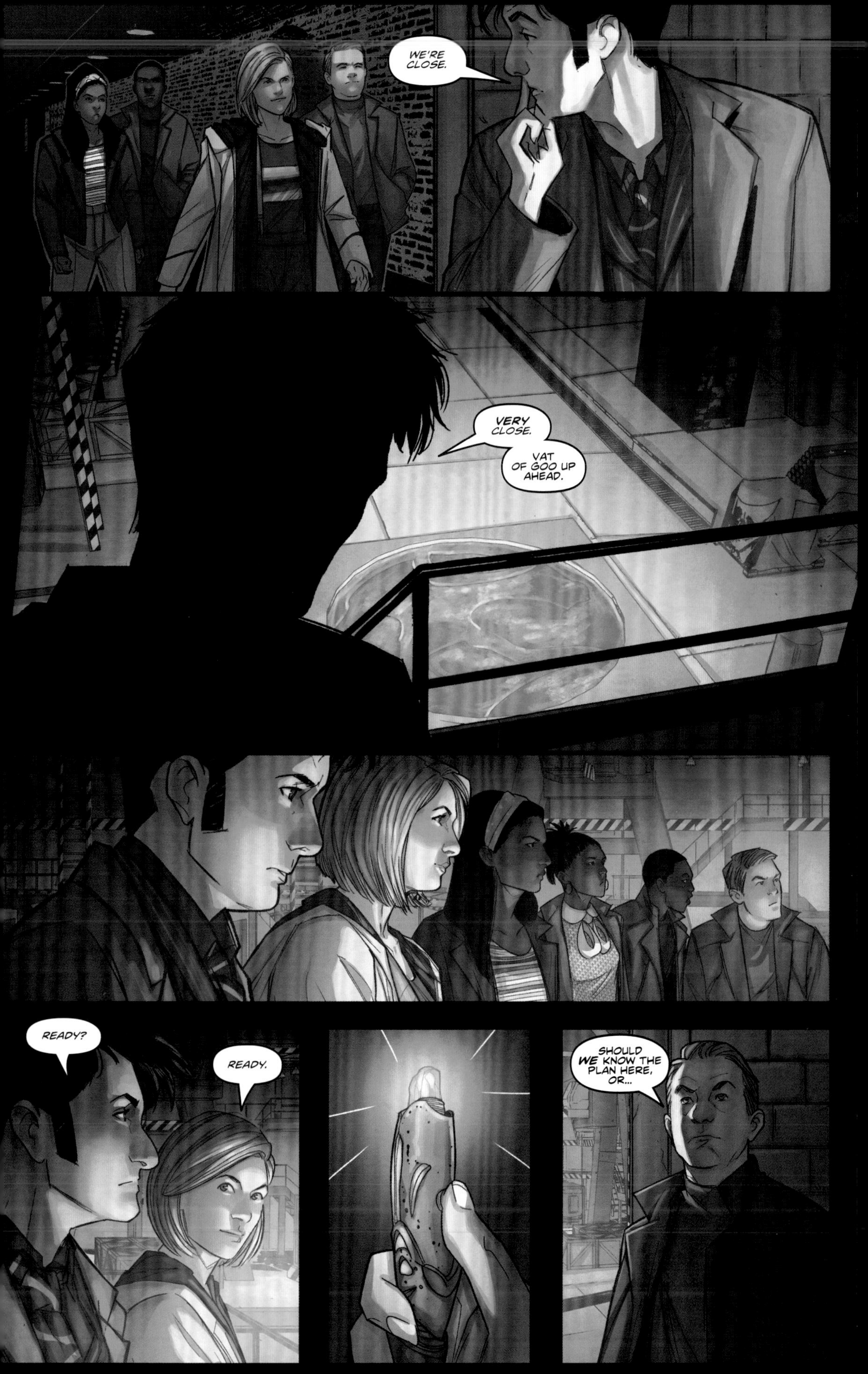
WE'RE CLOSE.
VERY CLOSE.
VAT OF GOO UP AHEAD.
READY?
READY.
SHOULD WE KNOW THE PLAN HERE, OR...

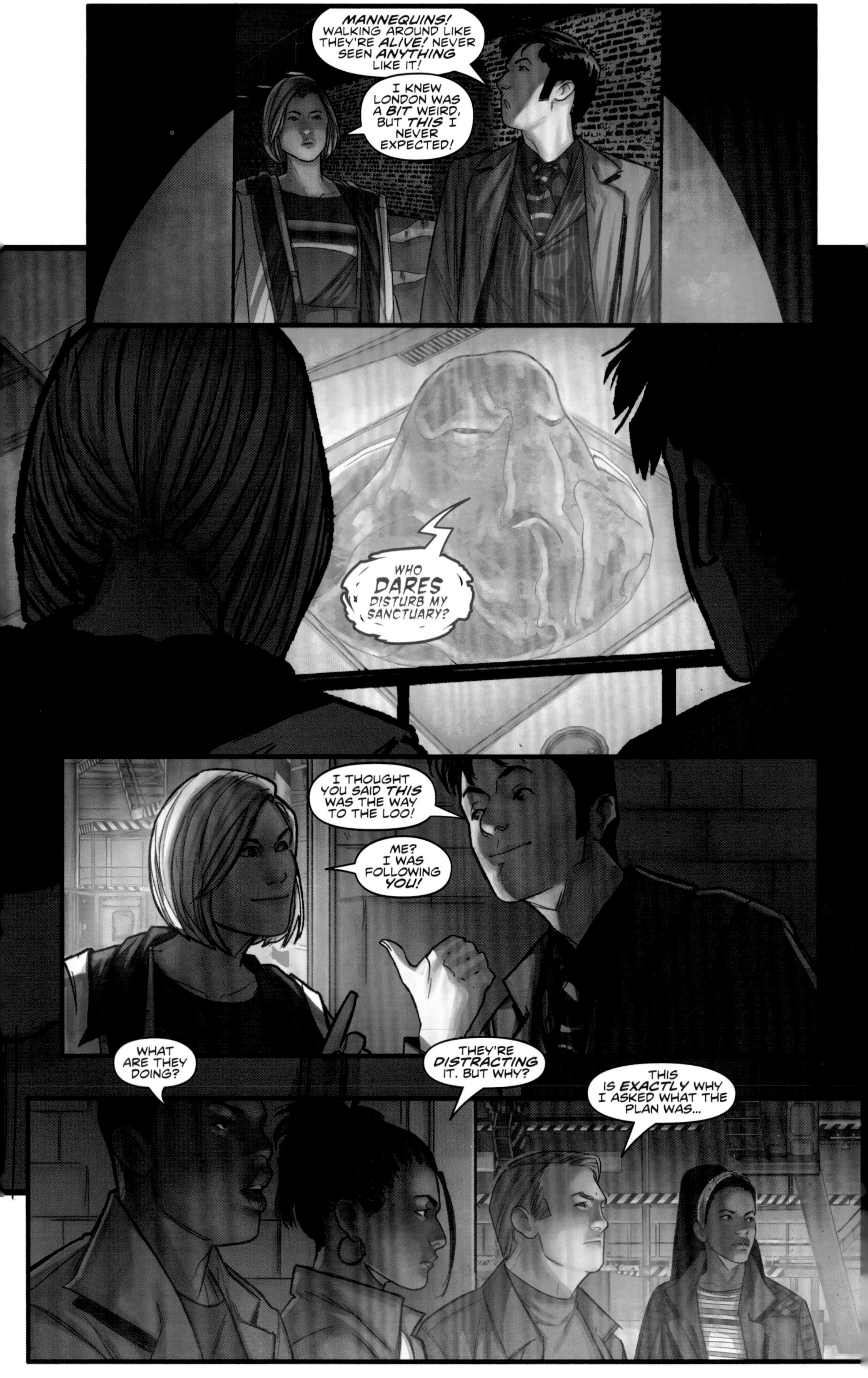
MANNEQUINS! WALKING AROUND LIKE THEY'RE ALIVE! NEVER SEEN ANYTHING LIKE IT!
I KNEW LONDON WAS A BIT WEIRD, BUT THIS I NEVER EXPECTED!
WHO DARES DISTURB MY SANCTUARY?
I THOUGHT YOU SAID THIS WAS THE WAY TO THE LOO!
ME? I WAS FOLLOWING YOU!
WHAT ARE THEY DOING?
THEY'RE DISTRACTING IT. BUT WHY?
THIS IS EXACTLY WHY I ASKED WHAT THE PLAN WAS...

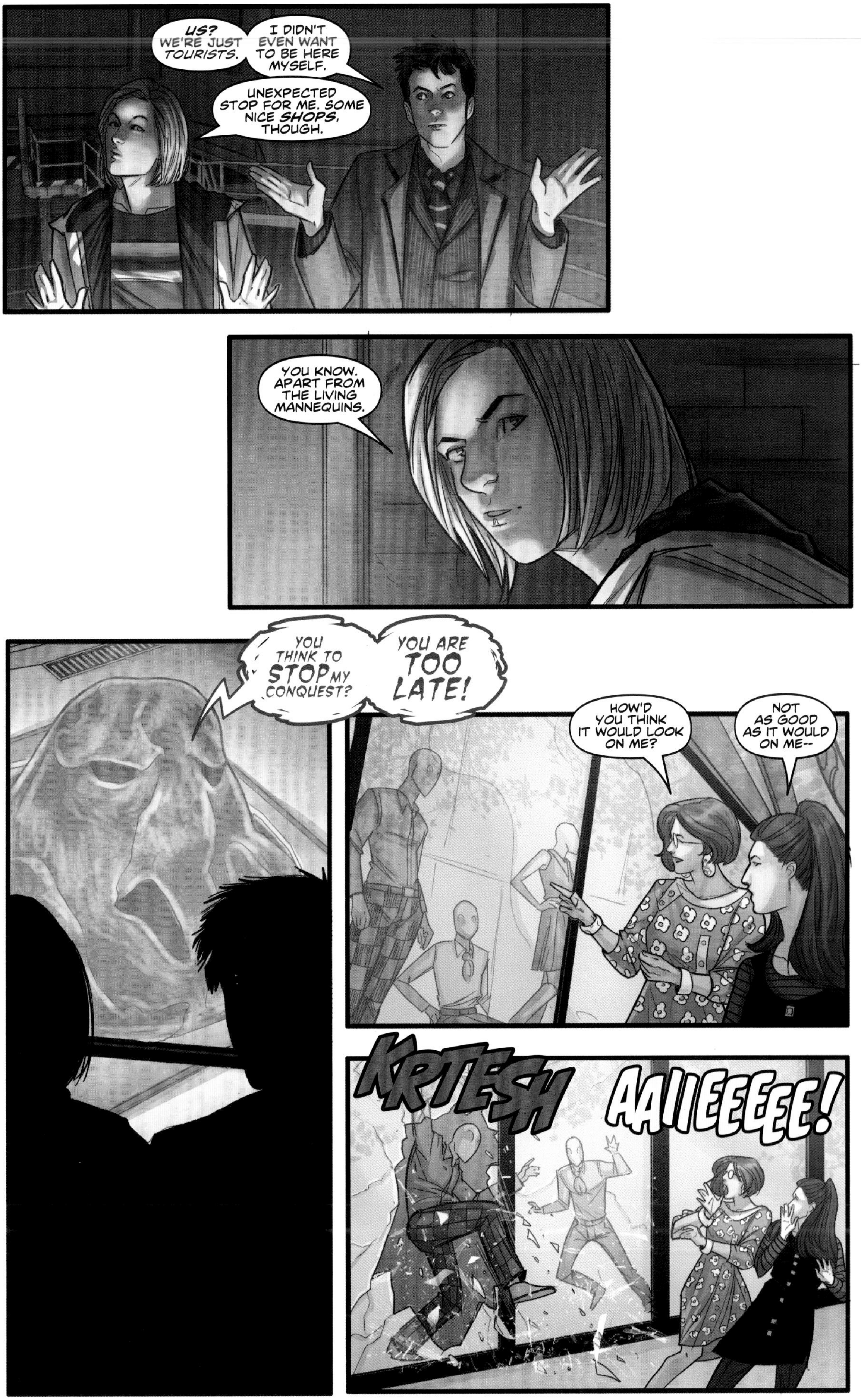
US? WE'RE JUST TOURISTS.
I DIDN'T EVEN WANT TO BE HERE MYSELF.
UNEXPECTED STOP FOR ME. SOME NICE SHOPS, THOUGH.
YOU KNOW. APART FROM THE LIVING MANNEQUINS.
YOU THINK TO STOP MY CONQUEST?
YOU ARE TOO LATE!
HOW'D YOU THINK IT WOULD LOOK ON ME?
NOT AS GOOD AS IT WOULD ON ME--
KRTESH
AAIIEEEEEE!

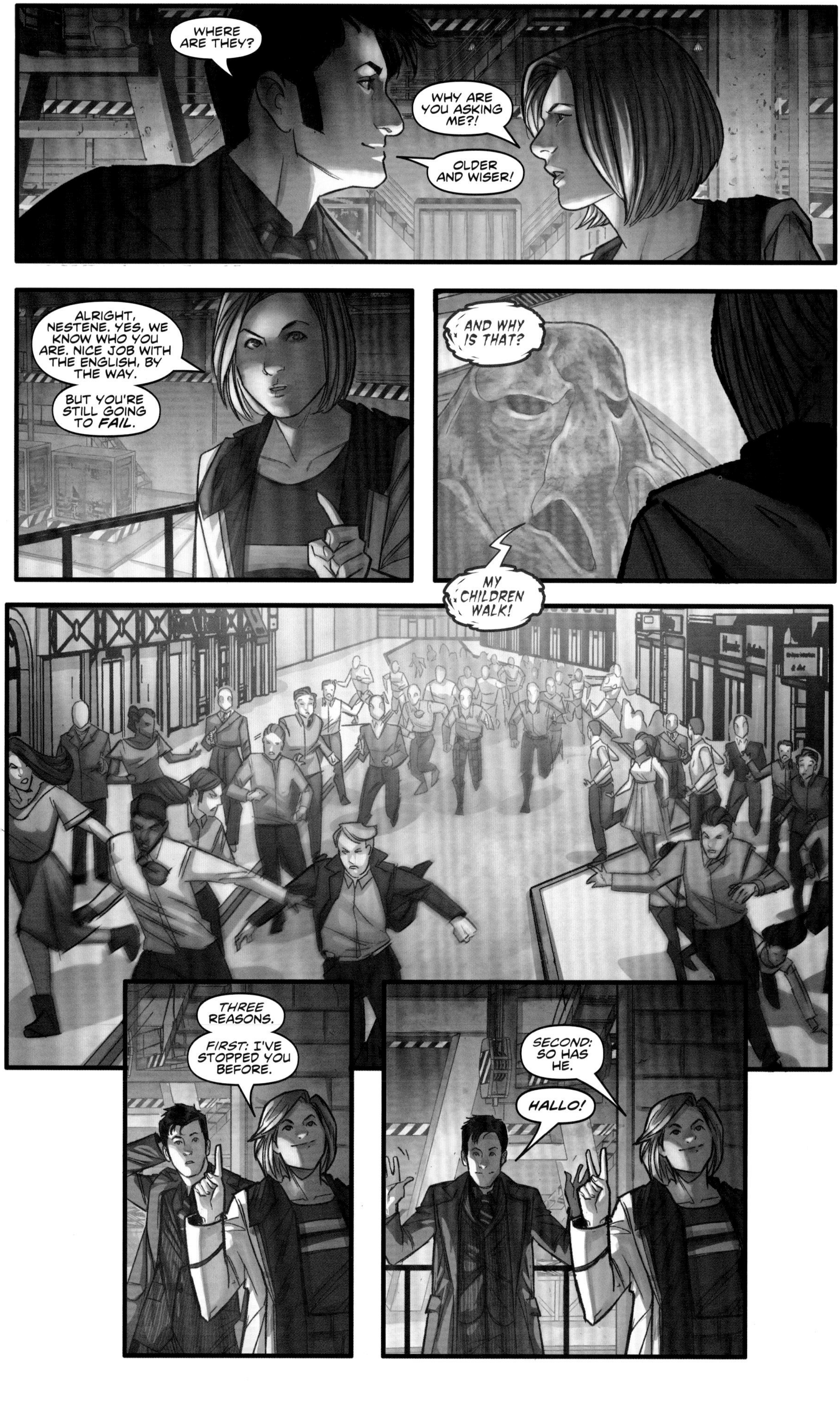
WHERE ARE THEY?
WHY ARE YOU ASKING ME?!
OLDER AND WISER!
ALRIGHT, NESTENE. YES, WE KNOW WHO YOU ARE. NICE JOB WITH THE ENGLISH, BY THE WAY.
BUT YOU'RE STILL GOING TO *FAIL*.
AND WHY IS THAT?
MY CHILDREN WALK!
THREE REASONS.
FIRST: I'VE STOPPED YOU BEFORE.
SECOND: SO HAS HE.
HALLO!

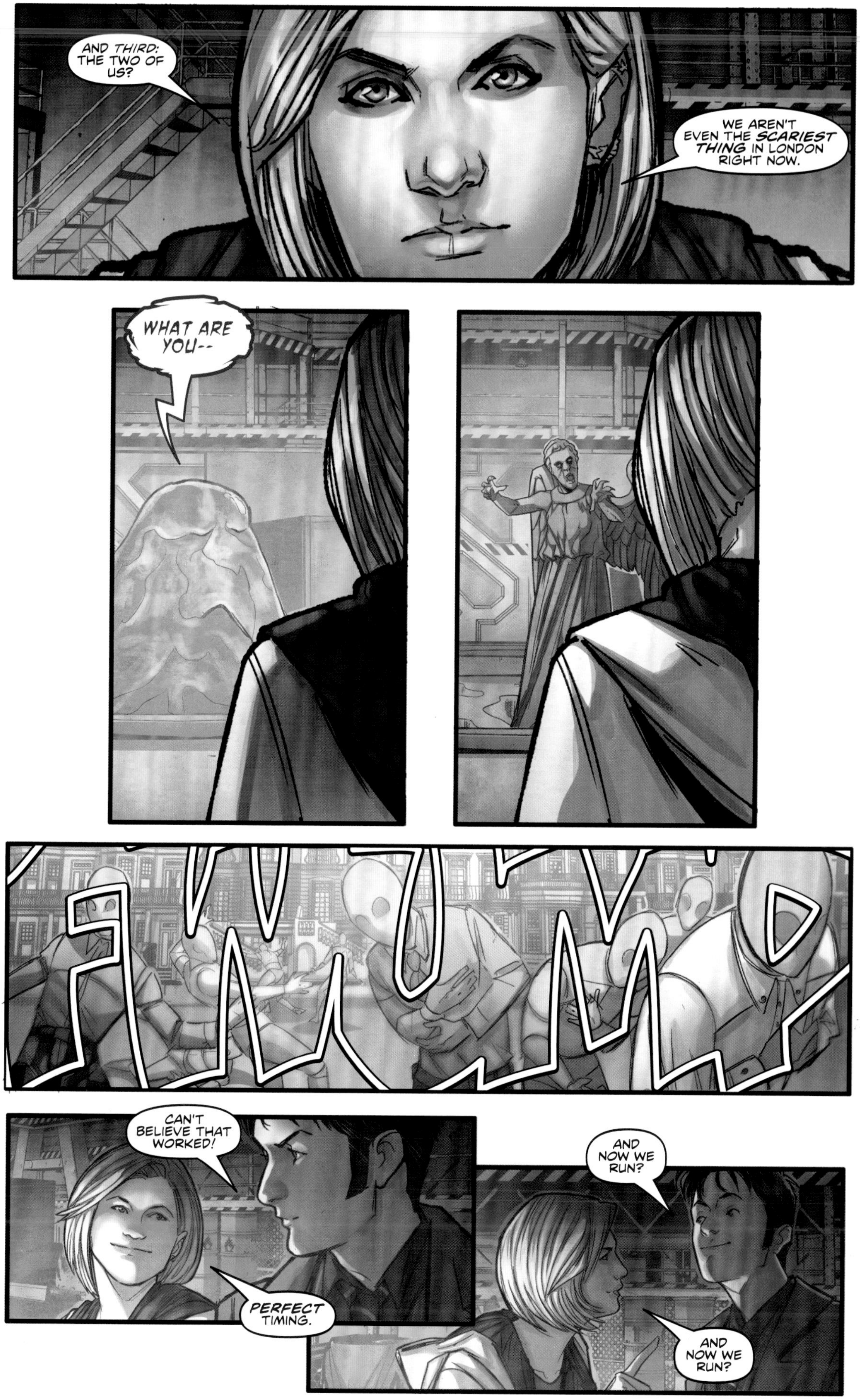
AND *THIRD*: THE TWO OF US?
WE AREN'T EVEN THE ***SCARIEST THING*** IN LONDON RIGHT NOW.
WHAT ARE YOU--
FWUMP
CAN'T BELIEVE THAT WORKED!
PERFECT TIMING.
AND NOW WE RUN?
AND NOW WE RUN?

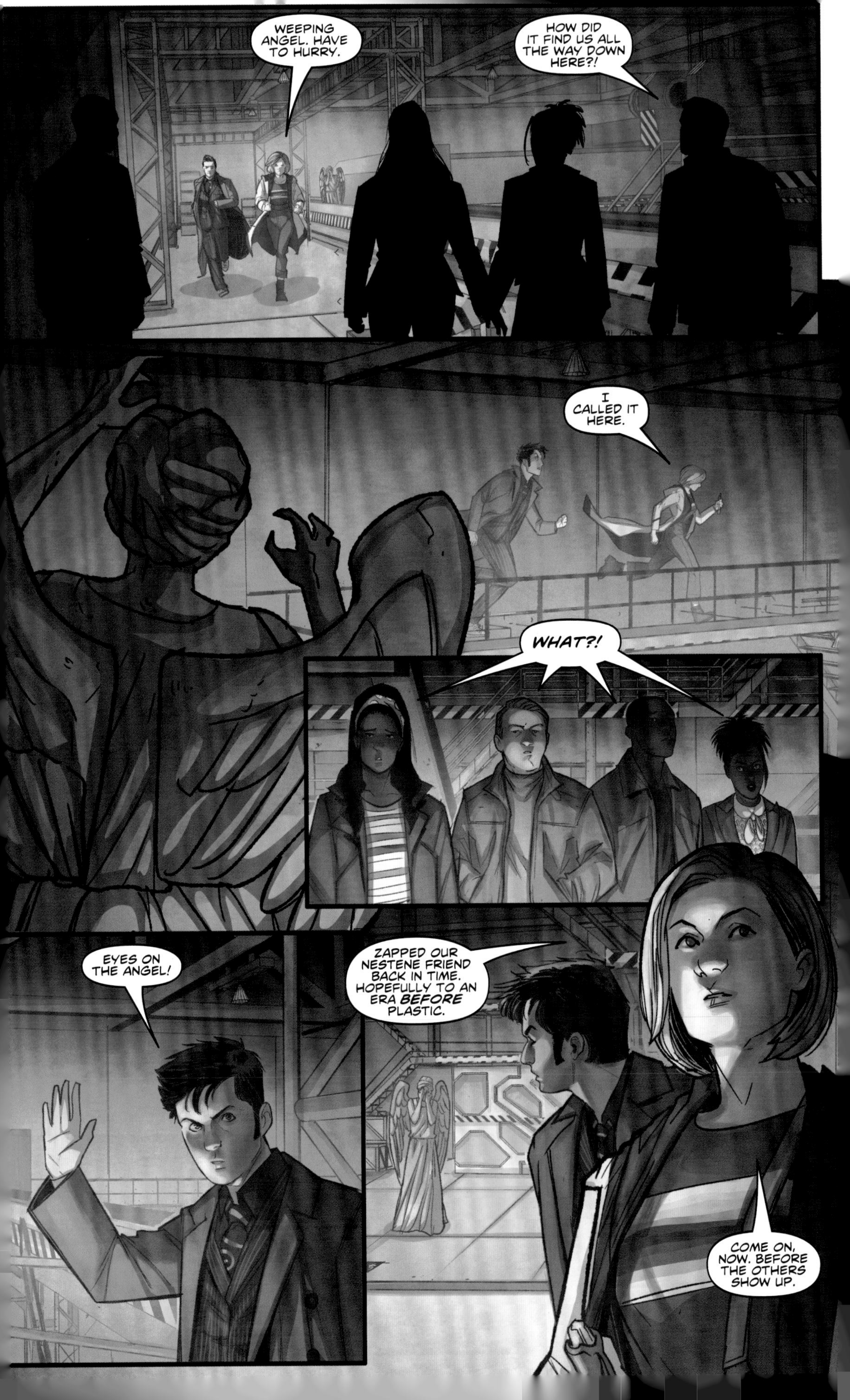
WEEPING ANGEL. HAVE TO HURRY.
HOW DID IT FIND US ALL THE WAY DOWN HERE?!
I CALLED IT HERE.
WHAT?!
EYES ON THE ANGEL!
ZAPPED OUR NESTENE FRIEND BACK IN TIME. HOPEFULLY TO AN ERA *BEFORE* PLASTIC.
COME ON, NOW. BEFORE THE OTHERS SHOW UP.

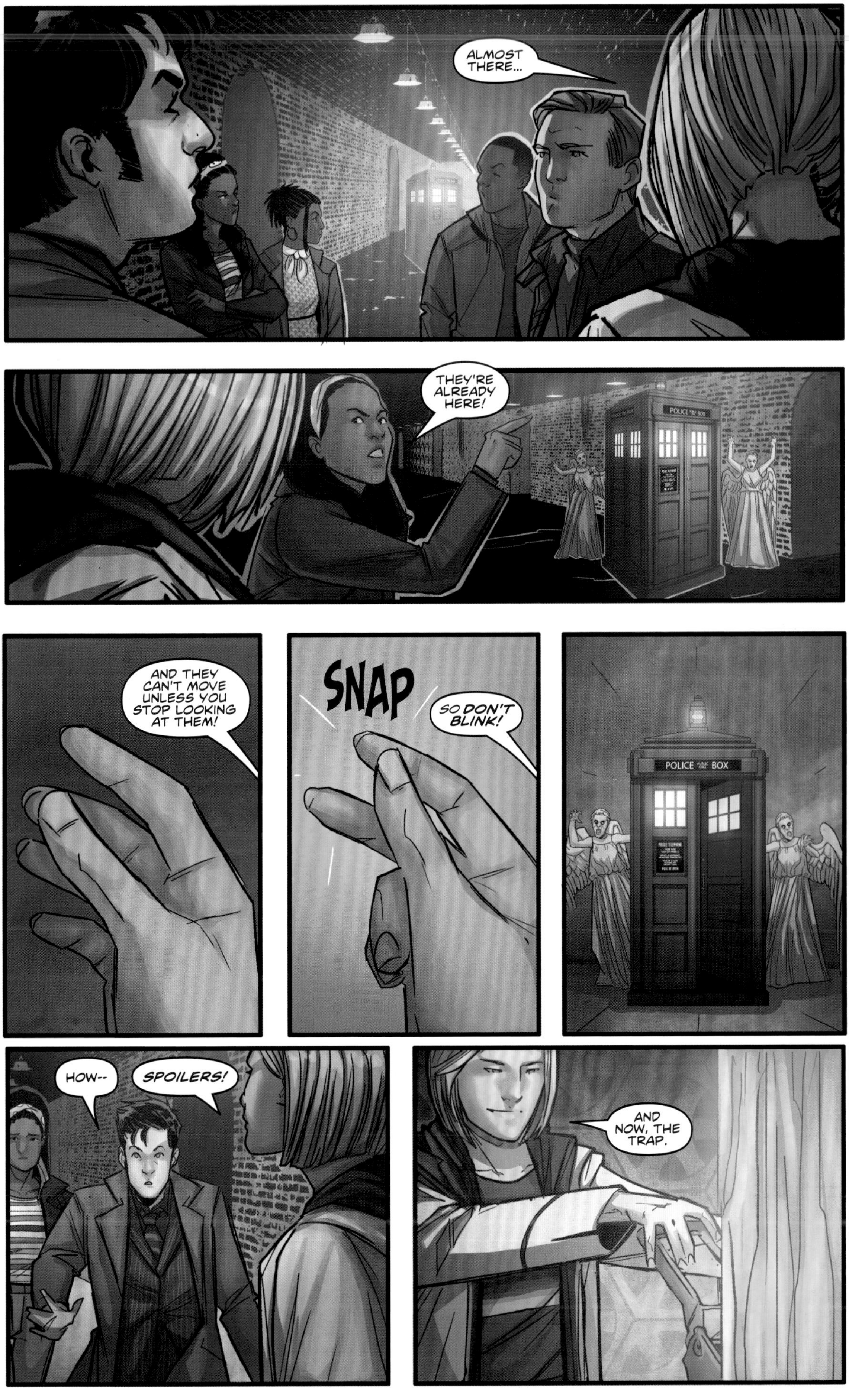
ALMOST THERE...
THEY'RE ALREADY HERE!
AND THEY CAN'T MOVE UNLESS YOU STOP LOOKING AT THEM!
SNAP
SO DON'T BLINK!
POLICE PUBLIC CALL BOX
HOW--
SPOILERS!
AND NOW, THE TRAP.

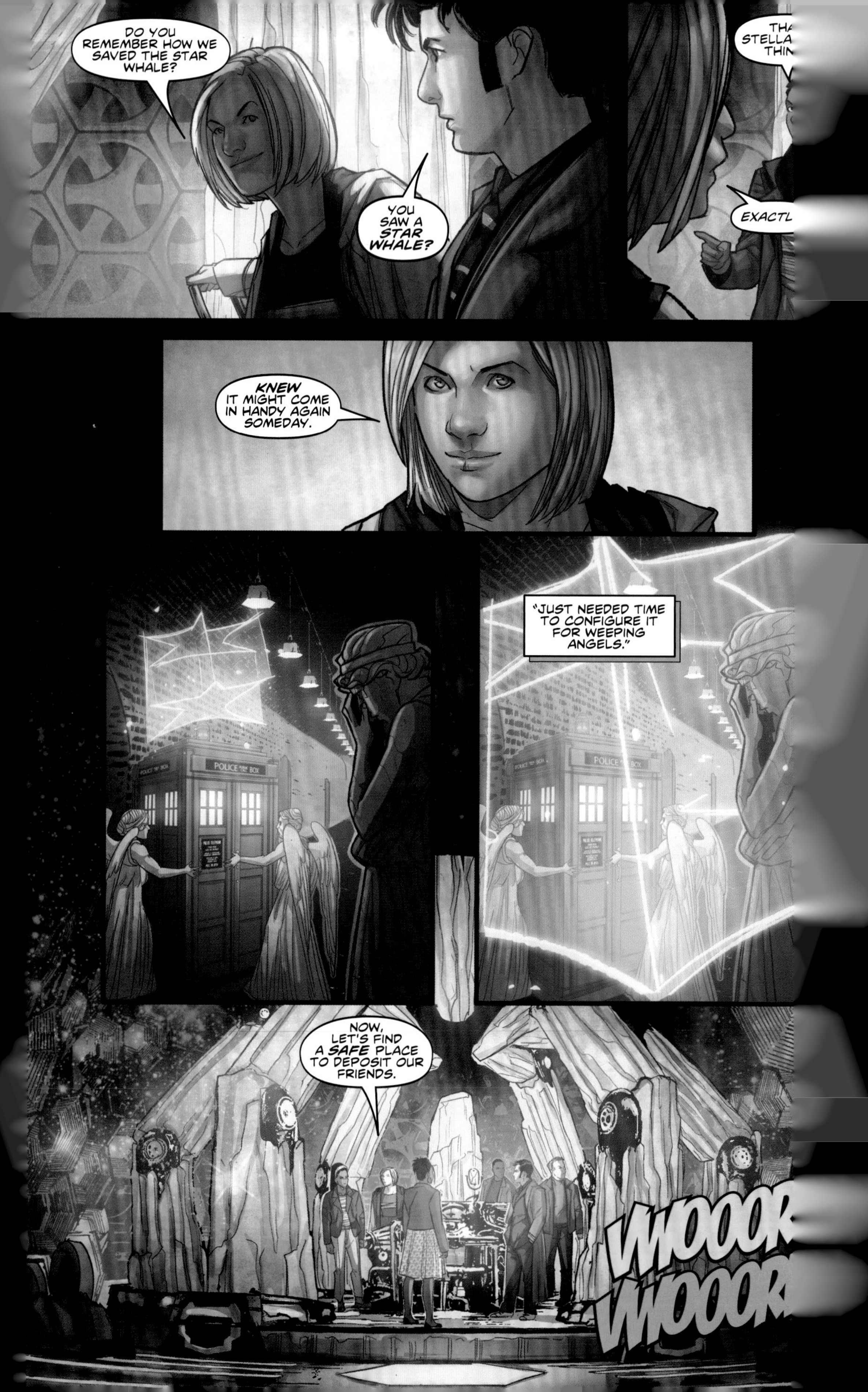

DO YOU REMEMBER HOW WE SAVED THE STAR WHALE?
YOU SAW A STAR WHALE?
THA STELLA THIN
EXACTL
KNEW IT MIGHT COME IN HANDY AGAIN SOMEDAY.
"JUST NEEDED TIME TO CONFIGURE IT FOR WEEPING ANGELS."
POLICE BOX
POLICE BOX
NOW, LET'S FIND A SAFE PLACE TO DEPOSIT OUR FRIENDS.
VWOOOR
VWOOOR

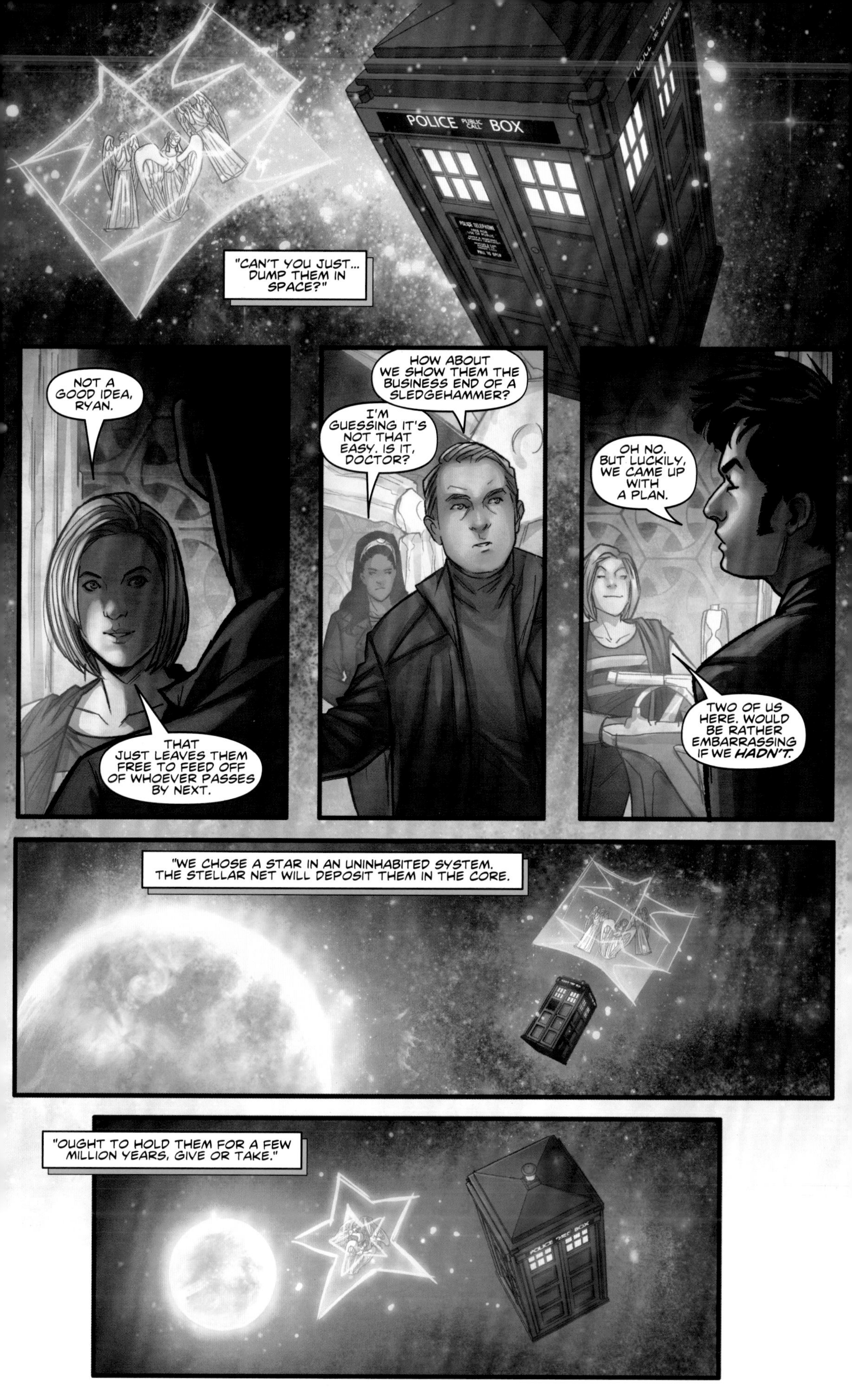
"CAN'T YOU JUST... DUMP THEM IN SPACE?"
NOT A GOOD IDEA, RYAN.
THAT JUST LEAVES THEM FREE TO FEED OFF OF WHOEVER PASSES BY NEXT.
HOW ABOUT WE SHOW THEM THE BUSINESS END OF A SLEDGEHAMMER?
I'M GUESSING IT'S NOT THAT EASY. IS IT, DOCTOR?
OH NO. BUT LUCKILY, WE CAME UP WITH A PLAN.
TWO OF US HERE. WOULD BE RATHER EMBARRASSING IF WE HADN'T.
"WE CHOSE A STAR IN AN UNINHABITED SYSTEM. THE STELLAR NET WILL DEPOSIT THEM IN THE CORE.
"OUGHT TO HOLD THEM FOR A FEW MILLION YEARS, GIVE OR TAKE."

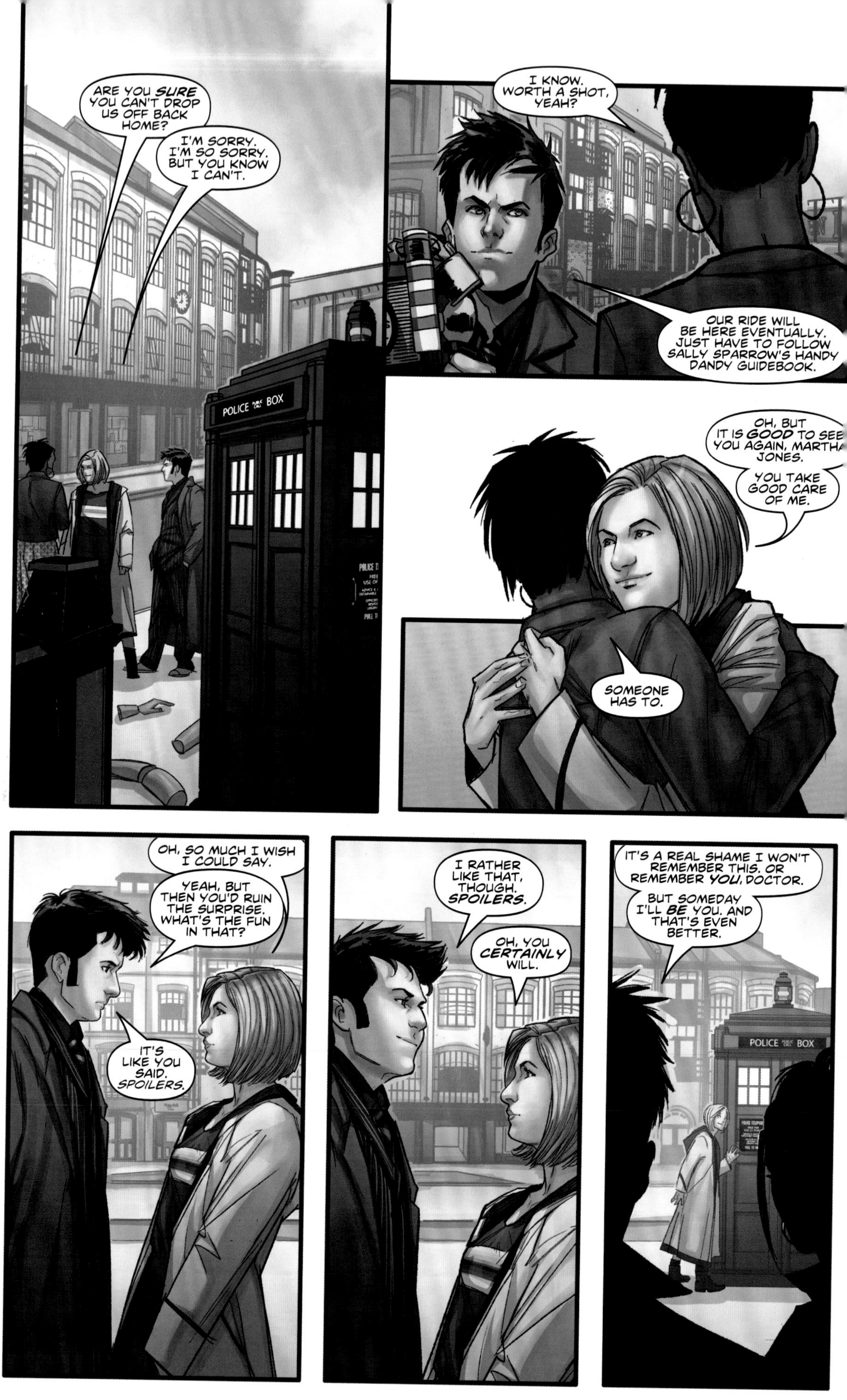
ARE YOU SURE YOU CAN'T DROP US OFF BACK HOME?
I'M SORRY. I'M SO SORRY. BUT YOU KNOW I CAN'T.
POLICE BOX
I KNOW. WORTH A SHOT, YEAH?
OUR RIDE WILL BE HERE EVENTUALLY. JUST HAVE TO FOLLOW SALLY SPARROW'S HANDY DANDY GUIDEBOOK.
OH, BUT IT IS GOOD TO SEE YOU AGAIN, MARTHA JONES.
YOU TAKE GOOD CARE OF ME.
SOMEONE HAS TO.
OH, SO MUCH I WISH I COULD SAY.
YEAH, BUT THEN YOU'D RUIN THE SURPRISE. WHAT'S THE FUN IN THAT?
IT'S LIKE YOU SAID. SPOILERS.
I RATHER LIKE THAT, THOUGH. SPOILERS.
OH, YOU CERTAINLY WILL.
IT'S A REAL SHAME I WON'T REMEMBER THIS. OR REMEMBER YOU, DOCTOR.
BUT SOMEDAY I'LL BE YOU. AND THAT'S EVEN BETTER.
POLICE BOX

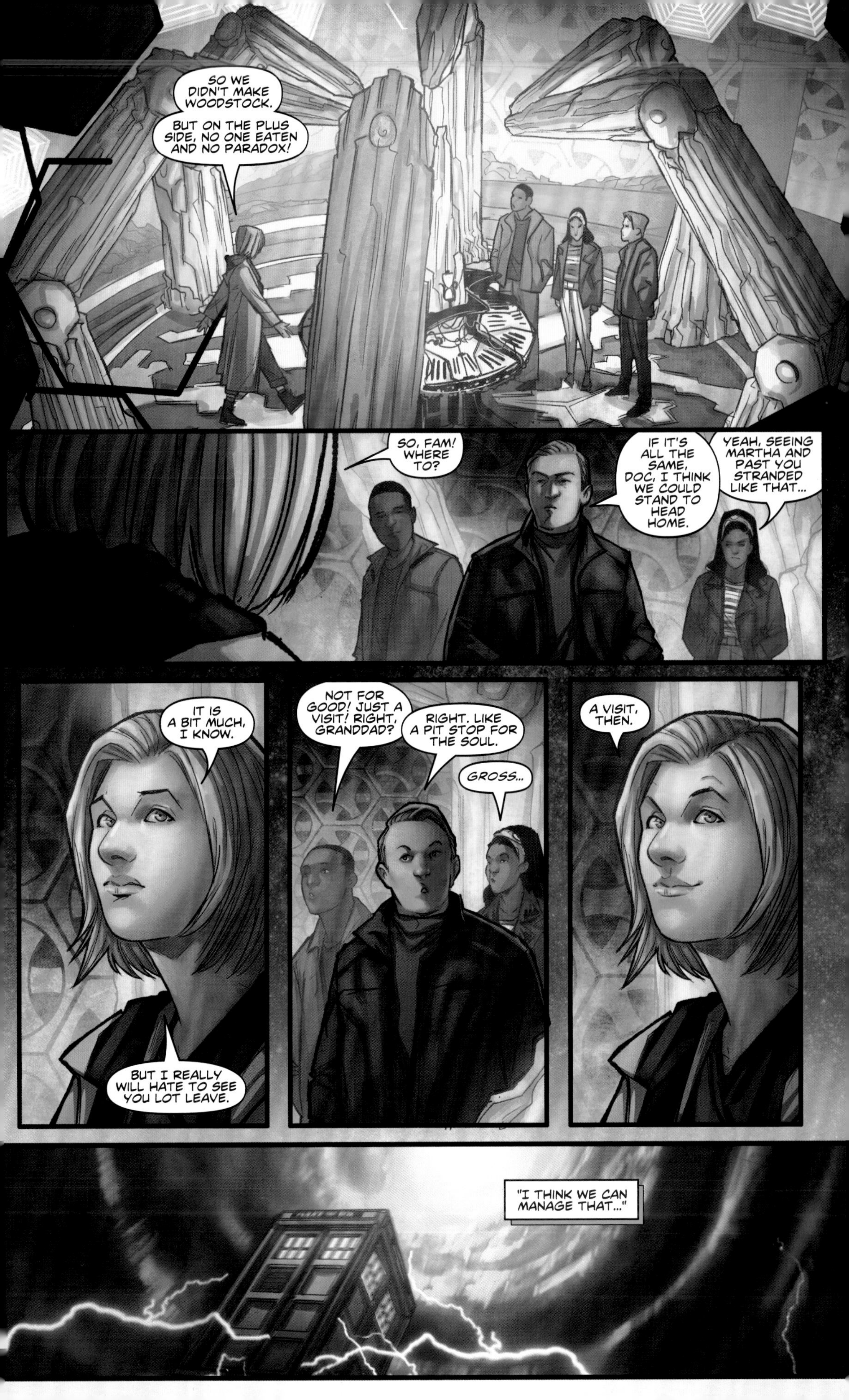
SO WE DIDN'T MAKE WOODSTOCK.
BUT ON THE PLUS SIDE, NO ONE EATEN AND NO PARADOX!
SO, FAM! WHERE TO?
IF IT'S ALL THE SAME, DOC, I THINK WE COULD STAND TO HEAD HOME.
YEAH, SEEING MARTHA AND PAST YOU STRANDED LIKE THAT...
IT IS A BIT MUCH, I KNOW.
BUT I REALLY WILL HATE TO SEE YOU LOT LEAVE.
NOT FOR GOOD! JUST A VISIT! RIGHT, GRANDDAD?
RIGHT. LIKE A PIT STOP FOR THE SOUL.
GROSS...
A VISIT, THEN.
"I THINK WE CAN MANAGE THAT..."

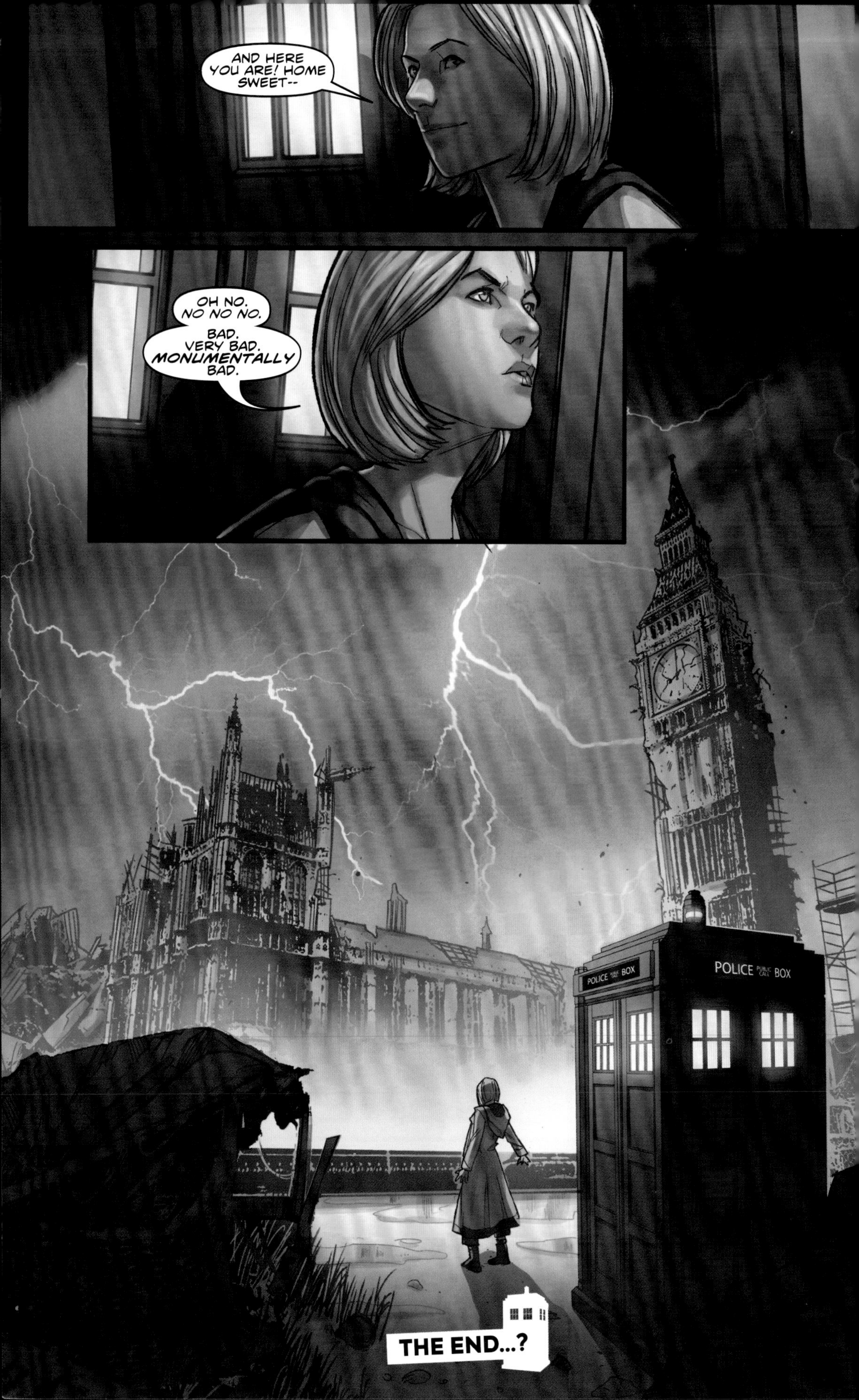
AND HERE YOU ARE! HOME SWEET--
OH NO. NO NO NO.
BAD. VERY BAD. MONUMENTALLY BAD.
POLICE PUBLIC CALL BOX
POLICE PUBLIC CALL BOX
THE END...?

BBC

DOCTOR WHO

THE THIRTEENTH DOCTOR

Covers Gallery

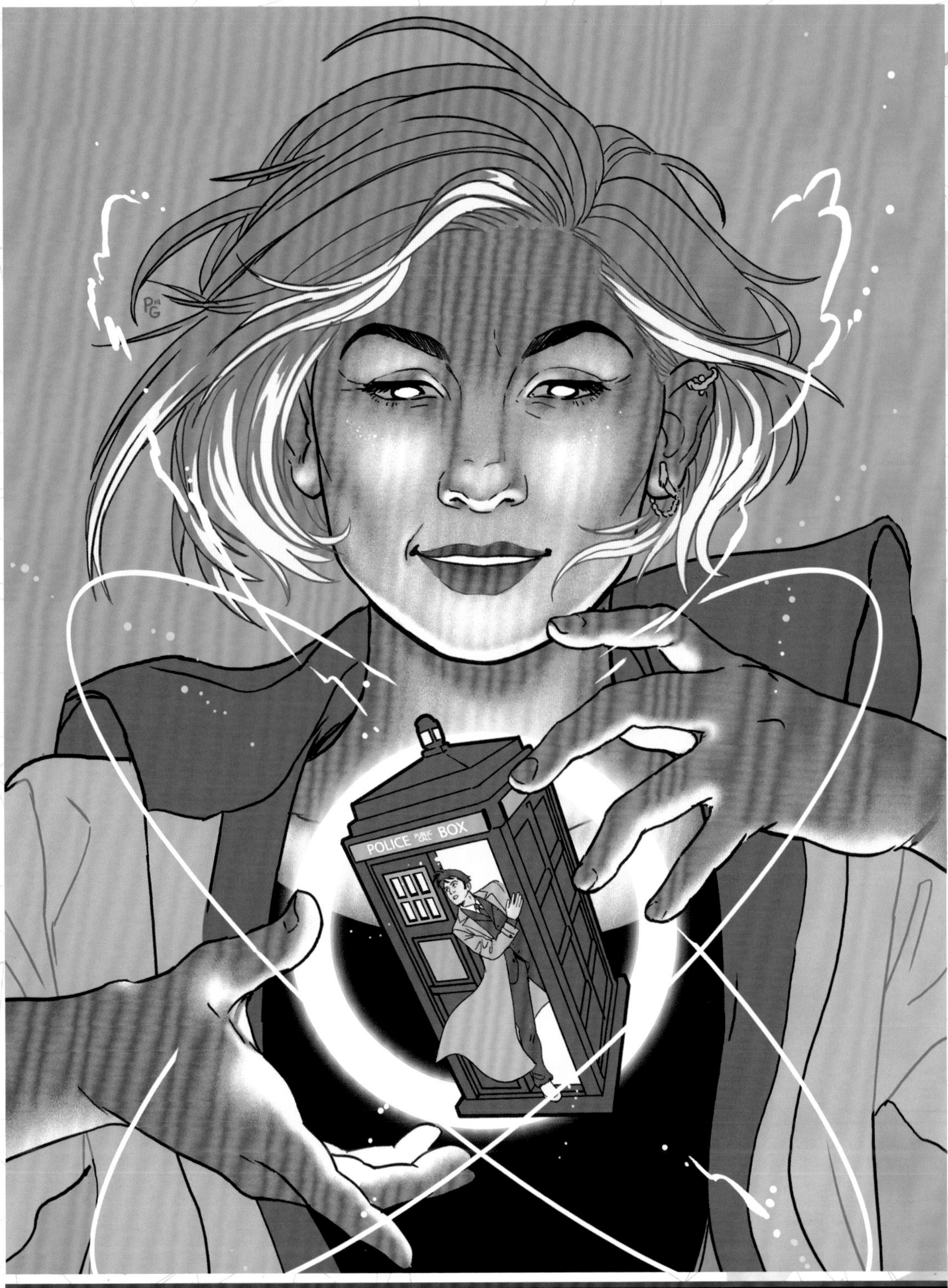
POLICE PUBLIC CALL BOX

ISSUE #2.1 COVER A • PAULINA GANUCHEAU

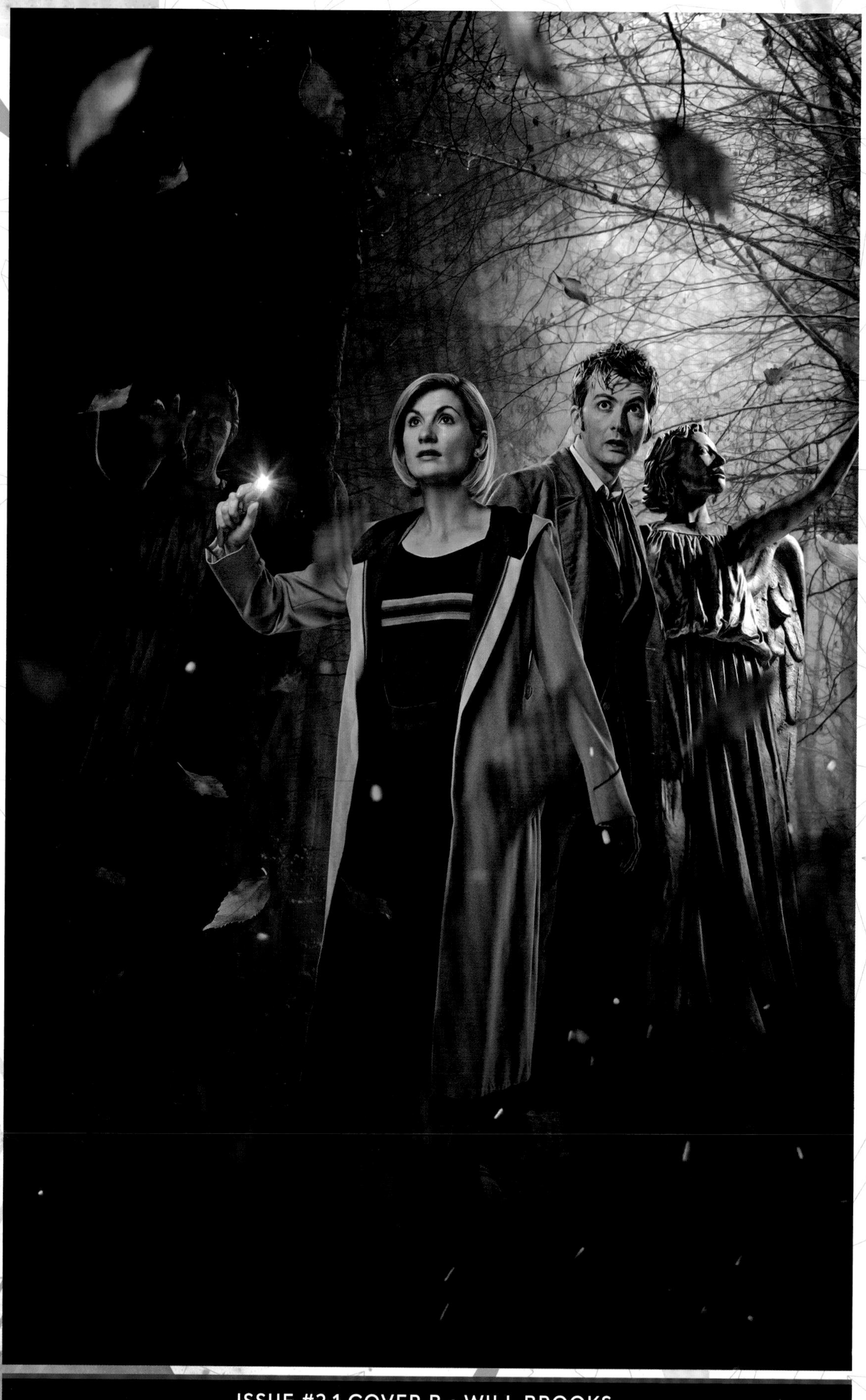

ISSUE #2.1 COVER B • WILL BROOKS

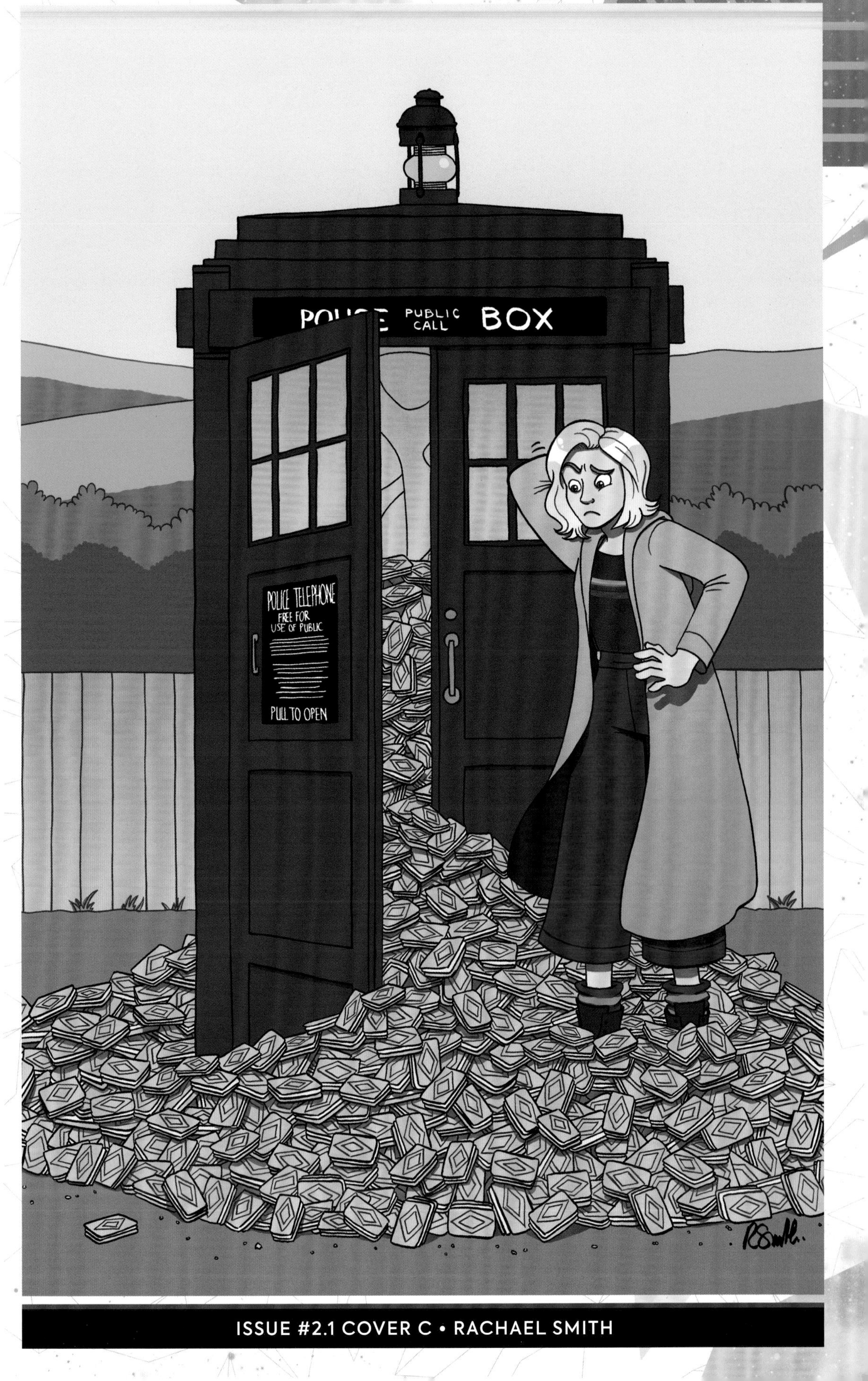
PUBLIC CALL
BOX
POLICE TELEPHONE
FREE FOR
USE OF PUBLIC
PULL TO OPEN

ISSUE #2.1 COVER C • RACHAEL SMITH

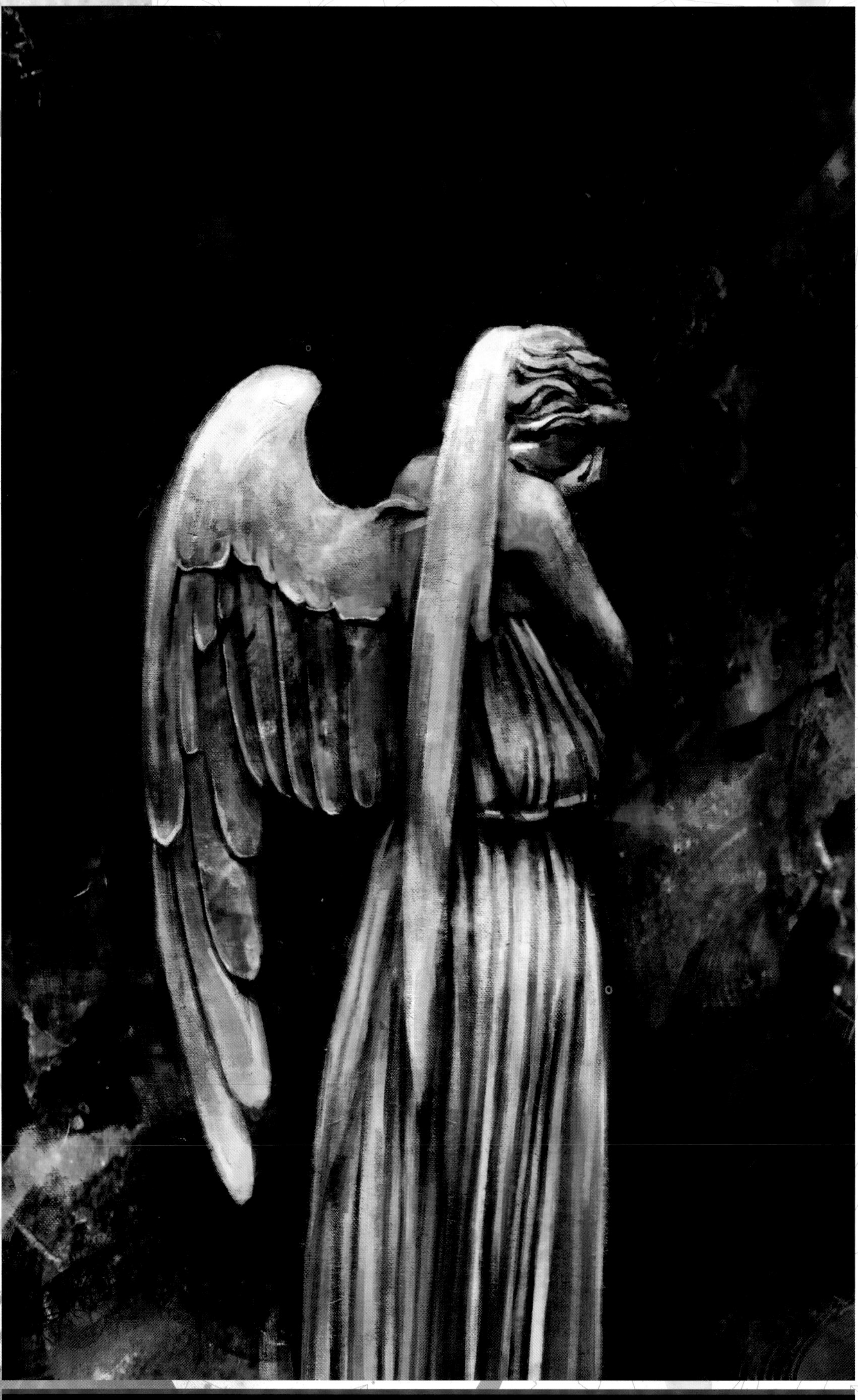

ISSUE #2.1 COVER D • ALICE X. ZHANG

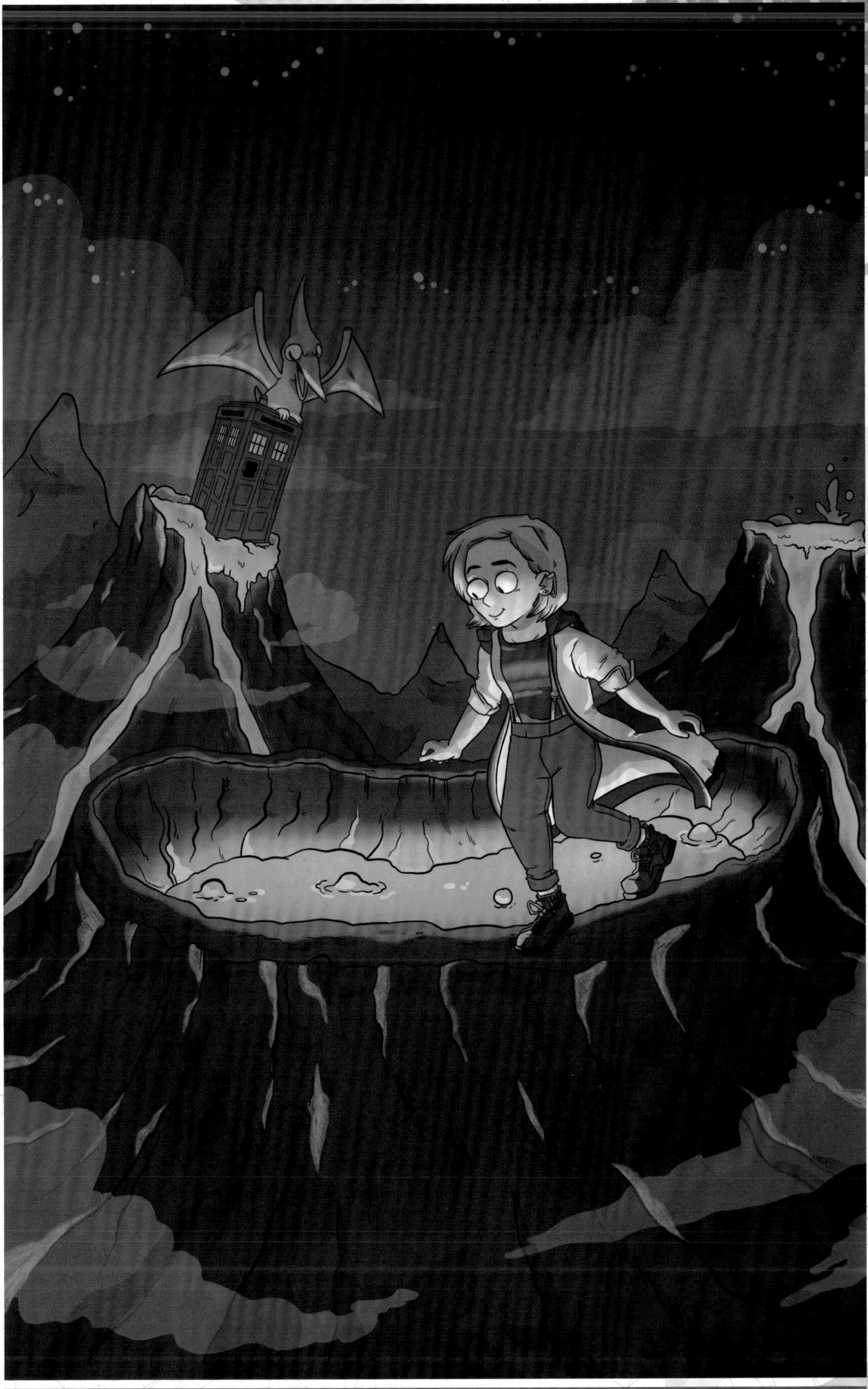

ISSUE #2.1 COVER E • SARAH GRALEY

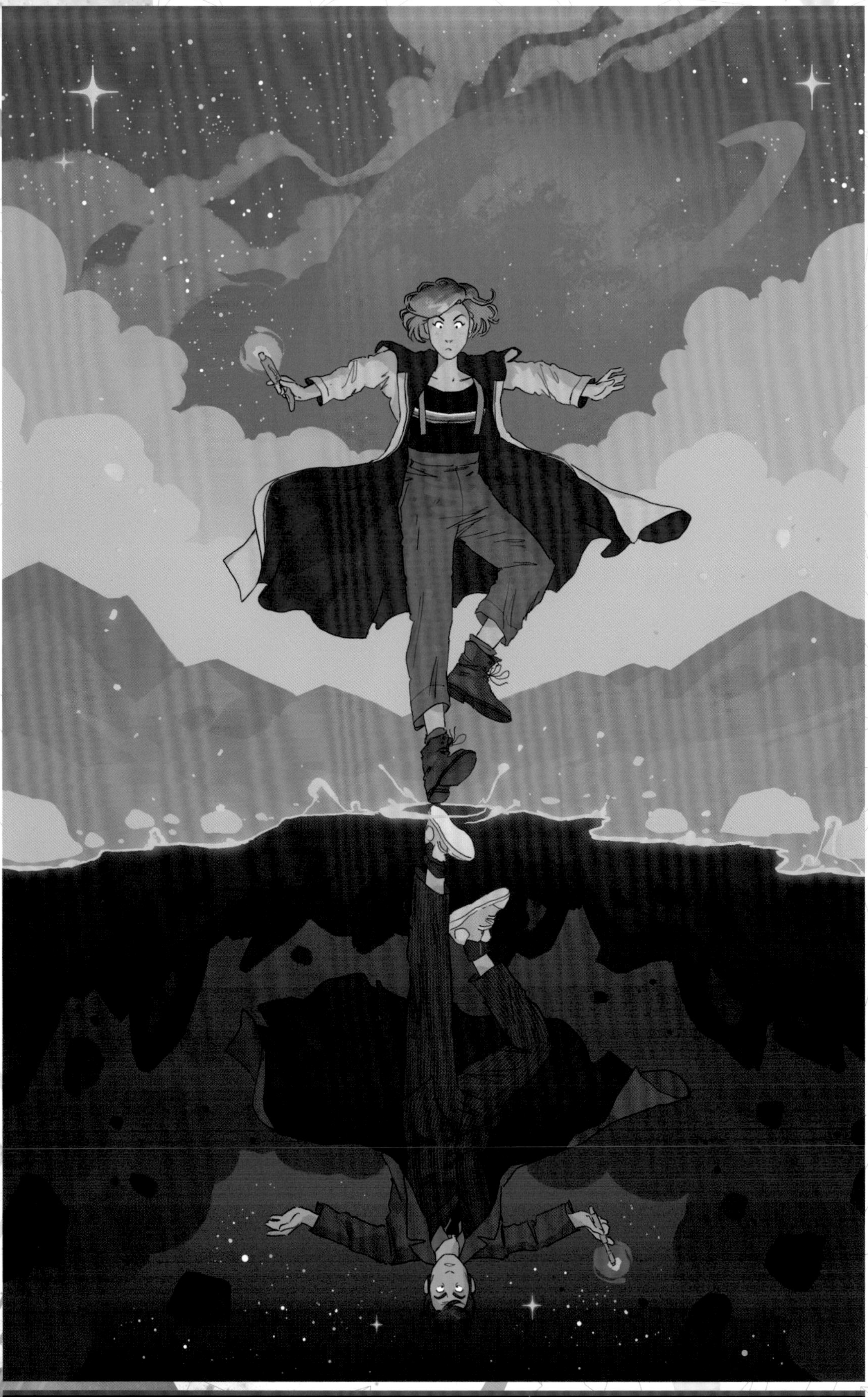

ISSUE #2.2 COVER A • HANNAH TEMPLER

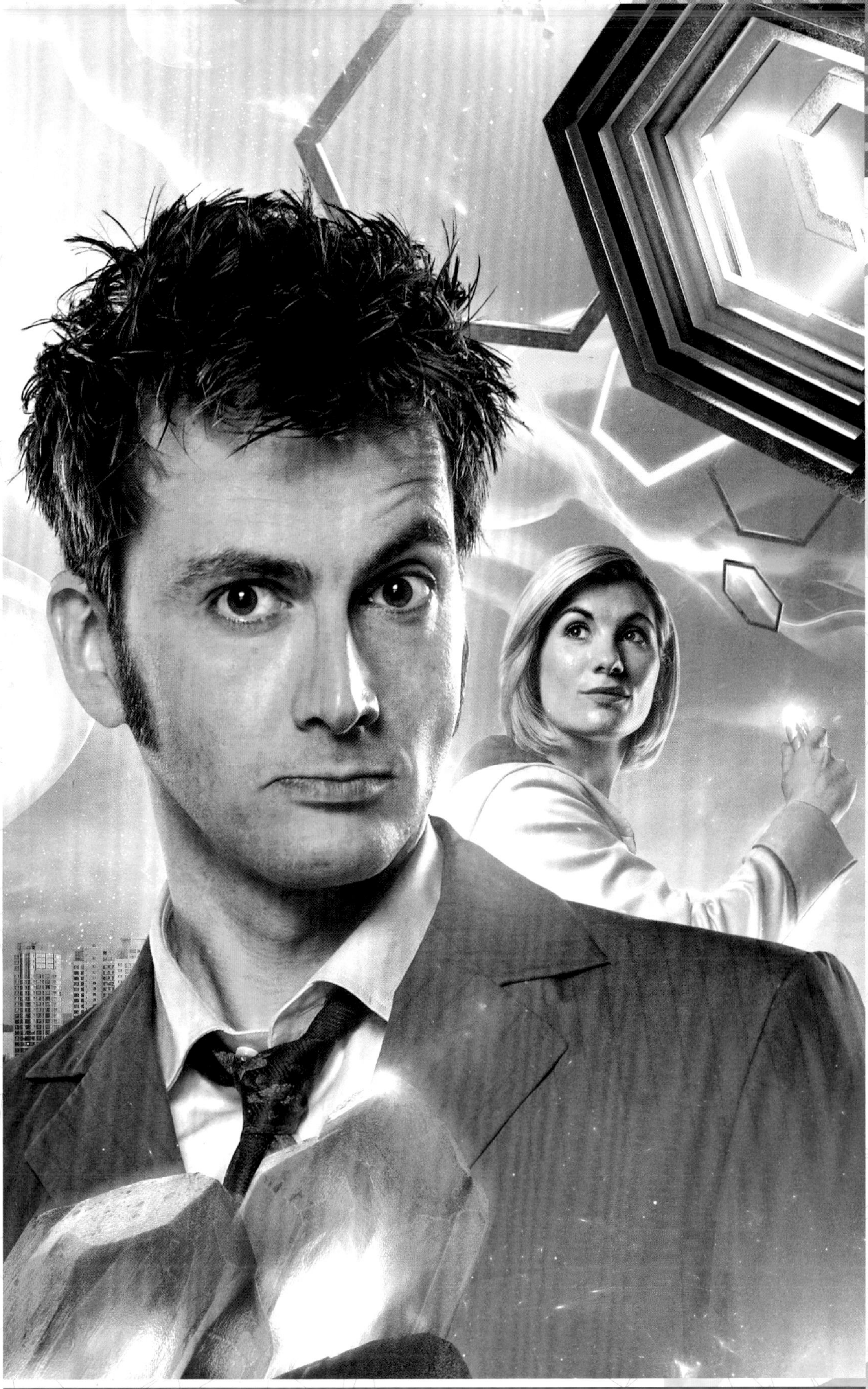

ISSUE #2.2 COVER B • WILL BROOKS

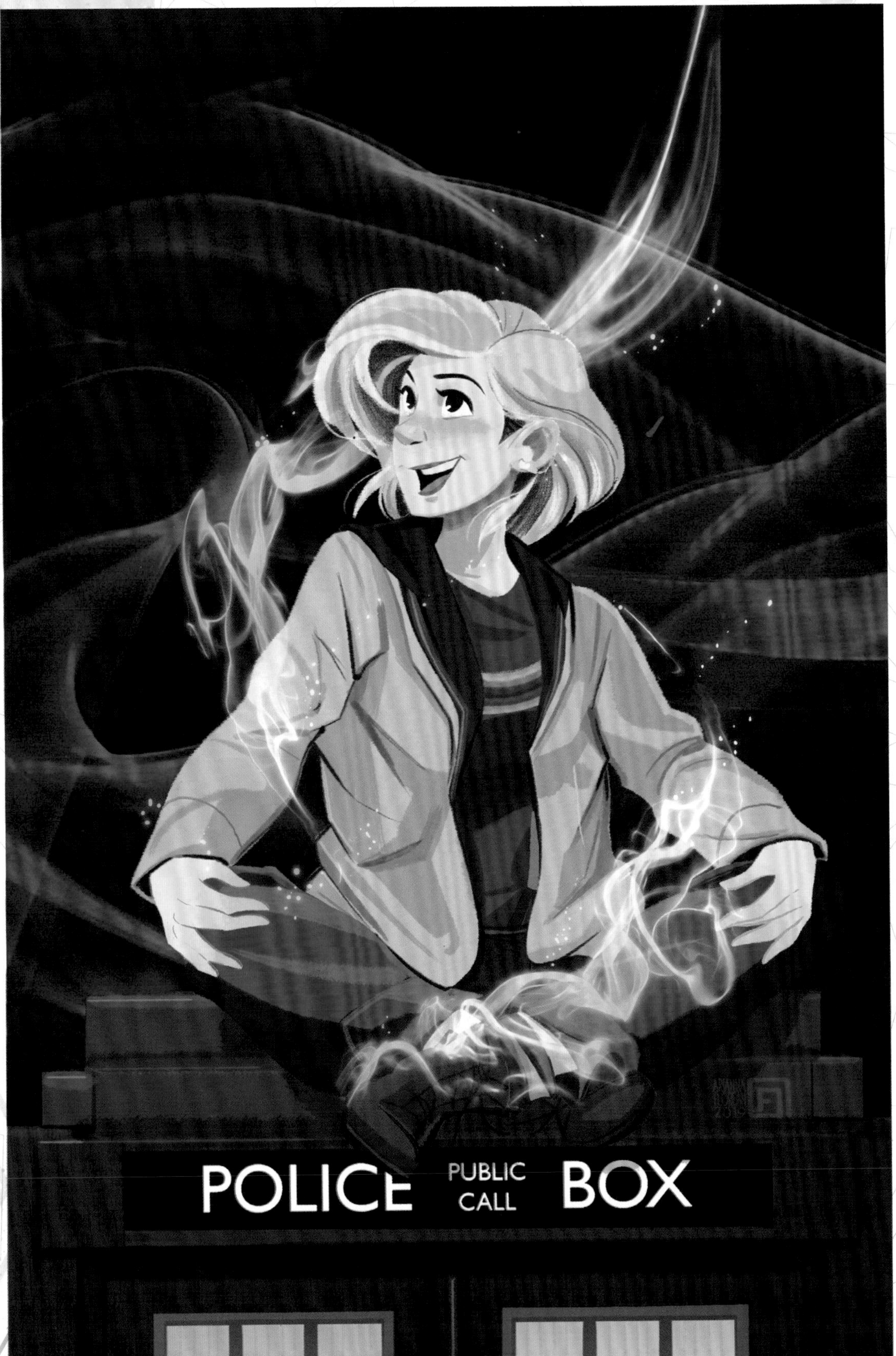
POLICE
PUBLIC CALL
BOX

ISSUE #2.2 COVER C • ARIANNA FLOREAN

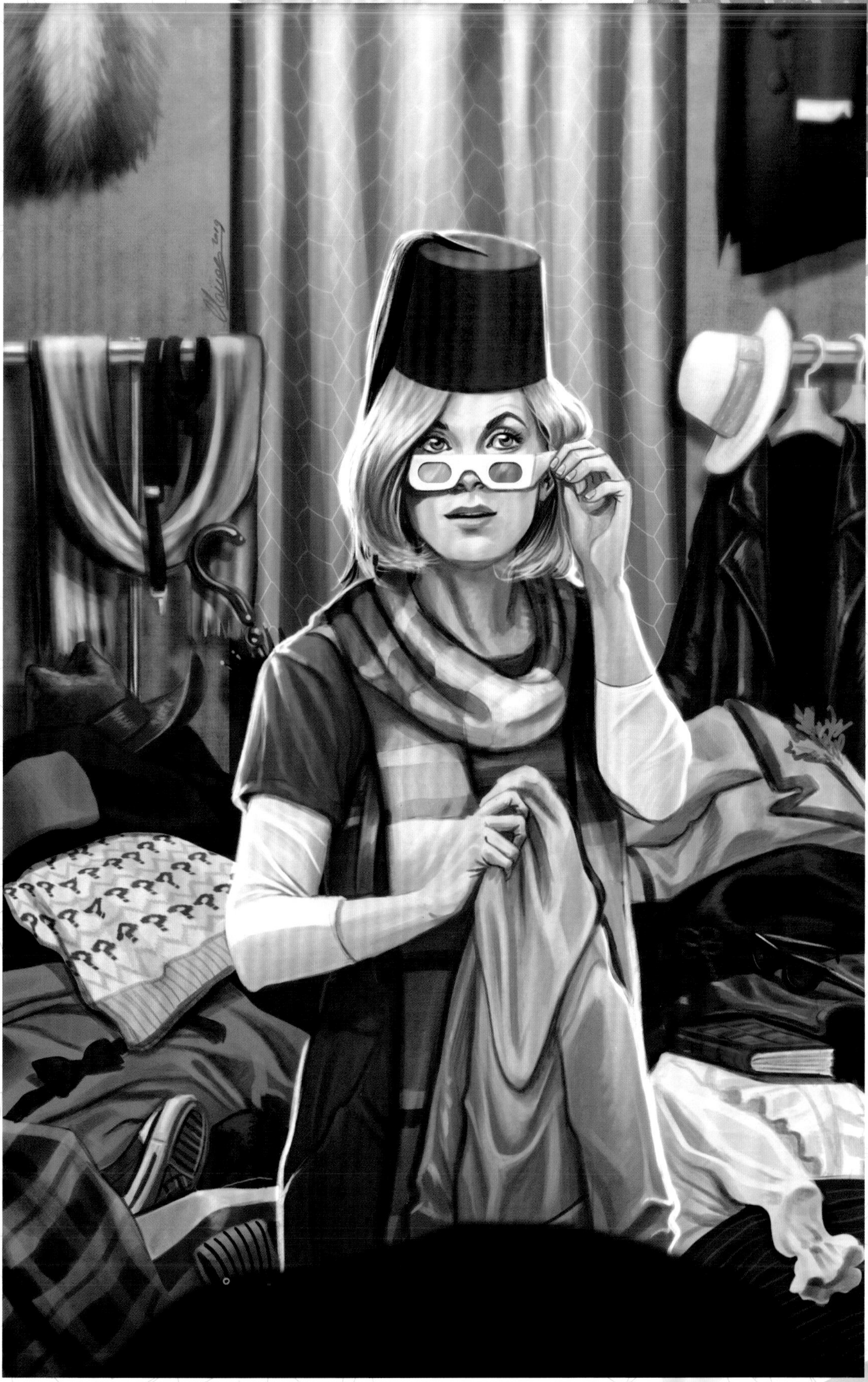

ISSUE #2.2 COVER D • CLAUDIA IANNICIELLO

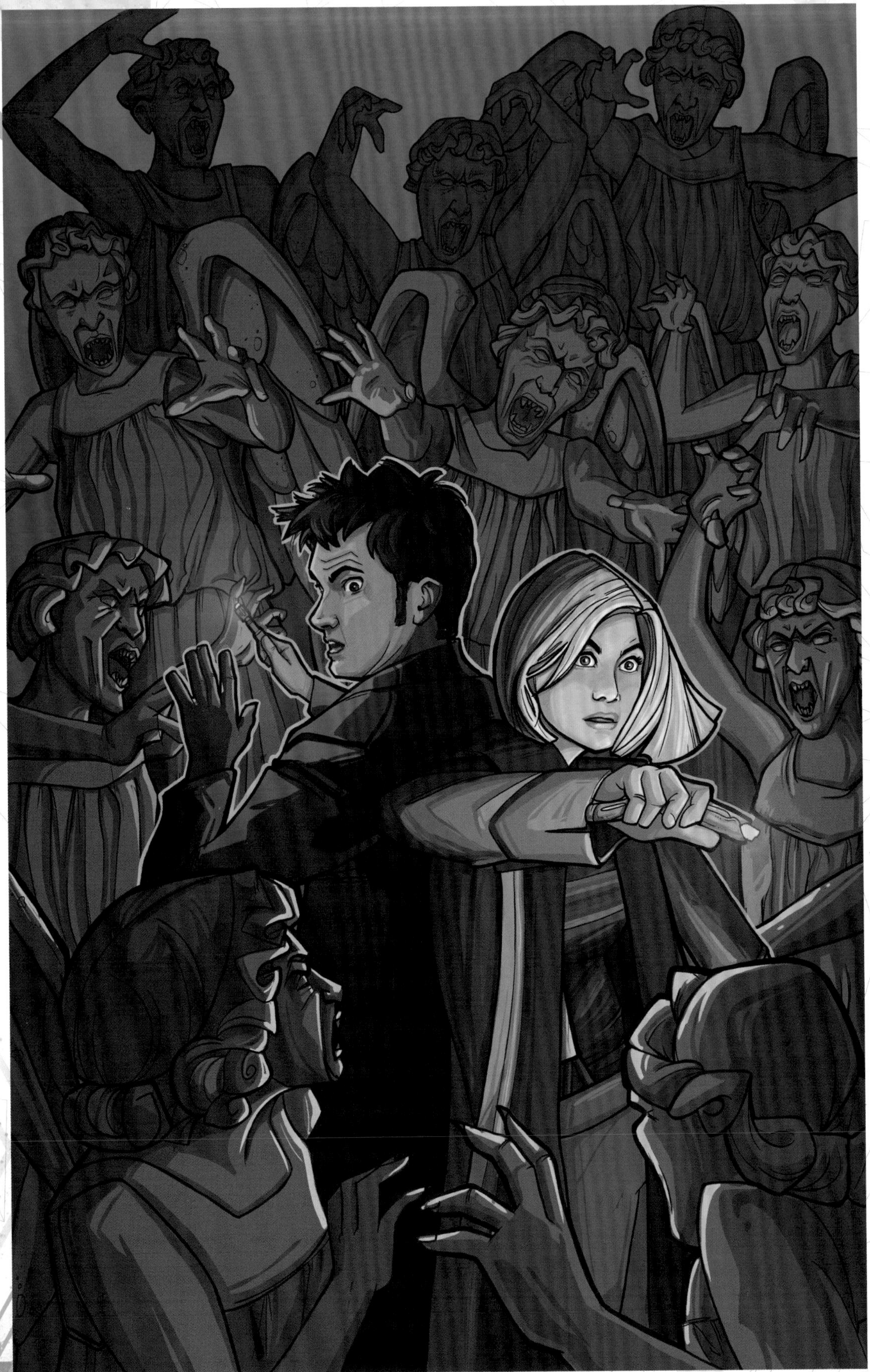

ISSUE #2.3 COVER A • KAREN HALLION

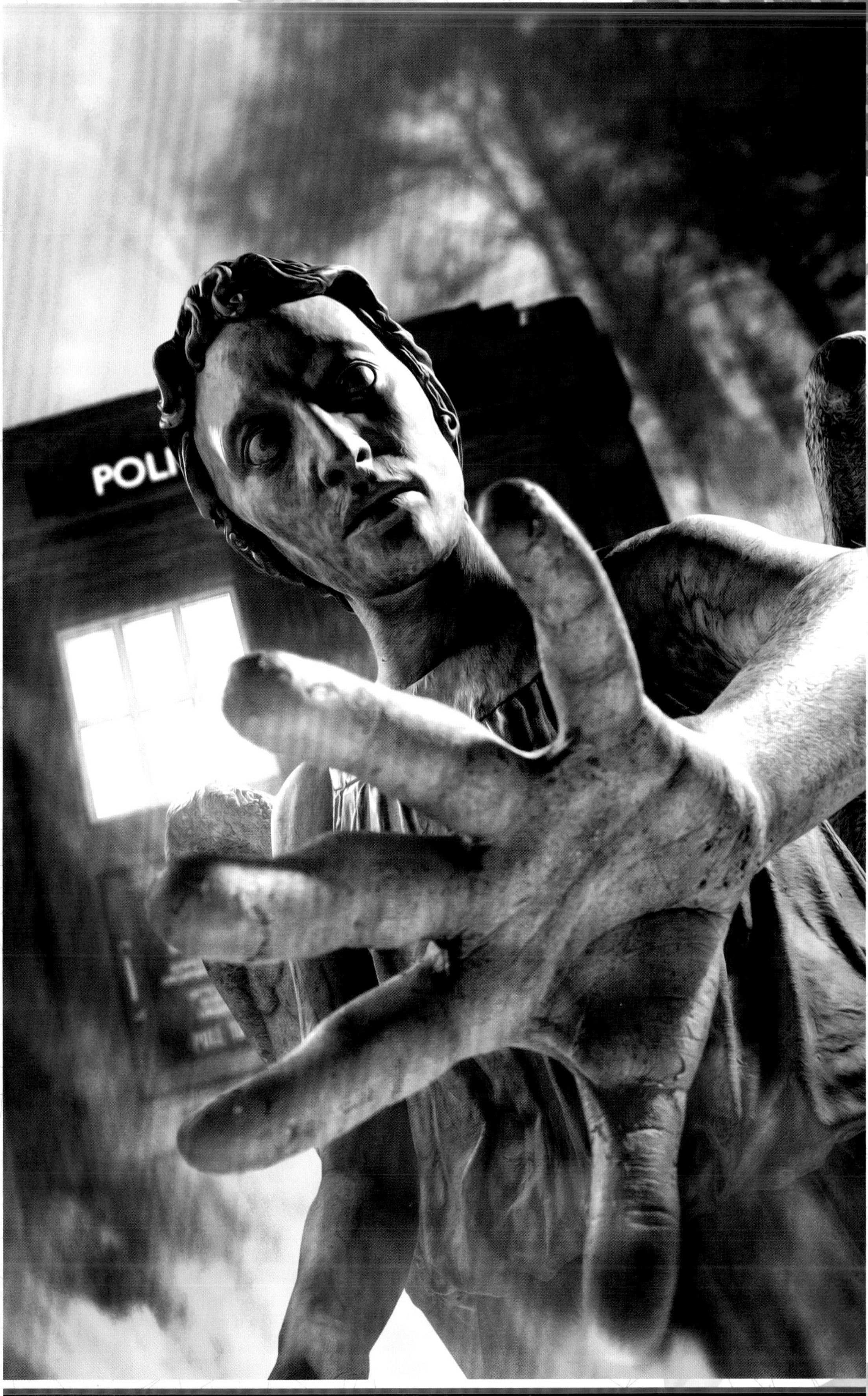
POLI

ISSUE #2.3 COVER B • WILL BROOKS

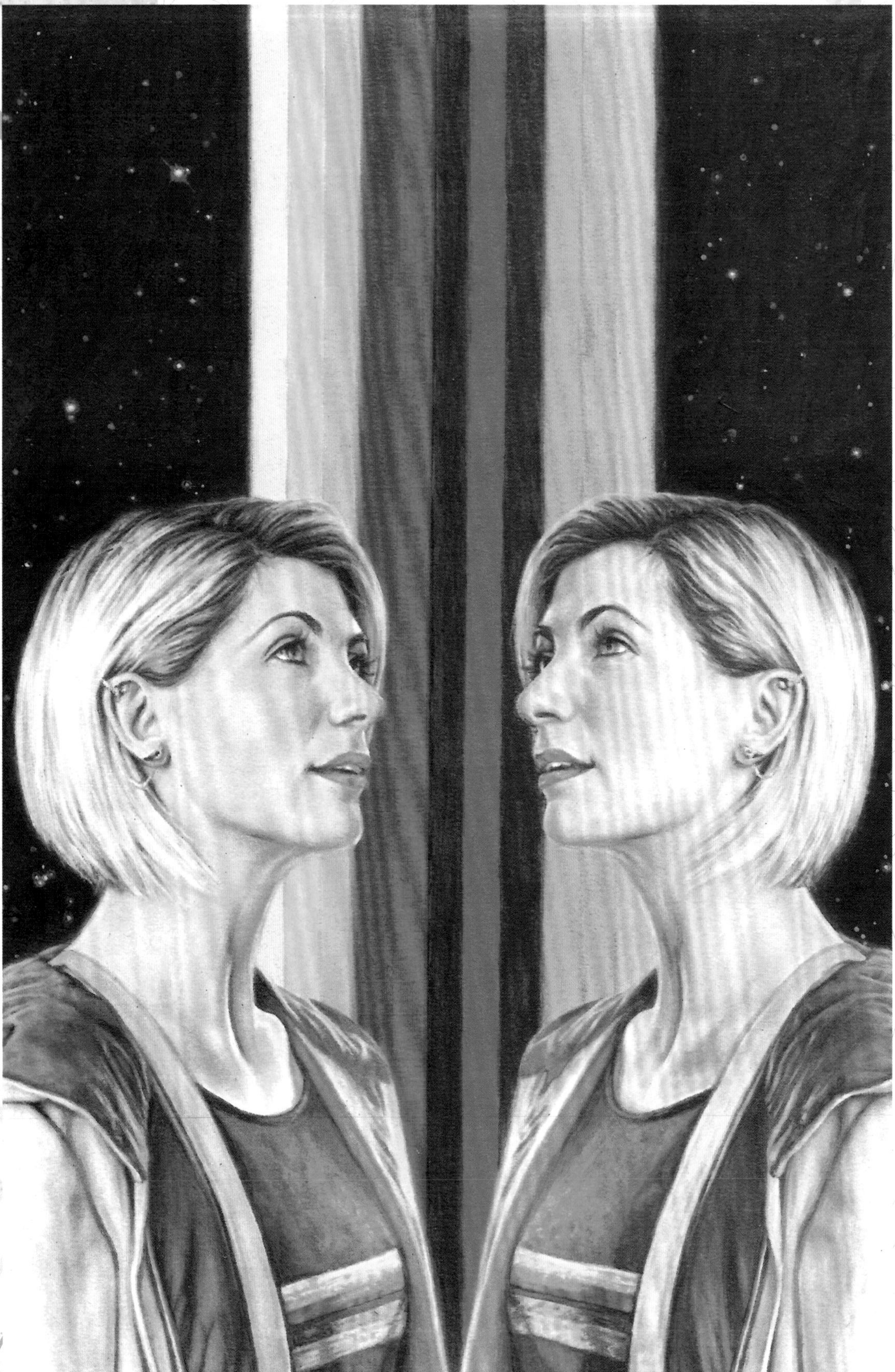

ISSUE #2.3 COVER C • ANDY WALKER

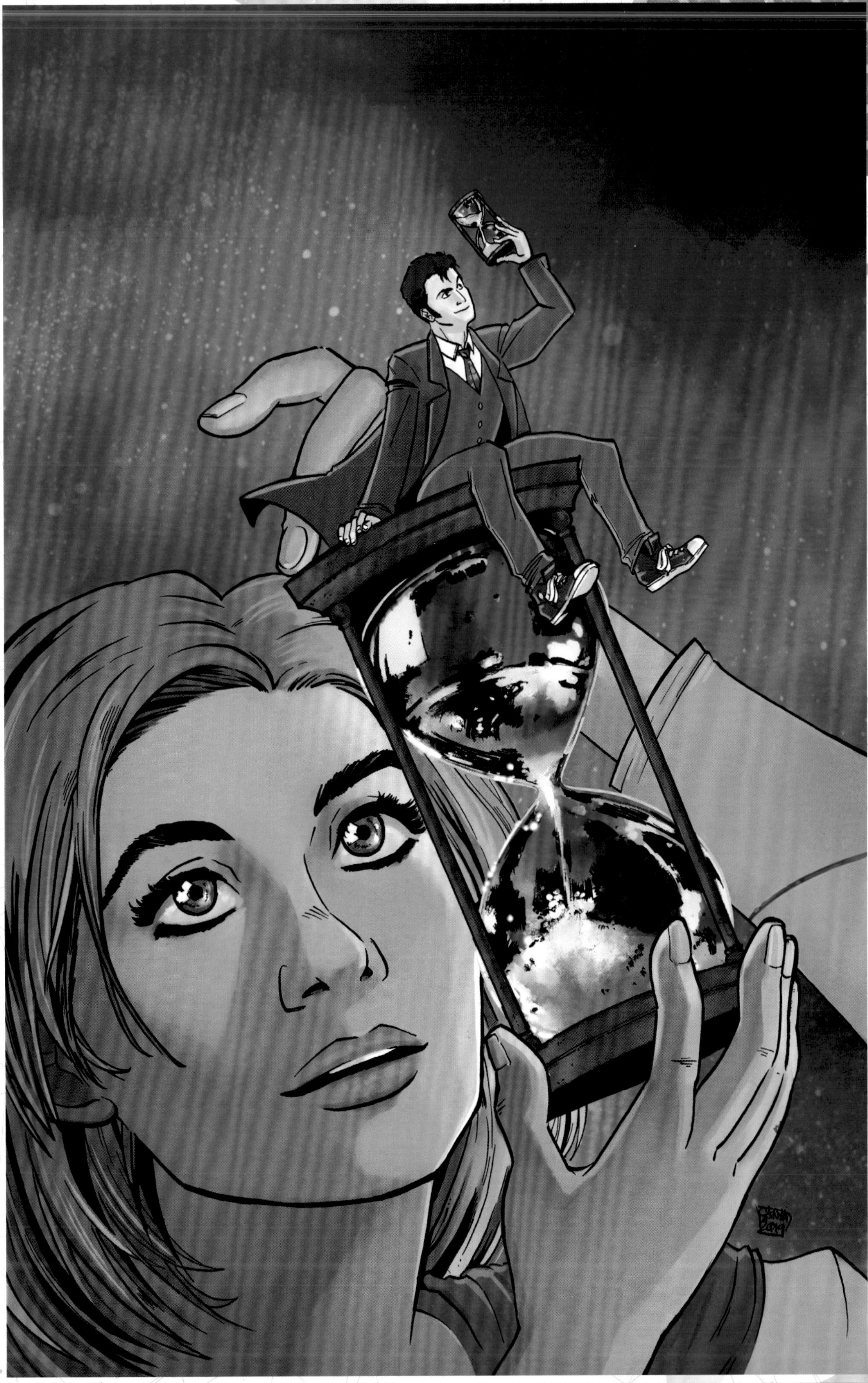

ISSUE #2.4 COVER A • SANYA ANWAR

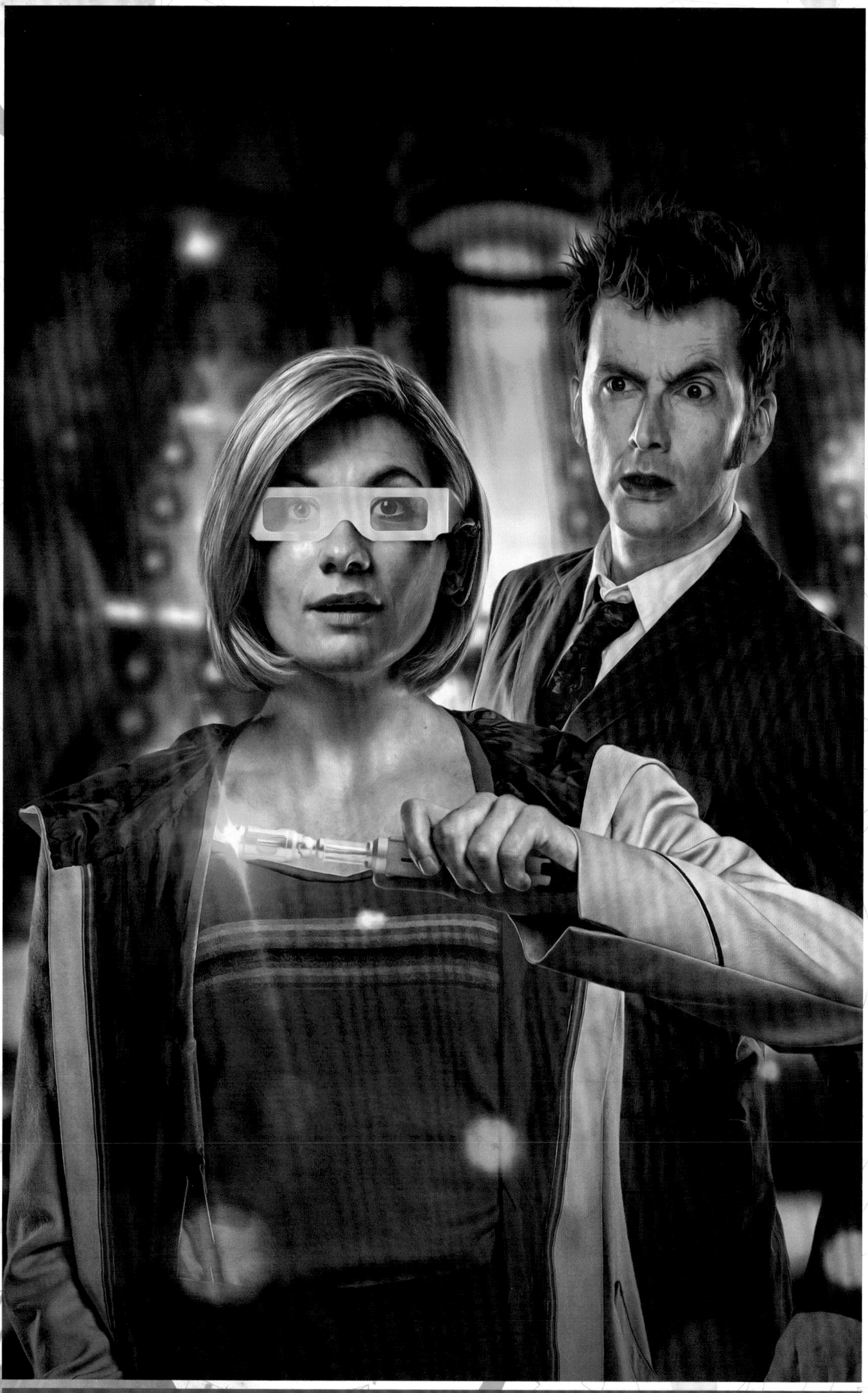

ISSUE #2.4 COVER B • WILL BROOKS

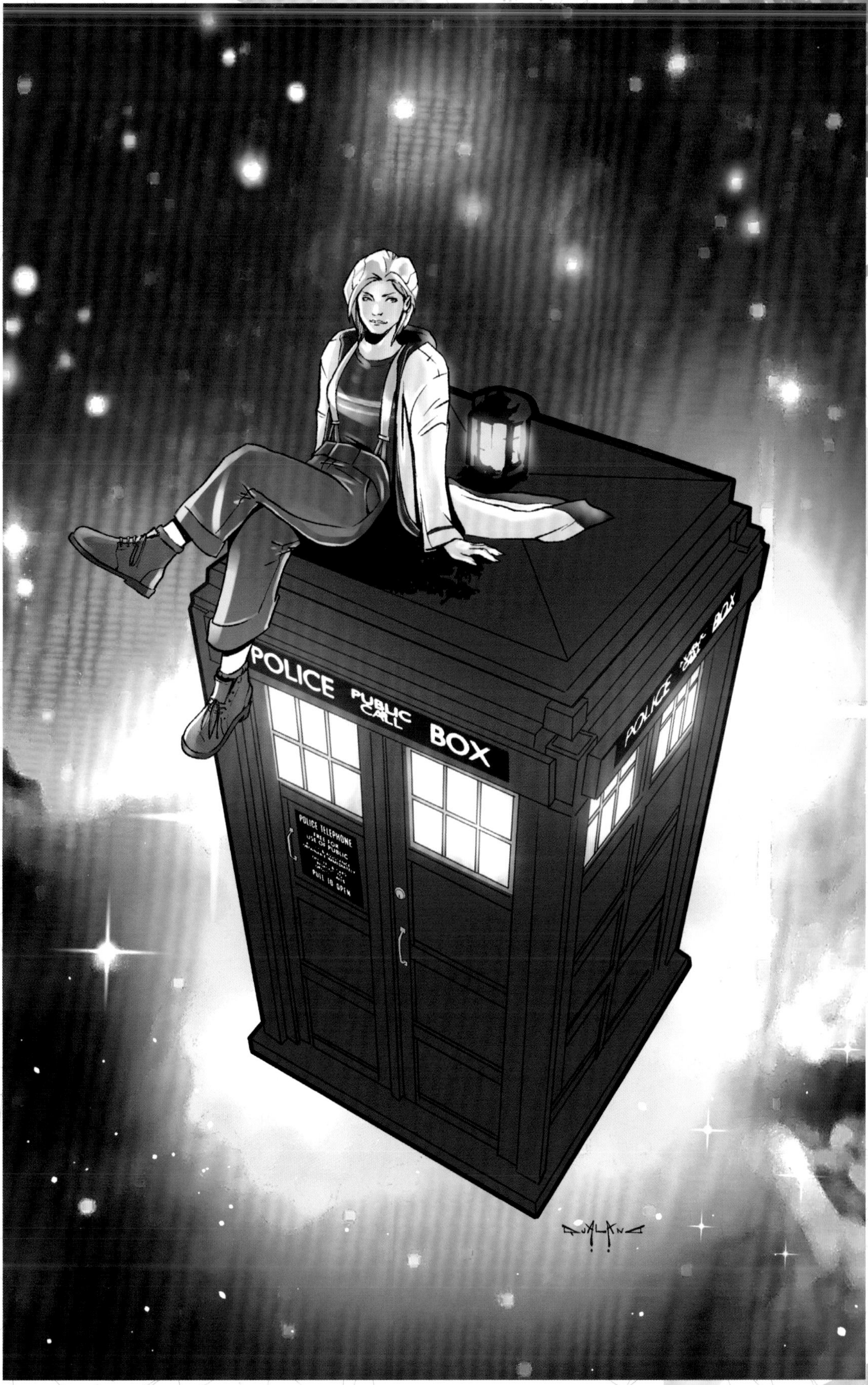
POLICE PUBLIC CALL BOX
POLICE TELEPHONE
PULL TO OPEN

ISSUE #2.4 COVER C • PASQUALE QUALANO

BBC

DOCTOR WHO

THE THIRTEENTH DOCTOR COLLECTIONS

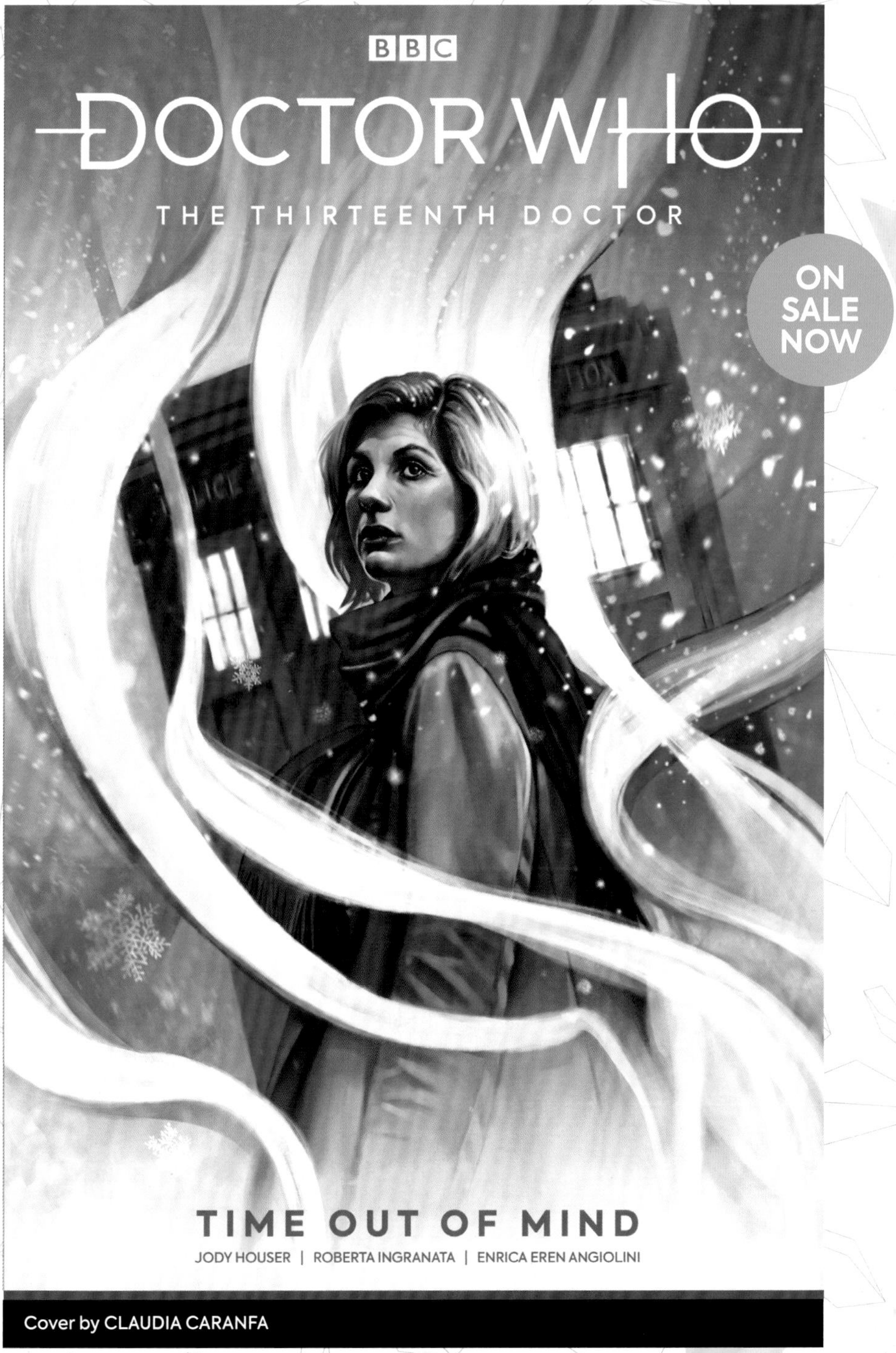
BBC
DOCTOR WHO
THE THIRTEENTH DOCTOR
ON SALE NOW
TIME OUT OF MIND
JODY HOUSER | ROBERTA INGRANATA | ENRICA EREN ANGIOLINI
Cover by CLAUDIA CARANFA

READER'S GUIDE

With so many amazing *Doctor Who* collections already on the shelves, it c[ould]
be difficult to know where to start. That's where this handy guide comes in!
And don't be overwhelmed — every collection is designed to be welcoming
whatever your knowledge of *Doctor Who*.

THE TWELFTH DOCTOR

VOL. 1:
TERRORFORMER

VOL. 2:
FRACTURES

VOL. 3:
HYPERION

YEAR TWO BEGINS! VOL. 4:
SCHOOL OF DEATH

VOL. 5:
THE TWIST

THE ELEVENTH DOCTOR

VOL. 1:
AFTER LIFE

VOL. 2:
SERVE YOU

VOL. 3:
CONVERSION

YEAR TWO BEGINS! VOL. 4:
THE THEN AND THE NOW

VOL. 5:
THE ONE

THE TENTH DOCTOR

VOL. 1:
REVOLUTIONS OF TERROR

VOL. 2: THE WEEPING
ANGELS OF MONS

VOL. 3: THE
FOUNTAINS OF FOREVER

YEAR TWO BEGINS! VOL. 4:
THE ENDLESS SONG

VOL. 5:
ARENA OF FEAR

THE NINTH DOCTOR

VOL. 1: WEAPONS OF
PAST DESTRUCTION

VOL. 2:
DOCTORMANIA

VOL. 3:
OFFICIAL SECRETS

VOL. 4:
SIN EATERS

Each comic series is entirely self-contained and focused on one Doctor, so you can follow one, two, or all of your favorite Doctors, as you wish! The series are arranged in TV season-like Years, collected into roughly three collections per Year. Feel free to start at Volume 1 of any series, or jump straight to the volumes labelled in blue! Each book, and every comic, features a catch-up and character guide at the beginning, making it easy to jump on board – and each comic series has a very different flavor, representative of that Doctor's era on screen. If in doubt, set the TARDIS Randomizer and dive in wherever you land!

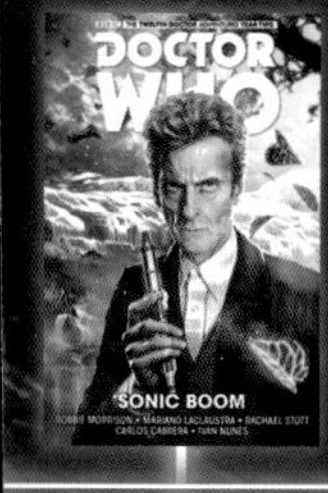
DOCTOR WHO
SONIC BOOM

VOL. 6:
SONIC BOOM

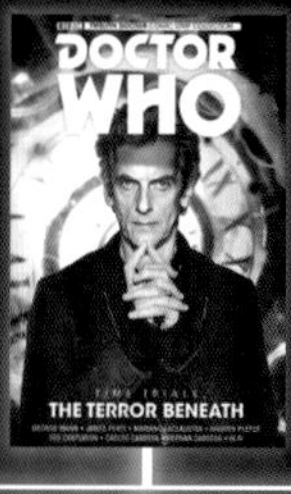
DOCTOR WHO
THE TERROR BENEATH

YEAR THREE BEGINS!
TIME TRIALS VOL. 1:
THE TERROR BENEATH

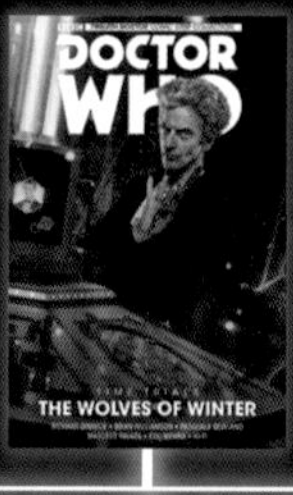
DOCTOR WHO
THE WOLVES OF WINTER

TIME TRIALS VOL. 2:
THE WOLVES
OF WINTER

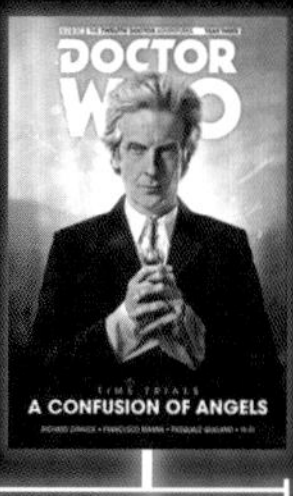
DOCTOR WHO
A CONFUSION OF ANGELS

TIME TRIALS VOL. 3:
A CONFUSION OF
ANGELS

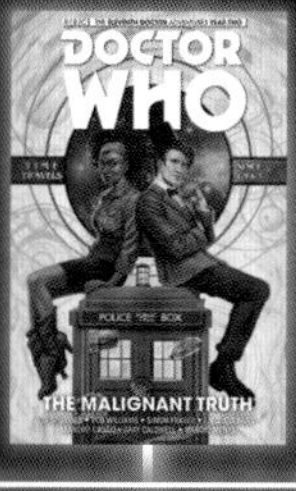
DOCTOR WHO
THE MALIGNANT TRUTH

VOL. 6:
THE MALIGNANT TRUTH

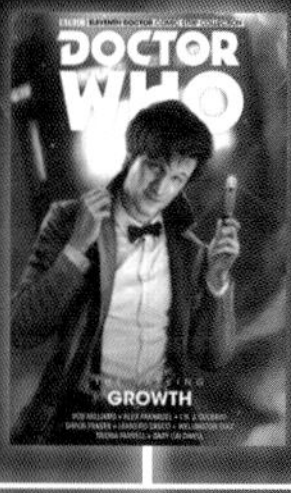
DOCTOR WHO
GROWTH

YEAR THREE BEGINS!
THE SAPLING VOL. 1:
GROWTH

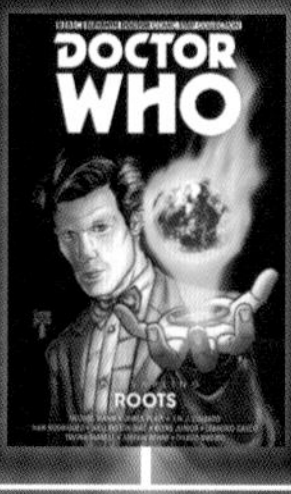
DOCTOR WHO
ROOTS

THE SAPLING VOL. 2:
ROOTS

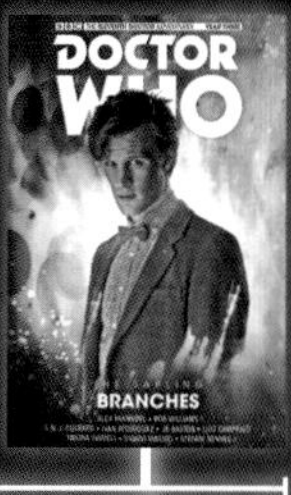
DOCTOR WHO
BRANCHES

THE SAPLING VOL. 3:
BRANCHES

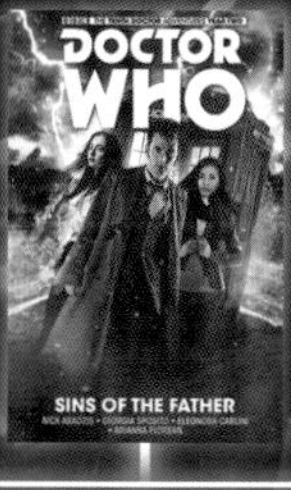
DOCTOR WHO
SINS OF THE FATHER

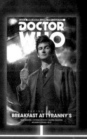

VOL. 6:
SINS OF THE FATHER

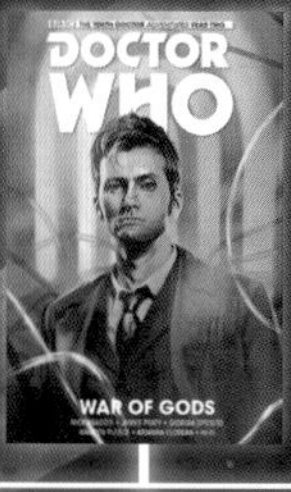
DOCTOR WHO
WAR OF GODS

VOL. 7:
WAR OF GODS

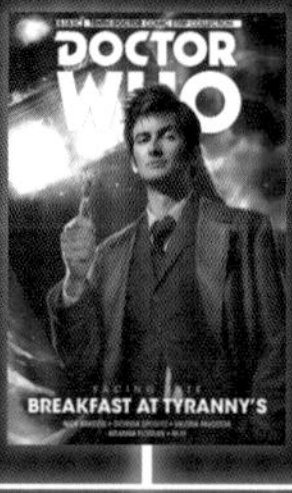
DOCTOR WHO
BREAKFAST AT TYRANNY'S

YEAR THREE BEGINS!
FACING FATE VOL. 1:
BREAKFAST AT TYRANNY'S

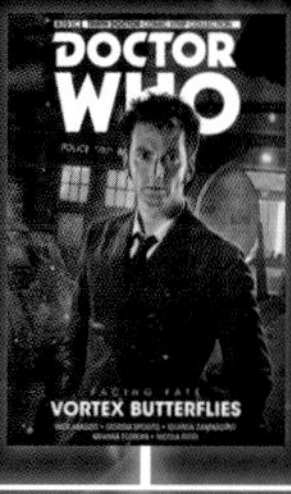
DOCTOR WHO
VORTEX BUTTERFLIES

FACING FATE VOL. 2:
VORTEX BUTTERFLIES

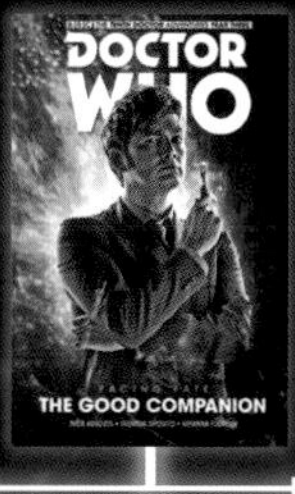
DOCTOR WHO
THE GOOD COMPANION

FACING FATE VOL. 3:
THE GOOD COMPANION

THE THIRTEENTH DOCTOR

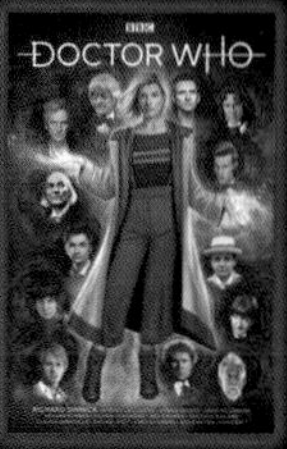
DOCTOR WHO

THE MANY
LIVES OF

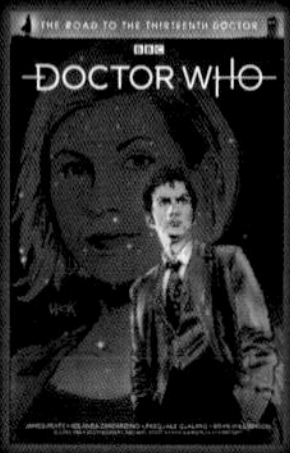
THE ROAD TO THE THIRTEENTH DOCTOR
DOCTOR WHO

THE ROAD TO THE
THIRTEENTH DOCTOR

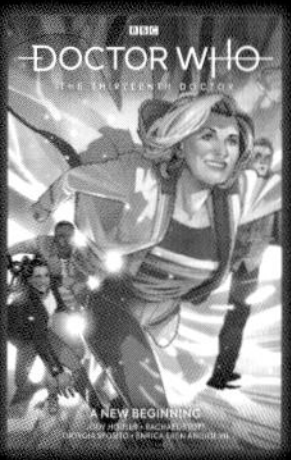
DOCTOR WHO
A NEW BEGINNING

VOL. 1:
A NEW
BEGINNING

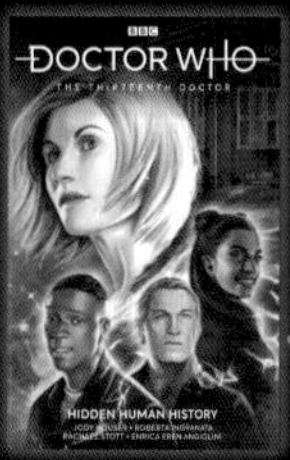
DOCTOR WHO
HIDDEN HUMAN HISTORY

VOL. 2:
HIDDEN HUMAN
HISTORY

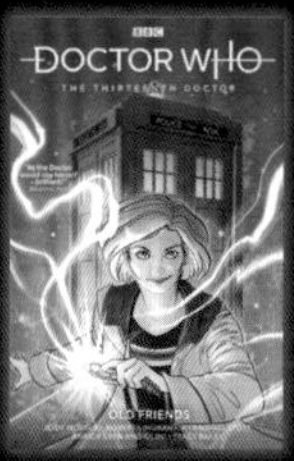
DOCTOR WHO
OLD FRIENDS

VOL. 3:
OLD FRIENDS

CLASSIC DOCTORS

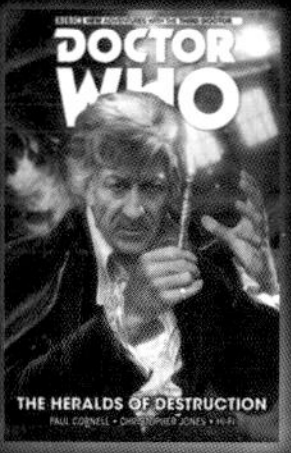
DOCTOR WHO
THE HERALDS OF DESTRUCTION

THIRD DOCTOR:
THE HERALDS OF
DESTRUCTION

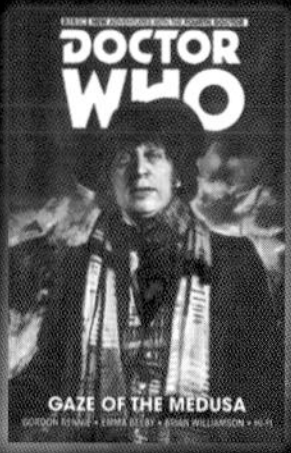
DOCTOR WHO
GAZE OF THE MEDUSA

FOURTH DOCTOR:
GAZE OF THE
MEDUSA

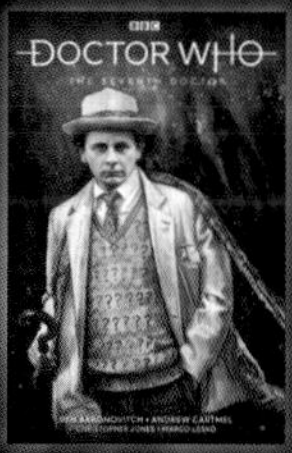
DOCTOR WHO

SEVENTH DOCTOR:
OPERATION
VOLCANO

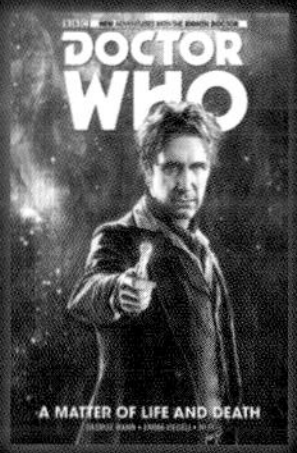
DOCTOR WHO
A MATTER OF LIFE AND DEATH

EIGHTH DOCTOR:
A MATTER OF LIFE
AND DEATH

MULTI-DOCTOR EVENTS

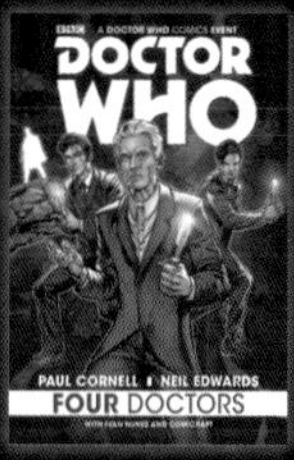
DOCTOR WHO
PAUL CORNELL • NEIL EDWARDS
FOUR DOCTORS

FOUR
DOCTORS

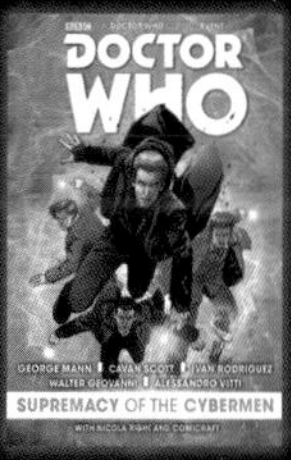
DOCTOR WHO
SUPREMACY OF THE CYBERMEN

SUPREMACY OF
THE CYBERMEN

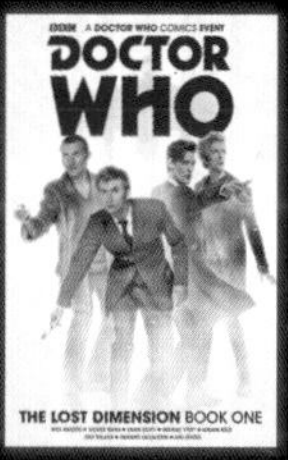
DOCTOR WHO
THE LOST DIMENSION BOOK ONE

THE LOST
DIMENSION
(BOOKS ONE & TWO)

BBC

DOCTOR WHO

A TALE OF TWO TIME LORDS

Biographies

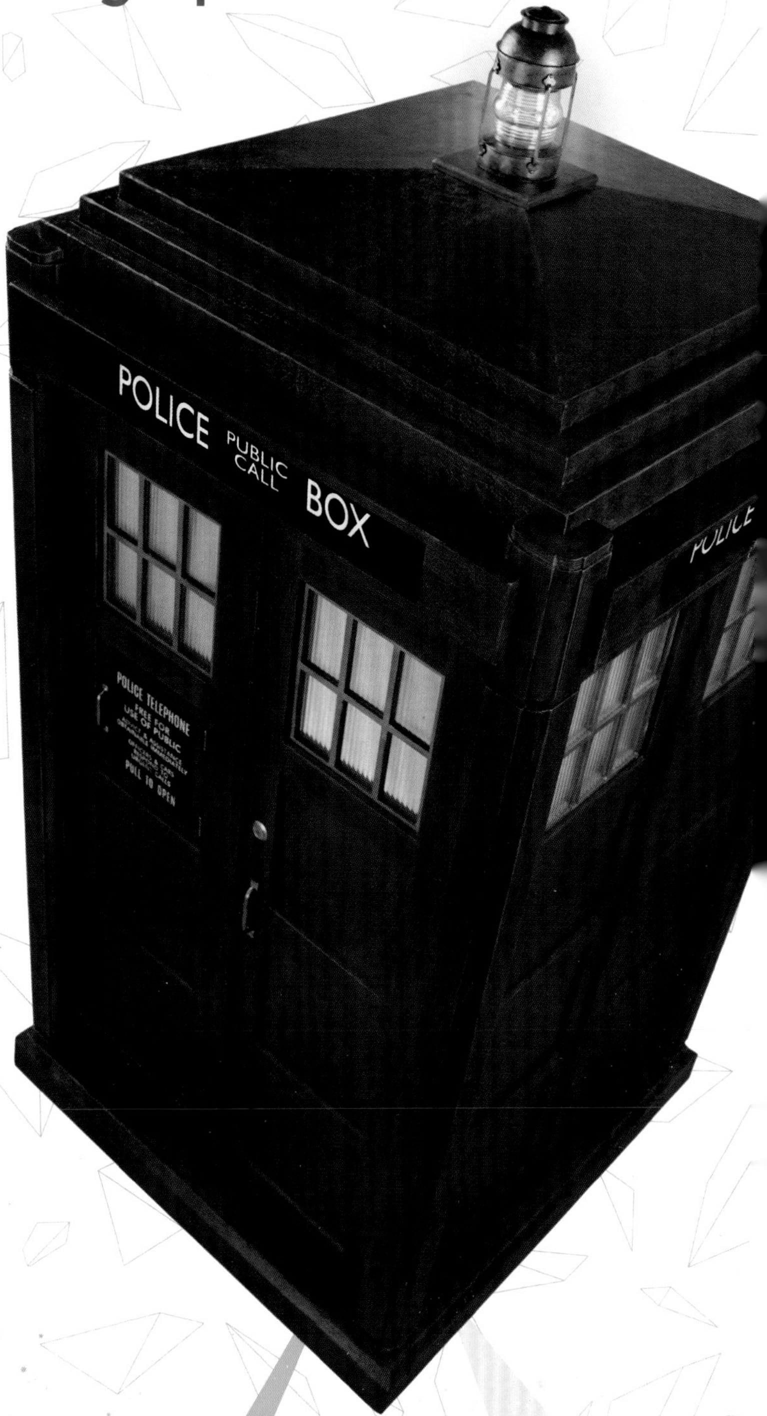
POLICE
PUBLIC CALL
BOX
POLICE TELEPHONE

Jody Houser

is a prolific writer of comics, perhaps best known for her work on *Faith* and *Mother Panic*. She has also written *Star Wars: Rogue One, Star Wars: Age of Republic, Amazing Spider-Man: Renew Your Vows*, and *Spider-Girls, The X-Files: Origins* and *Orphan Black*, and *Stranger Things, StarCraft*, and *Halo*.

Roberta Ingranata

is an Italian comic artist. She worked for various Italian publishers before making the leap to US comics. Titles she has leant her considerable talents to include the highly acclaimed *Witchblade* series, *Robyn Hood*, and *Van Helsing*.

Enrica Eren Angiolini

is a colorist and illustrator from Italy. Enrica's rich colors go from strength to strength, as demonstrated by her work on *Warhammer 40,000, Shades of Magic: The Steel Prince*, and her cover work for Titan Comics, and various other publishers.